What Kind of Country

by the same author

A Concise History of Irish Art
Orpen: Mirror to an Age
A Singer at the Wedding
The Song of the Nightingale
The Muted Swan
Running to Paradise

What Kind of Country

Country

Modern Irish Politics, 1968–1983

Bruce Arnold

JONATHAN CAPE
THIRTY BEDFORD SQUARE LONDON

First published 1984
Copyright © 1984 by Bruce Arnold

Jonathan Cape Ltd, 30 Bedford Square, London WC1

British Library Cataloguing in Publication Data

Arnold, Bruce
    What kind of country: modern Irish politics,
    1968–1983.
    1. Ireland — Politics and government — 1949–
    I. Title
    320.9417   DA963

ISBN 0-224-02046-3 (Hardback)
       0-224-02971-1 (Paperback)

Printed in Great Britain by
Thomson Litho Ltd, East Kilbride, Scotland

To my friends, colleagues
and collaborators in Ireland's
Third and Fourth Estates

Contents

Preface		xi
Prologue		1
1	The Challenges of Power, 1968–70	9
2	The Impact of Northern Ireland	16
3	Reaction in the Republic	27
4	'The Historic Unity of Our Country'	34
5	The Blaney Factor	42
6	'We Asked for Guns'	53
7	Arms and the Men	59
8	The Arms Crisis	64
9	The Arms Trials	74
10	The Aftermath	79
11	Cosgrave's Men	92
12	The Economy	99
13	Sunningdale	105
14	Security	117
15	Opposition	126
16	Commitments	130

vii

CONTENTS

17 Changing the Pilot   137

18 Charles Haughey   146

19 Unique Relationship   151

20 Garret Fitzgerald   162

21 More Instability   176

22 1982   183

23 The 'Unwanted' Election   195

24 'Programme for Government'   212

   Postscript   216

   Notes   219

   Index   233

Illustrations

PLATES

between pages 68–69
1 Violence on the street in Londonderry
2 Confrontation in the Bogside
3 Captain Terence O'Neill
4 John Hume
5 Ian Paisley
6 Jack Lynch at a press conference after the Arms Trial
7 Micheal O Morain
8 Jim Gibbons
9 Charles Haughey and Neil Blaney
10 Kevin Boland
11 Albert Luykx
12 John Kelly and Captain James Kelly

between pages 132–133
13 Liam Cosgrave
14 At the Sunningdale Conference
15 Liam Cosgrave and Edward Heath
16 Michael O'Leary
17 Justin Keating
18 Brendan Corish
19 Conor Cruise O'Brien
20 Mary Robinson, Richie Ryan and Garret FitzGerald
21 The wreckage of the car in which the British Ambassador, Christopher Ewart-Biggs, was killed

ix

between pages 196–197
22 Jack Lynch
23 Charles Haughey
24 Frank Cluskey campaigning
25 Desmond O'Malley
26 George Colley
27 Garret FitzGerald with Jack Lynch
28 The summit meeting at Dublin Castle between Margaret Thatcher and Charles Haughey
29 Dick Spring and Garret FitzGerald
30 Workers' Party deputies, Joe Sherlock, Proinsias de Rossa and Paddy Gallagher
31 Political leaders at the first meeting of the New Ireland Forum

PICTURE CREDITS

The author and publishers are grateful to the following for permission to reproduce photographs: Camera Press Ltd, no. 2 (photograph by Colman Doyle); Bob Hobby, nos 5, 18, 20, 22, 23, 24, 30, 31; *Irish Independent*, nos 3, 4, 7, 8, 9, 10, 11, 12, 14, 15, 16, 17, 19, 25, 26, 27, 28, 29; the *Irish Times*, nos 6, 13, and Popperfoto, nos 1, 21.

Preface

A special word of thanks is due to my newspaper, the *Irish Independent*, to the editors under whom I worked as a political commentator, Aidan Pender and Vincent Doyle, and to others within the group, particularly Bartle Pitcher, whose support and encouragement has been invaluable. At an earlier stage, Hector Legge, editor of the *Sunday Independent*, gave me particular support for which I will always be grateful. And I am also indebted to Nicholas Leonard, then editor of *Business and Finance*, for encouraging me to pursue political comment during the upheavals of the late 1960s and early 1970s.

Many politicians and journalists have given me help and advice, too many to name. Their friendship and support have been sustaining forces during certain vicissitudes. My wife, also a journalist, has been a patient and shrewd audience of my endeavour, not just in writing the book, but in the years of political reporting and comment which were its real genesis. I owe her a great debt.

B.A.

Dublin, 1983

'But in the end I understood this language. I understood it, I understand it, all wrong perhaps. That is not what matters. It told me to write the report. Does this mean I am freer now than I was? I do not know. I shall learn. Then I went back into the house and wrote, It is midnight. The rain is beating on the window. It was not midnight. It was not raining.'

Molloy. By Samuel Beckett

'...I have only to listen, it will show me my hiding place, what's it like, where the door is, if there's a door, and whereabouts I am in it, and what lies between us, how the land lies, what kind of country, whether it's sea, or whether it's mountain, and the way to take, so that I may go, make my escape, give myself up, come to the place where the axe falls, without further ceremony, on all who come from here...'

The Unnamable. By Samuel Beckett.

Prologue

In the aftermath of the November 1982 general election a story appeared in the *Irish Times* (Saturday, December 18) to the effect that my telephone, and that of another political journalist, Geraldine Kennedy of the *Sunday Press*, had been tapped by the outgoing administration. It had been done by warrant, involving the Police Commissioner and the previous Minister for Justice, as well as technicians from the police and the Department of Posts and Telegraphs. I already had some knowledge of this. It was confirmed by the Government, and permission was sought from me for a full investigation, which followed. It led, in January, to the resignation of the Commissioner for the Garda Siochana and his deputy, and the publication by the Minister for Justice, Michael Noonan, of three statements, one only of which, albeit the longest, concerned the tapping of the telephones of two journalists. A second covered the resignations, but a third — arguably the most interesting — revealed that police surveillance equipment had been demanded by the Minister for Justice, Sean Doherty, lent to the Minister for Finance, Ray McSharry, and used by him, covertly, to record a conversation with a Fianna Fail and former Government colleague, Martin O'Donoghue. The conversation was related 'solely to party political issues'.

The records of the Department of Justice showed that my phone had been tapped because 'Mr Arnold was anti-national in his outlook and that he might be obtaining information from sources of a similar disposition'. The warrant was sought 'for security purposes', and it was hoped from it 'to secure useful information concerning subversive activity which could not be obtained in any other way'.

In spite of the fact that Charles Haughey had, in the absence on holiday of his minister, been acting Minister for Justice during the period covered by one of the warrants, he denied all knowledge of the phone tapping; the real reason for it, in both Geraldine Kennedy's case and my own, which was politically motivated surveillance of our professional investigations into what was happening in and between political parties, and among politicians, was never clearly established.

For me, the anti-national accusation was a difficult one to deal with. As the events covered by this book show, Anglo–Irish relations occupy a significant position, both politically and emotionally, in Irish politics, even if they do not rate high priority in the opinion polls. Events such as Bloody Sunday, and the H-Block hunger strikes, can raise ancient animosities and provoke apparent hatreds which do not seem all that far beneath the surface. Their manifestation in the arena of political journalism is often muted, or of apparently negligible significance. The phone-tapping revelations made some sense, for example, of a bizarre series of personal attacks during 1982 by Fianna Fail politicians suggesting that I was a British spy, a view which still circulates within that party. Ludicrous at the time, the attacks subsequently subscribed to a malign and narrow logic about what 'anti-national' could be made to mean. It so happened, also, that the main purpose of a number of my articles in 1982 was threefold: critical examination of the internal divisions and poor performance of Fianna Fail, criticism of the negative attitude adopted by the Haughey Government to James Prior's Northern Ireland Assembly proposals, and criticism of the negative stance taken in Europe and at the United Nations on the Falklands. All, therefore, were critical of Fianna Fail. Any Irish subscriber, and there are many, to the idea that England's woes are Ireland's opportunity, or that an attack by an Englishman on Fianna Fail is an attack on Irish republicanism, had plenty of excuse for resenting what I was writing at the time. That sort of resentment, however, has been a rare phenomenon during more than twenty years of political journalism in my adopted country. With the exception of the 'Blow-In' speech, public manifestation has been absent; and private expression of what are really quite deep feelings, has been limited to periods of high tension, such as the H-Block hunger strikes.

The phone-tapping revelations provoked a crisis within Fianna Fail, another challenge against the party leader, which failed, and a re-examination of the events during an administration which had come to be regarded anyway as 'Grotesque, Unprecedented, Bizarre, Unbelievable' (GUBU). A new set of perceptions, another angle on participants, and an invitation to go back over the facts, was the broader effect of what had emerged; but within four months the opinion polls were showing the equalising in popularity of the country's political leaders, a decided wish on the public's part for a change of Government, and the inevitability, if and when this should come about, of a return to power of a team led by Charles Haughey not unlike the one which had run the country in 1982, abusing certain fundamental rights, and casting a dark shadow over the operation of democracy.

Because it was Ireland, the international press treated the phone-tapping issue quite superficially, except where it affected the survival of the leader of Fianna Fail, and the reputations of the former ministers directly involved in the scandal. The constitutional, human and civil rights aspects, as well as the implications for legal safeguards generally, were not addressed. Precisely because it was Ireland, and because it had happened to me, I was made to think again about the whole period covered by this book, already then the subject of substantial work.

Briefly, the conclusions were these: in common with many Englishmen, my first reaction to Ireland had been to identify it closely with my own country. This was reinforced for me by three things: the predispositions of literature, which had determined my coming in the first place, to study at Trinity College in 1957; secondly, a period of four years within the protected and largely, at that time, cosmopolitan environment of Dublin University; thirdly, by a life centred on the city of Dublin, which is also cosmopolitan to a degree that immunises its alien inhabitants from any real sense of an alternative and different Ireland elsewhere. After ten years, the sense of Ireland's foreignness becomes more clear; after twenty years it takes on a logical and finite form to which the individual, with a mixture of hope and despair, adapts. It is a refreshing mixture of variables over which the use of the English language, and the overlap of many of the more obvious English cultural traditions, throws a cloak of appearances which is essentially misleading. In a way that is only rarely ungenerous or threatening, one is not allowed to forget one's roots or origins. Like the intrusion of religion into different aspects of Irish life, questions about where you come from and why you came seem to provoke sustained curiosity.

As an added dimension to this rich and stimulating way of life which I had enthusiastically adopted, I was professionally drawn, more and more firmly, into what might be regarded, except for foreign correspondents, as the 'reserved territory' of Irish politics, and inescapably into the kind of confrontations between journalists and politicians which are part of the business of democracy. The starting point for this was simple and modest, working as *Guardian* correspondent during the 1960s. It was followed by more central involvement on behalf of different Irish publications, and then by ten years as parliamentary correspondent of the *Irish Independent*. The period, and the subject, exercised a fascination, and like a vortex drew me in. At best and at worst the people and the events made up a drama of sharp wit and raucous laughter, wild words and empty promises, occasional farce and infrequent fantasy. The country got itself governed, more or less. Packages of legislation were put together from time to time; exhortations about growth and development were supported by a long succession of documents; targets went awry; achievements were dissipated; Ireland came through one crisis in order to face another. This is not necessarily all that different from what happened in other countries over the same period; more raw, more ragged perhaps, taking its character from its leaders, but drawing most of its basic experiences out of the collective cauldron of world growth followed by world recession, Ireland had a 'good' decade in the 1960s, a 'bad' one in the 1970s. The scale of good and bad was different. There are certain isolating factors: an island beyond another island and on the western fringes of Europe; less wealthy, less developed, less populated; divided, and bitterly so; a revolutionary society, but deeply bred into Catholic and Protestant forms of conservatism; culturally self-conscious, yet aggressively proud of various artistic traditions. The more one delves, the more complicated becomes the story.

The choice of 1968 as a starting point has a number of justifications, the most sombre of which derives from Northern Ireland, and the beginning of the troubles which remain a permanent shadow over the fifteen years covered by this book. civil rights marches, which led to riots in Northern Ireland, raised in the South a number of fundamental political questions. They were about ideals and responses. They were also about the nature and quality of leadership, not just in Fianna Fail, the party then in power, but in Fine Gael and Labour as well.

Social, economic and political developments within the Republic were already challenging many of the most fundamental assumptions on which people were basing their lives. Moral and religious convictions, ideas about civil, human and constitutional rights, expectations about economic development, social reform, material well-being, the relationship of the country to the rest of the world, and the relationship of the country to its own individual citizens, were all challenged. The process was stimulating in some respects, horrifying in others. The twin political poles on the whole island, of republicanism and unionism, were tested as creeds and found wanting. That emptiness which is the abiding danger in political belief was discovered, often in painful circumstances. 'Republicanism', as a central political concept throughout the island, if an ill-defined one, was put to the test of actuality; instead of its meaning, which had always been the subject of endless and unlimited examination, its practical use, its working, its capacity to be used to resolve deep and otherwise intractable problems, were called in question — and in the process found wanting.

Unionism, the key political concept in Northern Ireland, went through the same process at the end of the 1960s and throughout the 1970s; it, too, failed; and it failed precisely those people who spoke most about it, and asserted the greatest faith in it. Out of these dual challenges evolved others. The relationship between Ireland, North and South, and Britain, changed from being a relatively static and backward looking set of political attitudes deeply bedded in history and enshrined in what seemed like finite form — an independent sovereign government in Dublin, a Northern Ireland parliament dominated for sixty years by Unionists at Stormont — and threatened to break down. Resolving the problems required real political initiative, sacrifice and imagination.

A further dimension was provided by Europe, and emphasised by the economic and social demands which grew out of the 1960s. Throughout that decade, Britain and Ireland had looked towards the E.E.C. in a positive way. Economically, the two countries had begun the process of coming together in a joint free trade area in preparation for entry to the community. This took place at the end of 1972, and became and remained the single most important economic factor for a decade. But it was not quite the economic paradise predicted by its most ardent proponents; the challenges and opportunities to which they had so frequently referred were treated differently, the challenges being tackled less seriously than was required, the opportunities seized on with more greed than prudence. Coincidentally, the western world entered the first of its oil crises within a year of Ireland's formal E.E.C. entry on January 1, 1973, and the cycle of recession began. It came at a peculiarly disadvantageous time. Unprecedented growth in the 1960s had created massive expectation; social behaviour, the nature of which was still dominated by the standards of a predominantly rural, conservatively Catholic and settled society, had given to Ireland the unique condition of an expanding birth rate and a naturally growing population.

In spite of emigration, which was still an accepted part of the complex Irish domestic economic system of budget-balancing, a young population was demanding more employment, more and better education, greater equality, a wider range of fundamental personal and civil rights, a better life. It was to be paid for by the State; and, if not the State, then Europe. Politicians had said that was the reason for going into Europe. They had also referred to change and sacrifice, to harder work and greater competition; but in a lower voice, and in less precise terms. And the resultant dichotomy became, at first, an imperceptible fissure in the country's social and economic texture, swiftly to develop, however, as the rude shock of market competition pressed home the reality of being part of Europe.

Some of the rights sought by a new generation of men and women were fundamental. One of them was concerned with contraception. In the McGee case a right under the Constitution to privacy in married life established a right for the individual to regulate the family. The repercussions of this were, and are, manifold. First, there are the implications of a written

Constitution. Constitutional case law, particularly during the 1960s, had developed and strengthened the Constitution as a vital and central feature of Irish life. It was firmly and increasingly shown to have practical relevance to the individual citizen, and to be more of an embarrassment than anything else to the politician. Secondly, it raised in a new form questions about the relationship of Church and State. In the McGee case the judiciary imposed on the legislature the obligation of passing laws protective of human rights, but potentially contrary to Roman Catholic teaching. The legislature failed lamentably to honour that obligation, not just in the aftermath of the McGee case, but subsequently as well. Thirdly, this set of developments invigorated the relationship of the individual with the State. It was not necessarily benign invigoration; a curious interdependence of laws and rights, presided over ostensibly by legislators and judges, a fact confirmed within the written Constitution, in reality represented a challenge to the individual and to a wide range of different interest groups, including the Catholic Church, who saw both threat and opportunity in the at times abstruse, yet highly-charged atmosphere surrounding constitutional conflict. On a number of specific occasions in the period 1968–83 the constitutional framework of the State was at issue, both in the rarified environment of the presidency and the Supreme Court, and in the combative environment of Dail and Senate.

It would be comforting to claim that Ireland came of age during this period, that the country learned by its experiences and by its mistakes, and advanced towards a more balanced, pluralist democracy, thereby making more attractive the idea of societies with often violently opposed religious views and starkly different ideas of loyalty and roots being able to come together in forms of agreement which might, one day, lead towards the unity so passionately espoused by so many. The evidence does not support the claim. The kind of country which had bred the mixed reactions to Northern violence in 1968–70, the arms crisis and the political wounds which derived from it, the odd handling of contraception, the even odder handling of the Pro-Life constitutional amendment, could not be said to have come of age. The lessons of this period are harsher and less evolutionary than that. What they are will be judged from the pages of this book.

I

The Challenges of Power, 1968–70

Ireland, North and South, was engulfed in crisis during 1968–70. The crisis in the Republic was provoked by the crisis in Northern Ireland, which in turn was set off by the civil rights campaign which, in the summer of 1968 had reached proportions sufficient to provoke confrontation between sections of the community, and with the police. But in both parts of the country the real causes were much deeper: the stagnation of political philosophy; abuse of power by political parties either permanently or persistently in office; inequalities of opportunity in societies benefiting from greater education, greater awareness and greater demand; and the provocative evidence, for the deprived, of achievement elsewhere: civil rights and student protests in Europe and America, during the 1960s, had created a climate of political optimism and political pressure.

In Ireland as a whole there was an in-built complication: Partition. Politicians in power in the Republic of Ireland saw it as a central handicap to advancement or the resolution of conflict, or blamed it as such, as they had done in the past. Politicians in power in the North rejected it, as a source of conflict and of crisis. Politicians in the South used it as a scapegoat, those in the North as an inadequate and insincere explanation of increasing violence, and therefore as something to be blamed as a contributory factor. In reality, partition had divided Ireland into a province of six counties in the North forming part of the United Kingdom, and an independent democratic republic in the south heavily dependent on the United Kingdom for trade and for the cultural spin-off of television, radio, a substantial part of magazine and newspaper consumption, the main source of books, and a certain common ground in other forms of art and information dissemination.

On the surface, the similarities between all three, in terms of life styles, were more apparent than the differences. But deep down, both in Northern Ireland and in the Republic, the societies which one assessed as being similar in broad terms, were frozen in moulds of antipathy and lack of mutual interest, suspicion and ignorance. When people in Northern Ireland looked at the South they had deep reservations about it. Members of the majority community saw the Republic as dominated by the Catholic Church, and a source of the republicanism which divided Northern society. Members of the minority community detected no serious understanding by southern politicians of their plight, and no genuine concern about it. And both North and South of the Border, the different views held about Britain were often equally unthinking, whether of the northern, Union Jack-flying loyalist variety, or of the southern 'Brit-bashing' republican kind.

What happened in one part of Ireland did interest some of the people in the other part all the time, and all the people just occasionally. But it was an uninformed interest, hardly productive of positive moves for better joint living. It tended in the opposite direction, towards an obsessional, hypnotic fascination which was to become a volatile source of energy as the different elements of crisis developed during a year, 1968, which historically and internationally has assumed a special importance. The Vietnam War protests in America, the student riots in Paris, the rising in Czechoslovakia, and events in Ireland, make of 1968 an *annus mirabilis* for the twentieth century comparable to — though on a much smaller scale than — 1848 during the nineteenth.

The manifestation of civil rights demands in Northern Ireland during 1968 sparked off a reaction in the Republic of Ireland which was concerned with a number of things, among them power, republicanism, violence, religious faith, culture, the Constitution and constitutional change, the operation of democracy; but not, ironically, civil rights. Glib voices would claim that the Republic had already jumped the hurdles which civil rights activists were lining up in front of a reluctant Unionist Government at Stormont in 1968. And to some extent this was true; electoral gerrymandering and inequalities over housing were not quite of the same order of distortion in the Republic as in Northern Ireland. The crisis in the South was still there; only it was different, in its origins, its direction, and its outcome. Civil rights issues were marginal. Events in Northern Ireland were also marginal. Concern about the welfare of the people of Northern Ireland, in their crisis, was selective, emotional, but at heart passive. The real issue in the crisis which developed in the Republic was power. The challenges of power were central: who had it, who exercised it, and who decided on its transfer.

Equally central, both to the crisis, and to the difference between Northern Ireland and the Republic of Ireland, were the political realities surrounding the party in power throughout the 1960s: Fianna Fail, the republican party. Unlike the Unionists in the North, they did not enjoy a permanent guarantee of power although they came close to it. They were the largest party; and, since their first acquisition of power in 1932, had governed for thirty of the previous thirty-six years. They were also inherently more professional at that time, and politically more astute, than either of the Opposition parties. But power had undoubtedly corrupted many of the ideals and objectives of Fianna Fail, increasingly so since the departure of Eamon de Valera as party leader in 1959.

The challenges of the 1960s had been economic and social, and Fianna Fail had responded imperfectly to them. The party had provided an essentially *laissez-faire* Government in an essentially conservative country. There had been heavy dependence on a growth economy, in many respects passively reliant on international economic expansion, in so far as that growth was allowed to filter through to Ireland from Europe and the United States. There was a reluctant admission that the protectionism of the previous thirty years had to be abandoned, first by the creation of a free trade area with Britain, then by Ireland's entry into the E.E.C. But there was even greater reluctance about tackling the fundamental reforms of agriculture and industry which would turn membership of an international open-market economy to Ireland's advantage. The efforts made by a few to harden off an over-protected and fledgling industrial structure, largely founded on a grant-based philosophy, not just to withstand the shock of competition, but to benefit from it, were intense, but met with apathy and resistance on all sides. Industrial relations were bad generally in the late 1960s, and daily news was dominated by a series of major industrial confrontations and strikes which reflected equally badly on management and on trade union practice.

Economic policy, throughout the decade, had been dependent on a series of economic programmes for development which had set sensible enough targets, and had been underpinned by correct public service and political exhortations about what needed to be done, and how it should be done. Nevertheless, the economy generally was far from ready for the trade pacts and agricultural deals which were being negotiated after the signing of the Anglo-Irish Free Trade Area Agreement of 1965. This set a ten-year timetable for the elimination of Irish tariff barriers against British imports, and was overtaken eventually by the joint entry of both countries into the E.E.C. By 1968, Government preoccupations, economically speaking, were related to electoral considerations.

Jack Lynch had succeeded Sean Lemass as Taoiseach (Prime Minister) in November 1966, less than eighteen months after the June 1965 general election. By 1968 he was thinking about the next, and his first, general election. Both he and those around him were concerned primarily with staying in power. Jack Lynch's own concern was obvious enough: he still had to prove himself electorally. The party's concern with power was equally understandable. Fianna Fail was coming to the end of its third consecutive period in office, the difficulties of remaining there were manifest, and the apparent threat from the Opposition parties more substantial than was the reality.

A key, if complex issue in 1968, illustrative of the electoral obsessions within Fianna Fail, and of the fairly reprehensible self-interest of the party in power, was related to the country's Constitution. It serves to illustrate the prevailing political tone. In August 1966, before resigning, Sean Lemass had set up an all-party committee of Dail and Senate 'to review the constitutional, legislative and institutional basis of government'. The committee, in its report published in December 1967, had made some recommendations which were unanimous, and some which contained arguments for and against. Perhaps the most important of the former, for Ireland North and South, was the recommendation which referred to Article 3 of the Constitution, and proposed replacing the wording about 'the re-integration of the national territory', with something less provocative. Of the non-unanimous recommendations, arguably the most controversial concerned proportional representation, the electoral system used in the Republic since independence. There had already been an attempt by Fianna Fail, at the time of the 1959 presidential election, to do away with it, and introduce the straight vote system. And this had been firmly rejected. Now, in 1968, another attempt was made. Blatantly ignoring the areas of unanimous agreement, the Fianna Fail Government put before the people, in the form of a referendum on October 16, 1968, the replacement of proportional representation by the 'straight vote' system, in single-member constituencies. The people wisely rejected the proposal by a 3:2 ratio, though there were areas in the country where Fianna Fail had an absolute majority in favour of the change. In itself it was political opportunism of an obvious kind, and widely condemned as such in advance of the electoral verdict. More seriously, it brought to an abrupt end the all-party approach to constitutional change. The committee, whose report had been an 'interim' one, never met again. Agreed constitutional reform became a political impossibility. And any general debate on broad constitutional reform, which would have been relevant to North–South accord later, was ruled out by the dishonest, unilateral manner in which Fianna Fail handled potential constitutional change between 1967 and 1969.

The Fianna Fail response to the failure of the referendum was immediate: Kevin Boland, the minister responsible, introduced an Electoral Amendment Bill, redrawing the constituencies throughout the country in a gerrymander designed to favour Fianna Fail in the coming general election. The legislation dominated Dail activity during the autumn and winter of 1968, and then moved to the Senate at the end of February, to be gone over again with fresh arguments about its electoral unfairness. This is the context in which events in Northern Ireland began to unfold during the summer and autumn of 1968; this is the context in which Fianna Fail had to respond to those events.

'Fianna Fail, the republican party' has always claimed two fundamental policy objectives: the restoration of the Irish language, and the reunification of the country. Progress by 1968 was negligible in both areas. Only a tiny minority had any enthusiasm for Irish as the first official language; an even smaller number actually used Irish as their own natural first language. Equally, a tiny minority of people were actively looking towards a united Ireland, and the majority of those who were, believed in achieving their aims by illegal rather than legal means. The rest merely talked about it.

Between 1968 and 1970 new political groupings emerged in Northern Ireland, bringing together those opposed to the Unionist majority. The basic groundwork was also laid for an alternative government in the South. A prime minister was forced to resign in Northern Ireland. Two ministers were dismissed in the Republic and then brought before the courts on conspiracy charges. The seeds of sustained terrorism in Ireland were sown, giving birth, through a divided Sinn Fein and a divided Irish Republican Army, to the Provisionals. There were deaths, through rioting, on the streets of Derry and Belfast. British Government ministers imposed reforms on the Northern Ireland administration, and began the process by which the Republic's role in Northern affairs was grudgingly to be recognised. The British Army took over security in the North. United Nations intervention was called for by the Republic, and blocked by Britain on grounds of non-interference in Britain's internal affairs, with strong support from Belfast politicians and Army chiefs. Gradually, the unevenly balanced three power bases on which Ireland rests – Dublin, London and Belfast – became a force which was to alter and underwrite politics for the foreseeable future. The shift in the relative strength of these power bases was central to the political realities which emerged between two dramatic developments: the rise of the civil rights movement in Northern Ireland, the first marches and the first riots in the late summer of 1968, and the cauterising aftermath of the second Arms Trial in Dublin in October 1970.

Like all such events, the processes leading up to them, and the results deriving from them, lead backward and forward in time. Indeed, both in the context of Captain Terence O'Neill's fight for survival in Northern Ireland during the first half of 1969, and in the context of the interpretations of republicanism in the South which are bound up in the arms crisis of 1970, we witnessed passions and actions whose roots were centuries old. Yet in a vivid and precise way the two years which ended the decade of growth and expansion in Ireland and ushered in the doubts, the reversals, the deaths and the despair of the 1970s, are crucial to any understanding of modern Ireland. The events still echo around us. Many of them still overshadow the future.

2

The Impact of Northern Ireland

On August 24, 1968, the first civil rights march was held in Northern Ireland. It was entirely peaceful. Yet it marked a watershed between the uncertain and ineffective protest about political inequality in the North leading to social, economic and electoral deprivation, and the concerted agitation which took its form and direction from the events of that summer afternoon. The march was from Coalisland to Dungannon, a distance of three miles. It was organised by the Campaign for Social Justice in Northern Ireland, based in Dungannon, and by the Northern Ireland Civil Rights Association, which was an umbrella organisation that had grown out of the various housing action committees, as well as other groups seeking reforms in Northern Ireland.

For the majority of members and supporters, housing was the key issue; and it was specifically the abuse of local authority housing allocation in Caledon, another village near Dungannon, that led to the first civil rights march. Two Catholic families had squatted in houses in Kinard Park. One family was ordered out, and the house was given to a single, 19-year-old Protestant girl employed by a local Unionist councillor. Briefly, the house was then taken over by a Nationalist M.P. at Stormont, Austin Currie, with considerable publicity surrounding the event, and the injustice which had been highlighted became the specific focus for the Dungannon march.

The march was led by Austin Currie, Gerry Fitt, a Republican Labour M.P. with a seat both at Stormont and Westminster, and by Betty Sinclair, a prominent Northern Ireland trade unionist who was chairman of the Civil Rights Association, and also a declared Communist.

A counter-demonstration was organised by the Protestant community. The Home Affairs Minister, William Craig, ordered the police to prevent any trouble. As a result they re-routed the march, stopping it from entering the market square in Dungannon town centre. There was a confrontation between the march-leaders and the police, but the marchers then accepted the order to disperse, and, after singing 'We Shall Overcome', they went away quietly.

All of this was widely and effectively reported in the southern newspapers, and Irish television deployed news-covering resources in work that was comparatively new and challenging. Confrontation and protest swiftly came to dominate television screens in an immediate and shocking way, and gave the 'troubles' a stark realism which had been denied to earlier confrontations in Northern Ireland. To some extent, the media became part of the process which sustained and motivated the political events, and this had equally dramatic effect on both sides. The apparent success of peaceful demonstration provoked swift retribution from militant Unionists.

The next march, on October 5, in Derry, was entirely different. Again blocked by Protestant Unionists, who were supported by a Home Affairs Office ban on the march, with police determined to uphold it, the demonstration turned into a major riot which went on through the night and into the early hours of the following morning, Sunday. With a brief truce for worship, it continued into the early hours of Monday morning.

There had been swift escalation from a civil rights campaign to marches, followed by confrontation and police intervention, leading to riots, injury, damage to property, looting; it would only be a matter of time before shooting and death would be added. Northern Ireland was facing a major crisis, and the whole world knew about it in vivid and horrifying detail.

Whatever may have been their longer-term aspirations, or their more fundamental judgments about the cause of disaffection within Northern Ireland, none of the politicians who had led the Catholics as they gathered at the Waterside Station, across the River Foyle from the centre of Derry on that ill-fated Saturday at the beginning of October, saw the ending of partition either as a realistic political objective, or as something that would make the slightest difference to the plight of the poor in Northern Ireland. All of them, together with the civil rights activists who were not associated then with party politics, were bent on reform. Principally concerned with housing and with jobs, over both of which the Protestant Unionist majority exercised discrimination in favour of their own kind, the demands of the civil rights movement in Northern Ireland also included a universal suffrage in local elections to replace the proprietorial voting system unique to the North in the British Isles, and an impartial redrawing of constituencies.[1] They wanted a points system for local authority housing, legislation on job discrimination, and certain security changes, including the disbanding of the B Specials[2] and the repeal of the Special Powers Act.[3]

Politicians in the South had a very blurred understanding of this, many preferring the republican 'solution' of unity in place of putting basic wrongs right. For some, such as Conor Cruise O'Brien, the civil rights phenomenon itself was nothing new, since he had been involved in American civil rights campaigning in the 1960s. Nor was he inhibited by ideological beliefs within the Labour Party[4] which he had recently joined, from emphasising the issues connected with basic human rights, and condemning any muddling of these with pleas for a solution to Northern Ireland through the reunification of the country. With the exception of a few, notable among them John O'Connell, a Dublin deputy with strong republican leanings, O'Brien's view prevailed increasingly strongly within the Labour Party.

The attitude was similar in Fine Gael,[5] where there was far greater emphasis on social and economic issues, and where divisions in the party tended to be on a Left–Right basis, with militant republican running a poor third. The Fine Gael Party leader, Liam Cosgrave, was widely and correctly seen as a 'law and order' man. A former army officer, and the son of the country's first prime minister, W. T. Cosgrave, who had been in power between 1922 and 1932, Liam Cosgrave was as reticent about the positive value of widespread reform as he was about any form of militant action outside the obsessively respected 'institutions of the State'. While politically he recognised the importance of paying lip-service to the reunification of Ireland, he was enough of a political realist to grasp the

18

impossibility of achieving it in the foreseeable future, and the very serious problems it would produce for the Republic. The same realisation, though from a different standpoint, coloured the thinking of Garret FitzGerald, the leading liberal within Fine Gael and one of the party's choices as eventual successor to Liam Cosgrave. But with Fine Gael not in power, and himself one of his leader's main opponents, the relevance of his views was limited. Nevertheless, he was responsible, with Paddy Harte, and in close liaison with John Hume and Austin Currie, for the restatement of Northern Ireland policy, and for the presentation of proposals which contained the seeds for power-sharing in the North as a way out of the political impasse. The Fine Gael approach was swiftly supported by Labour; subsequently by Fianna Fail.

It was Fianna Fail, rather than the two Opposition parties, that faced real difficulties in coming to terms with the events taking place in Northern Ireland. And their problems were numerous. They were in power and had been for more than ten years; they faced an election, which they wanted to win. They had to react to an unprecedented set of events in Northern Ireland which were provoked by an uncomfortably youthful, Left-wing, reformist movement. Their past record was, to say the least, unhelpful in the circumstances. Their current obsession with a nakedly selfish electoral device — the proportional representation referendum — was also unhelpful. At heart, Fianna Fail had problems over the basic principles of reform. In term of civil liberties in the South, their performance was far from enlightened. Emergency powers, imposed at the beginning of the Second World War, were still technically in force. Justice and law and order enforcement were distinctly authoritarian. There was still heavy censorship of films, while the censorship of literature was only just emerging from the absurdity of Powell, Orwell and Salinger being banned writers. The periodic intrusion of Church into State affairs was an accepted way of life. Housing and jobs, where they formed part of the complex and far-flung State patronage, may not have been sectarian — there were too few Protestants, and they were generally too well protected — but were often subject to party preferences. From the highest appointments downward an essential principle, voiced by Donogh O'Malley in 1968, prevailed generally, and this was to give party preference where possible.

For such a party there were two courses open: one was to accept the reformist motivation driving the civil rights movement and opposition politicians in Northern Ireland, and support it; the other was to fall back on the fundamental objective of a united Ireland as an answer to all difficulties, ignoring interim solutions, and piecemeal changes.

The latter of these two courses was the one taken by Neil Blaney, Minister for Agriculture, and more tacitly supported by others within Fianna Fail, including Charles Haughey and Kevin Boland. The former was the line adopted by Jack Lynch, and one that prevailed both before and after the arms crisis of May 1970. The key to political events in the Republic, where they concern Northern Ireland and Anglo-Irish relations as they affect the North, is to be found in this simple and straightforward parting of the ways that emerged within Fianna Fail during the closing months of 1968, and lasted, in various forms, for the next fourteen years.

This division within Fianna Fail came about as a result of Northern politicians persuading the Fianna Fail leader to abandon the shibboleth of partition in favour of realistic reforms. At an early stage in the autumn of 1968 they achieved this objective. It was then necessary, for political reasons, deliberately to obfuscate the real wishes and intentions of the Government in the South, as well as its interpretation of the problems of Northern Ireland, with statements which catered for strongly held, if ignorant, sentiments within the Fianna Fail Party, whose name, for electoral purposes, is always represented in full as 'Fianna Fail, the Republican Party'.

If this need is a constant factor with every leader of the party, it was particularly so with Jack Lynch in 1968 because he was electorally an untried force. Moreover, he did not come from an Irish political family. He could not claim a father who had fought in the G.P.O. or had been imprisoned, or otherwise victimised for his republicanism, at any time between 1918 and 1932. A mild, pipe-smoking Corkman, with an avuncular attitude and a slow, contemplative manner, Lynch had been a reluctant Fianna Fail candidate in 1948, chosen for his national reputation in Gaelic games. He has six all-Ireland medals in a row, for hurling and Gaelic football, between 1941 and 1946. Married, but without children, his lifestyle was modest. He was a tailor's son, and dressed impeccably. Furthermore, his strongest opponents in the party did enjoy the questionable asset of republican atavism, and included such men as Neil Blaney, who were all too ready to give expression to militant criticism of partition, as though its demise would work an instant and total metamorphosis upon the people of the North.

Jack Lynch therefore faced a complicated task. Understandably, the Derry riots of October 5–7 provoked Lynch to say that the root cause was partition. He repeated the same line on the Tuesday night in Clonmel, after the benefit of security reports and the regular Government meeting. The speech is a good example of the manner in which southern politicians had for years wrapped up the 'problem' of Northern Ireland in the partition blanket:

> In commenting briefly at Kilkenny on Sunday on the incidents in Derry City I expressed the hope that the root causes of such demonstrations would soon be eliminated, so that people of different religions and political persuasions and convictions would be able to live together in peace and harmony, free to exercise and enjoy their lawful democratic rights. The people of Ireland know what these root causes are. I know them. The Northern Ireland Prime Minister, Captain O'Neill, knows them. The British Prime Minister, Mr Wilson, knows them also. Partition is the first and foremost root cause. And partition arose out of British policy. The methods necessary to maintain partition against the wishes of the vast majority of the Irish people and local majorities in areas like Derry City – that is, gerrymandering, discrimination in jobs and housing, suppression of free speech and the right of peaceful protest – could not be continued without the political and huge financial support received from Britain. I trust that the efforts of all men of goodwill, North and South, will be directed towards the creation of healthy and wholesome community relations in the Six Counties, not only to eliminate discrimination and bigotry and to establish the full and free exercise of democratic rights, but to eliminate the root cause of dissension among Irishmen in the North – that is the partition of our country against the wishes of the overwhelming majority of the Irish People.

It was 'soft' republicanism compared with other versions in Fianna Fail — and it must be remembered that the main purpose of Jack Lynch's speaking engagements at the time were to campaign on behalf of the electoral changes on which there was to be a referendum — but it was undeniably a line of argument peculiar to the Republic of Ireland, and one that, in its ambivalence, was unhelpful to the civil rights movement and offensive to the Protestant majority in Northern Ireland.

It so happened that the Northern Ireland Nationalist leader at that time, Eddie McAteer, who had been injured by the police during their attack on the civil rights marchers in Derry on the previous Saturday afternoon, was on his way to Dublin for talks with the Taoiseach. He was accompanied by Gerry Fitt. These talks took place on Wednesday, October 9. Jack Lynch, as well as politicians from other parties, was told what was needed for Northern Ireland, and it did not include the ending of partition. The emphasis was on reform. The sympathy of the people in the South for the victims of police brutality in Northern Ireland was sought, but the Government's role, as expressed by Gerry Fitt, was seen essentially in terms of pressure on the Labour administration under Harold Wilson at Westminster to bring in speedy reforms in Northern Ireland. The key to this was for Britain to abandon a 'gentleman's agreement' then seen as obstructing necessary reforms; this was the Westminster convention of non-intervention in Northern Ireland affairs. Direct intervention was seen by Fitt and McAteer, and those they represented, as the correct course of action to bring about the fundamental changes which even the relative liberal, Captain Terence O'Neill, was afraid to introduce because of the Right wing of his own party.

Jack Lynch's response to the demands of Northern politicians representative of the minority was a positive one. It was also a response which he delayed, possibly deliberately, in order to draw from the militant republicans within Fianna Fail *their* recipe for the North. This came in a strongly-worded speech by Neil Blaney on Friday, November 8, 1968. It was in the form of an attack on the Northern Ireland Prime Minister, Captain Terence O'Neill, who was described as one who 'can only speak for a mere bigoted junta in six of its [Ulster's] counties, a junta that has made his liberal image a shameful sham.' Like a gust of chilly wind, shivering across the surface of calm water, Neil Blaney's contribution indicated the potentially deep-seated differences and tensions within Fianna Fail. It was a deliberate attack, not so much on O'Neill as on Jack Lynch himself, and it reflected the pressures within Government.

With equal deliberation, Jack Lynch, on the following Monday evening, November 11, 1968, ostensibly and significantly at a meeting of the Fianna Fail Party's National Executive in Dublin, carefully reversed the priorities which had been at the heart of Fianna Fail's Northern Ireland policy. Paying lip-service to party objectives on the ending of partition he nevertheless set it firmly aside in favour of reform in Northern Ireland. The speech was directed far more widely afield than just to the Fianna Fail organisation, nor was it just towards nationalist opinion in Northern Ireland, but towards the Unionists, and towards politicians in Britain. But the message for his own party was an important one. Only incidentally a rap over the knuckles for his recalcitrant Minister for Agriculture, more fundamentally it was a serious warning to others within Fianna Fail who, without possessing either Neil Blaney's knowledge of Ulster and the North or his outspokenness in pursuing a 'hard' republican line, were tending towards the voicing of militant, 'united Ireland' objectives. Lynch emphasised reform and cross-Border co-operation. The most he would say about partition was that it would continue to arouse 'deep feelings and emotions in people and it is natural that expression will be given to their emotions.'

By late 1968 Northern Ireland looked as though it might stabilise, principally on the basis of undertakings from the Unionist Government about reform. These were implicit in the television address by Captain Terence O'Neill on December 9 in which he said, 'Ulster stands at the crossroads'. His appeal, aimed at moderate opinion generally, obtained a positive response from the Northern Ireland Civil Rights Movement, which was favourably disposed towards a moratorium on their protest marches. The movement wanted to see if brave action would follow brave words. Then, just before Christmas, the more militant People's Democracy announced a march which would cross Ulster, from Belfast to Derry, beginning on New Year's Day. The make-up of People's Democracy was radical, youthful, impatient, inexperienced, uncompromising and ideological. It did not want to reform society from within, but to change it more fundamentally from without, sweeping away the elements which had failed; and they were to be the judges of what those were. It was more truly revolutionary in the changes on which it set its sights. Numerically small, its actions were counter-productive in holding together and managing, in political terms, the civil rights goodwill which was forcing the pace in Northern Ireland. Its march, however, was to have a fundamental, if negative impact on the progress of reform, and on the survival of O'Neill. It unleashed malign forces on both sides in Northern Ireland, dividing society there more firmly and thereby laying the ground for the rise of terrorism. And in the South the impact of the march had similar results during 1969, both on perceptions about Northern Ireland, and on the conflicting views about what the Republic's responses should be.

The main confrontation on the march came on the fourth day, at Burntollet Bridge, where the students and demonstrators were ambushed by Protestant extremists led by Ronald Bunting. It was an organised and brutal attack. Those engaged in the ambush wore white armbands to identify themselves to each other, and to the police, and carried clubs and stones. The attack was watched by a far from impartial R.U.C. force. Despite the ambush, the march was not stopped. It continued on into Derry, depleted and shocked, and then disintegrated into an afternoon and evening of essentially sectarian rioting.

Politically, Captain Terence O'Neill was faced with growing rifts within the Unionist Party. Brian Faulkner, his deputy and Minister for Commerce, resigned from the Government on January 23, 1969. Two days later William Morgan, Minister for Health and Social Welfare, also resigned, to be followed by a junior minister. Open expression of a desire for leadership change emerged, and speculation about O'Neill's chances of survival. It became clear that he was losing control of his party and his Government. *In spite of* actual and promised reforms on the one hand, and *because* of such reforms on the other, he was presiding over the steady polarisation of Northern Ireland society. The civil rights movement was becoming more militant; so, too, were Protestant and Unionist organisations. Terence O'Neill was unfairly the victim of hatred from both sides. Equally unfairly, he had become the symbol to Catholics of precisely what he was not: an unregenerate Unionist, and to Protestants also a symbol of what he was not: the ally of Catholics and a traitor to both the Protestant faith and the Union.

This was the background to the general election which he called on February 4, 1969. It resolved nothing. Ironically, Terence O'Neill claimed that it would be 'the most democratic election the North has ever had', and went to say that Northern Ireland would 'never be the same again'. It wasn't. But hardly in the way he had meant. He was looking for a vote 'loud and clear' in favour of progress, and he claimed that the election would decide the destiny of the Unionist Party. For the first time in its history, that party held a Sunday press conference to conclude its campaign. Public comment by a member of the Southern Government on the Northern Ireland election came when Neil Blaney defined the contest as being about reunification, and urged 'Irish' voters in the North to withhold their support from candidates who favoured the Union with Britain.

The result was a very qualified success for Terence O'Neill's Unionist Party. The party won its predictable majority, but the general feeling was that O'Neill himself could not survive for long as leader. One comment, on the day of the result, Tuesday, February 25, came from the secretary of the Northern Ireland Labour Party, Sam Napier, who was pessimistic about O'Neill's chances of survival, and saw him being replaced by Brian Faulkner, the former Minister for Commerce in O'Neill's Government. 'I think there will first be a caretaker premier, and then Mr Faulkner will take over, although I don't think at the moment he could unite the party.' It was an accurate prophecy.

In the aftermath of the general election Terence O'Neill's control over the Unionist Party was marginal. A vote of confidence at a full meeting of the Unionist Council, on March 31, 1969, was won by 338 to 263, not really sufficient in the prevailing political climate. Demonstrations, with violence, continued during the spring. Fears of a new campaign by the I.R.A. were increased by a major explosion at the Castlereagh electricity installations outside Belfast[6] at the end of March, and this was followed by further acts of sabotage during April. In April, also, Bernadette Devlin won the Mid-Ulster seat at Westminster, and brought directly into parliament there her forceful,

People's Democracy radicalism. At the end of April the Unionist Parliamentary Party agreed, by 28 votes to 22, to support the principle of one man, one vote in local elections.

By the end of April, 1969, O'Neill believed that his ability to govern had been almost totally undermined. At the same time he had solid and irreversible reforms already behind him, and the reality, still, of majority consent within his own party, in spite of the dismissal of William Craig the previous December, and the resignation of Brian Faulkner, on January 23, 1969. Then James Chichester-Clark, Minister for Agriculture, resigned. It was believed by many that this was orchestrated by Terence O'Neill to pre-empt the possibility of the Unionists on the Right taking over control of the party.

Chichester-Clark was the 'moderate' predicted by Sam Napier, and seen by O'Neill and others as capable of holding the party together without abandoning the reforms still necessary if Northern Ireland was to survive as a self-governing democracy. O'Neill had seen the alternative danger of the party falling into the hands of the Right, represented to a certain degree by Brian Faulkner, who could count on the support of William Craig and those opposed to O'Neill, and who was also, in O'Neill's view, ambitious enough for power to compromise dangerously on the reforms which were essential.

On April 28 O'Neill announced his resignation. 'It is all part of political life', he said later. 'You either succeed or you fail. I failed.'[7] On May 1 the Unionist Parliamentary Party met and elected James Chichester-Clark as its leader by 17 votes to 16. His opponent was Brian Faulkner, who subsequently committed himself to serving in Government if asked.

3

Reaction in the Republic

The fall of O'Neill was an occasion for genuine regret by the majority, though not all, of the Government in the Republic. In a statement, Jack Lynch voiced this feeling, and re-emphasised the urgent need for reforms 'so that fundamental human rights and freedoms may be enjoyed by every citizen in the Six Counties area, discrimination in every form ended, and peace and harmony restored'.

In terms of Fianna Fail's political self-interest the fall of O'Neill and other events in the North remained marginal rather than central, in spite of the deep and growing public concern. Whatever the brave words, the real political obsessions were elsewhere.

In a more personal and circumscribed way, the victimisation which brought O'Neill down struck sympathetic chords among at least some Southern politicians. Jack Lynch's reaction was consistent with his own public policy stance, and the one which had been pursued, with some difficulty by the Government in the South since mid-October, 1968; this was based almost exclusively on maintaining the pressure for reforms and saying nothing that might worsen relations. O'Neill had been genuinely admired, not only by Lynch but also, before him, by Lemass, who, as early as January 1965, had gone to Northern Ireland to meet the premier and to initiate a modest programme of cross-Border co-operation. Apart from the necessary genuflections at party conferences and at the graveside of dead heroes to the idea that 'Ireland unfree would never be at peace', and that partition was the root of all Irish evils, Lemass had set a tone emphasising economic co-operation as a by-product of economic growth and development in the Republic, and had left it at that. Lynch's basic belief was the same. A major worry was that Northern Ireland would upset the economic progress of the 1960s. O'Neill's departure sharpened that concern. But other, and more jaundiced eyes were gazing northward.

Looked at from the South, the Northern Ireland election of February 1969, and the events leading to O'Neill's resignation, had seemed remote for a number of reasons, and the interjection of Neil Blaney's call to Irishmen not to vote for the Union with Britain was typical of the sterile interpretation put on events in the North by some of the very few southern politicians who regarded themselves as informed, and claimed concern. Coming from Donegal, Blaney was given to describing himself, quite accurately, as an Ulsterman and a Northerner, and in due course his stance was to isolate him completely in Irish politics. But he really had few points of contact with the main non-Unionist political drive in Northern Ireland between the late summer of 1968, and the aftermath of the Northern Ireland elections in 1969. The main reason was the very issue on which he, as well as other politicians in the South, felt so passionately: partition.[1] He was representative of a widely held and inherently superficial view that the ending of partition was a political possibility, without actually doing anything about it.

This was at the very heart of the crisis in politics in the Republic of Ireland in 1969. It involved Northern Ireland marginally, rather than centrally. It was really about internal perceptions in the Republic, about traditional beliefs, worn-out political creeds, sterile versions of republicanism, ancient antipathies towards Britain, the undertow of sectarianism, the incompatibility of reform and change with the myths and fears on which so great a part of political life seemed to depend.

Southern politicians were profoundly challenged by what was happening in Northern Ireland, and were found wanting. With a few exceptions, they understood little of what was happening. They failed to recognise what Terence O'Neill was trying to do, or the magnitude of the Unionist Party problems with which he had to contend. They misunderstood Ian Paisley, classing him as a political firebrand, a fundamentalist monster reborn from the seventeenth century.

Neil Blaney was the most vocal 'republican' voice in the Fianna Fail Government; he was also the most directly involved minister, travelling through Northern Ireland on his way to and from his constituency, and in touch with many people in the Northern Ireland nationalist community. Kevin Boland, Minister for Local Government, was committed in terms of ideals and principles derived from a curiously naive view of Fianna Fail and national politics. In other words, he saw events in the North, in 1968 and 1969, as the 'opportunity' for achieving unity. These were the two main public exponents of the alternative, 'hard-line' approach on Northern Ireland. They were also, incidentally, threats to Jack Lynch's leadership, though not overtly so; they believed they 'controlled' him, and were not slow in spreading this belief among journalists and television commentators.

Though Neil Blaney was the most public of Jack Lynch's challengers, and Kevin Boland the most principled, Charles Haughey was undoubtedly the most dangerous, because he was the most powerful. Consistently, since Lynch had replaced Haughey's father-in-law, Sean Lemass, as leader in 1966, Charles Haughey had seen himself as the real man of power in Fianna Fail, and had canvassed and encouraged this view of himself within the party and among friends in the press, radio and television. It was decidedly not a confrontation about republicanism, as it was in the case of both Blaney and Boland, but a confrontation related to dynamic leadership in the sphere of economic and social policy, and the general running of the country. And when it emerged, in May 1970, that Charles Haughey was a closet-republican, the majority of people in the country were amazed. His whole public image had been based on economic and other ministerial skills, and on dynamism as a political leader: good analysis and swift, firm decisions. In a Government which could not be described as a galaxy of stars, he stood out.

To many within the Fianna Fail Party Haughey was seen then as the natural challenger, rather than successor, to Lynch. To a few, including himself, he was the alternative leader already, if not actually the man who wielded real power, by virtue of his key role as Minister in the most powerful department, Finance. He was hard-working, aggressive, decisive. He was privately successful, a wealthy man, with a large estate, who rode to hounds, owned racehorses, was a patron of the arts, and remarkably attractive to, and effective with, the press. Within a given circle he was dismissive of his leader's capabilities, and within the Government itself there were lines of demarcation loosely drawn between a small group of ministers, including Haughey, who were seen to have their hands firmly on the reins of power, and the rest, presided over by the Taoiseach. These ministers were in due course to be at the centre of the arms crisis; but in the second half of 1968, their public image was of a far more mundane kind. Together with Blaney, Charles Haughey was directly involved in the Anglo–Irish Free Trade Area Agreement talks during 1968, and they were seen collectively as handling the major problem areas of the Irish economy. Both, in addition, were regarded as key party organisers, together with Boland, who, as Minister for Local Government, was responsible for the constituencies.

Between them, these three could be said to have a reasonably strong hold over party organisation and essential areas of policy. It was by no means as strong, however, as they themselves believed, nor as strong as was indicated to those closest to them, as well as to certain political commentators. There was therefore a somewhat distorted view of the balance of power within the Fianna Fail and, more important, in the Cabinet of 14 over which Jack Lynch presided. Haughey's own availability to members of the press, cultivated assiduously and with skill, created an impression of dynamic leadership from a small group within the Government, led by himself, and lack of effectiveness elsewhere. The reality was rather different.[2]

Jack Lynch faced his first general election as leader of Fianna Fail in the early months of 1969. Even without the events in Northern Ireland, he had to tread very carefully indeed. The electoral rebuff sustained by Fianna Fail over the proportional representation referendum had been substantial. 'The Third Programme for Economic and Social Development', on which hopes for the economy in 1969 (and, more subtly, for electoral success) had been based, had cut little ice. And the budgetary realities of 1969 were sufficient to create gloom over prices, incomes, and the deficit of £50m on the country's balance of payments. There was widespread industrial unrest, following a very damaging strike of maintenance men. There were tensions between the farmers and the Minister for Agriculture over the less than satisfactory trading terms which were emerging as part of the Anglo–Irish Free Trade Area Agreement. And this tension was worsened by the fact that basic disagreement between Lynch and Blaney over Northern Ireland policy was echoed in disagreement between them over agricultural policy. Lynch had made known publicly his view that the National Farmers' Association, led by T. J. Maher, had the right of consultation, on matters of concern, with the Minister 'at all reasonable times'. Yet repeatedly in early March such meetings, requested by the farmers, were turned down by Blaney.

Almost the only thing that seemed to favour Lynch was the fact that the two Opposition parties were organised neither in policy terms, nor in terms of leadership or personalities; when they should have been harrying the Government in preparation for the contest, they were dealing with internal discord. More seriously, they had no agreed platform *of any kind* as between Labour and Fine Gael; consequently, there was no convincing alternative government on offer.[3]

On Wednesday, May 7, 1969, Charles Haughey introduced what was essentially a 'Social Welfare' Budget, though by far its most memorable feature was the provision of income tax relief on works of artistic or cultural merit for writers, painters, sculptors and composers. On May 21, exactly a fortnight later, the 18th Dail was dissolved by President Eamon de Valera, on Jack Lynch's advice, and a general election fixed for June 18, giving a full, 28-day campaign.

In his dissolution statement Lynch spoke of avoiding a 'protracted period of political uncertainty'. 'An atmosphere of relative calm is happily prevailing in the country', he said, and it was the right occasion 'without undue distraction or diversion' to elect a government for another full term. E.E.C. membership 'as a continuation of economic and social progress', together with the 'steady and firm' leadership of the country by a united party in a period of potential political instability, constituted Lynch's main platform.

If it was Jack Lynch's first general election as leader, the same was true of Liam Cosgrave. The only veteran leader was Brendan Corish, whose electoral assets lay in the new candidates he had attracted to the Labour Party, namely Conor Cruise O'Brien, Noel Browne, David Thornley, Justin Keating and Michael D. Higgins, and whose main electoral handicaps were the two awkward facts of a perhaps too determined Left-wing set of policies, and no coalition arrangement with Fine Gael.

Although the Fianna Fail director of elections was Charles Haughey, and ostensibly the main organisational work was in the hands of Neil Blaney and Kevin Boland, the principal burden of country-wide campaigning was undertaken by Jack Lynch, who became the first Fianna Fail leader to visit every constituency during the course of a general election. A slow start led to a somewhat troubled middle period in the campaign for Fianna Fail, when there were rows and differences in individual constituencies, notably Limerick and Louth, and when the controversial question of Charles Haughey's land deals, while a member of the Government, led him to make a lengthy statement and to give a press conference.[4] To some extent, the dual focus of the campaign seemed to rest on Charles Haughey and Conor Cruise O'Brien; the former symbolised Fianna Fail's image of private enterprise, the attraction of capital, and the steady economic expansion of successive governments; the latter represented the new, radical voices in opposition, demanding greater state intervention on jobs and prices, the extension of social democracy, and the control of building land. Somewhere in between was Fine Gael, a free enterprise party which also wanted a more just society. The O'Brien–Haughey confrontation, made more real by the fact that they were running against each other in the same Dublin constituency, was the subject of immense three-day profiles of each man in the *Irish Times* during the final week of the campaign.

There was a high turnout of voters on June 18. Compared with 1965, the Fianna Fail first preference vote dropped from 47·8 per cent to 45·6 per cent. Fine Gael increased their support marginally from 33·9 to 34·1, and the Labour Party, with its highest number of candidates, 99, saw its vote go up from 15·4 per cent to 17 per cent, its highest share since 1932. It was subsequently to decline steadily, to almost half that figure, in the following ten years.

The re-drawing of constituencies had deprived the opposition parties of the legitimate fruits of their endeavour. The Labour Party's leftward move had damaged its hopes in rural constituencies while helping it in Dublin, and the net outcome was a loss of three seats, down to a total of 18 seats. This was further depleted, almost immediately, by the death of Sean Dunne, on June 25. For Fine Gael, the absence of any proposed deal for a coalition arrangement with Labour handicapped their basically sound 'Just Society' policy stance, and they gained only three seats. Jack Lynch had a comfortable overall majority of five seats. He called it 'a great victory'.

When the 19th Dail met on Wednesday, July 2, 1969, Lynch made no major changes in his Government of 14, one less than the constitutional maximum.[5] No less than four maiden speeches were made straightaway: by Garret FitzGerald, Conor Cruise O'Brien, Justin Keating, and David Thornley. One of the senior ministers, Kevin Boland, defied an instruction from Jack Lynch to shorten his speech, and gave an extensive address, defending his electoral gerrymander. Tempers, and even the procedures of the House, were upset. Lynch himself was one of the few to keep calm; he referred to the need for a man carrying a full jug to 'walk aisy', and then, giving the Labour benches a hard stare, declared that an empty jug had its own dangers. The 'empty jug' was certainly a good deal noisier than the Fine Gael Party, and at that stage was more alarming in its apparent strengths. Yet Jack Lynch was electorally quite secure for a full term in office, and strengthened substantially against any further challenges from within his own party.

The Dail was set to adjourn for the summer recess on July 24. The Republic of Ireland contemplated the contrasts between Northern Ireland and itself with obvious self-congratulation. Whatever economic and social problems there were to be solved, they were of markedly less magnitude than those faced by the Six Counties, and by the British Government in tackling problems which showed no signs of lessening, and which were less likely to be resolved by a Unionist administration led by James Chichester-Clark, who had succeeded O'Neill, without increased pressure from Westminster. In such circumstances Jack Lynch could confidently regard himself as well placed for the future. He had completed the first half of this watershed year in Irish politics on a positive note of political and personal success. He had taken on and defeated all external challenges to his authority within the Republic, and this had strengthened him in facing such internal challenges as might now emerge. They were to be substantially greater than anyone could envisage.

33

4

'The Historic Unity of
Our Country'

A curious peace prevailed during the first six weeks in which
James Chichester-Clark was in charge. In the Republic it tidily
allowed for the general election, in which Northern Ireland was
largely ignored, its civil rights demonstrations temporarily
forgotten. In the North the new premier was given time to settle
in. He was a dull leader. Eton, the Irish Guards, and a comfortable landowning background, epitomised traditional Unionism, with its strong links with the Conservative Party in
Britain, and underlined how much at odds this was with the
lives and prospects of so many of those within the Six Counties
who were marching, on the one hand, but also counter-demon-
strating on the other.

The first test came swiftly enough. The anniversary of the
Battle of the Boyne, July 12, fell on Saturday in 1969. In spite of
the previous year's experiences, Orange organisations were
permitted to march, and rioting broke out in Derry, Dungiven
and Lurgan. On both sides there was shooting, and two people
were wounded by police.

Then the first death, as a result of Northern Ireland civil
rights campaigning, occurred on July 14, 1969, following an
incident in Dungiven. It was an unfortunate by-product rather
than the deliberate result of police brutality. Intermittent sectarian clashes followed in Derry and Belfast. At the beginning
of August there was serious rioting in Belfast. British troops in
the North were on alert. Chichester-Clark held daily Cabinet
meetings. Harold Wilson went on holiday, leaving James
Callaghan, his Home Secretary, to summon the Northern
Ireland premier to talks in London.

Fears now centred on the Apprentice Boys' August 12 March in Derry. Chichester-Clark was afraid to ban it, since, if the ban was defied, there could be a general breakdown of law and order. James Callaghan, and the British Defence Minister, Denis Healey, were relying on the relatively small British Army presence under General Sir Ian Freeland, and the R.U.C., deeply distrusted in Derry, which had already been the scene of some of their worst excesses. But the Army was not deployed.

On the Catholic side the emphasis was on defence of the Bogside in the light of fears, rumours and specific threats of Protestant and R.U.C. 'revenge' or punishment for the events of January and July. The Derry Citizens' Defence Committee had been formed, barricades had already gone up on the morning of Tuesday, August 12, and petrol bombs had been prepared.

What followed, during the rest of that week, in Derry first, in what became known as *The Battle of the Bogside*, and then in Belfast, was the worst period of rioting so far. Savage from the start, it was sustained relentlessly on both sides. By Thursday it had spread elsewhere in Northern Ireland, notably to Armagh and Belfast, and the moving in of the British Army had become inevitable.

For the Government in the Republic, the policy adopted and sustained for almost a year, seemed now irrelevant. Under strong pressure from Charles Haughey, Kevin Boland and Neil Blaney, with support from Brian Lenihan, Sean Flanagan and the new Minister for Defence, James Gibbons, Jack Lynch was persuaded to harden his line on Northern Ireland, and to deliver a television address on August 13, 1969, which included the commitment of the Irish Government, for the first time, to positive action on the North:

> The Irish Government can no longer stand by and see innocent people injured and perhaps worse. It is obvious that the R.U.C. is no longer accepted as an impartial police force. Neither would the employment of British troops be acceptable nor would they be likely to restore peaceful conditions, certainly not in the long term. The Irish Government have, therefore, requested the British Government to apply immediately to the United Nations for the urgent dispatch of

a Peace-Keeping Force to the Six Counties of Northern Ireland and have instructed the Permanent Representative to the United Nations to inform the Secretary General of this request. We have also asked the British Government to see to it that police attacks on the people of Derry should cease immediately.

Very many people have been injured and some of them seriously. We know that many of these do not wish to be treated in Six County hospitals. We have, therefore, directed the Irish Army authorities to have field hospitals established in County Donegal adjacent to Derry and at other points along the Border where they may be necessary.

Recognising, however, that the re-unification of the national territory can provide the only permanent solution for the problem, it is our intention to request the British Government to enter into early negotiations with the Irish Government to review the present constitutional position of the Six Counties of Northern Ireland.

These measures which I have outlined to you seem to the Government to be those most immediately and urgently necessary.

All men and women of goodwill will hope and pray that the present deplorable and distressing situation will not further deteriorate but that it will soon be ended firstly by the granting of full equality of citizenship to every man and woman in the Six Counties area regardless of class, creed or political persuasion and, eventually, by the restoration of the historic unity of our country.

The statement was a composite one, reflecting opposed views within the Government in more or less equal proportions. Reliance on the United Nations was consistent with Ireland's commitment to it, even though Jack Lynch must have known that the proposal would be rejected. Moderates in the Government would have supported, however, this piece of cosmetics, just as they would also have supported the continued emphasis on the need for reform. Stronger meat was demanded by militants, and delivered in the form of the decision to set up field hospitals, and in the request for 'early negotiations' on Northern Ireland's constitutional position, leading 'eventually' (the insertion of which word being typical of Jack Lynch's capacity to soften and ameliorate hard-line sentiments) to unity.

Many wild and exaggerated assertions have been made about that statement, about the atmosphere out of which it was born, the effect it had in Northern Ireland and elsewhere, and its internal impact on the Fianna Fail Government and Party. From it, certainly, and from the Government meeting the previous day, Tuesday, August 12, at which it was redrafted from an earlier statement, derived the arms crisis which was to surface eventually in early May 1970, nine months later, and lead to the Arms Trial in Dublin the following September and October, and the direct and unsuccessful challenge to Jack Lynch by Charles Haughey.

What the television statement did not include were the other Government decisions supposedly made on that day. One was the setting up of a four-man sub-committee of the Government to deal with certain aspects of Northern Ireland affairs. Three Ministers from Border constituencies were on it: Neil Blaney and Joseph Brennan (Donegal) and Padraig Faulkner (Louth); in addition there was Charles Haughey, Minister for Finance, because of his alleged knowledge of, and interest in, Northern Ireland. Neither the Minister for Justice, Micheal O Morain, nor the Minister for Defence, Jim Gibbons, who was new to the Government, were on the sub-committee. It was set up for the purpose of gathering information. It had no other function but to gather facts, and report back. It failed to do this, and became the vehicle for other, less clearly defined functions. Charles Haughey was also given, or assumed, direct control over a relief fund for Northern Ireland. It was also decided that the Government would undertake an international propaganda campaign.

Taken at face value, almost all these decisions were faulty. The sub-committee neither worked properly, nor reported back to the whole Government. It repeatedly allowed outside information to be passed to individuals within the Government who did not then pass it on. It gave authority to a theoretical decision-making process which was unconstitutional. The decisions distanced Jack Lynch from the factions within his Government. They relieved those who wanted relief from direct involvement in the Northern Ireland question, and they gave a self-asserted *carte blanche* to those who did want such involvement. That Government meeting set in train a whole sequence of astonishing errors and misjudgments It almost immediately provoked Kevin Boland to resign, but he reversed his decision the next day without the fact becoming public knowledge. It led to four political careers being partially or completely blighted. It provoked a most serious political crisis. And, of the multitude of questions which were subsequently raised, many still remain unanswered, and indeed never will be answered.

Cause and effect are curious factors in politics, however. Given one interpretation of that Government meeting, then Jack Lynch could be said to have lost control and not regained it properly until the autumn of 1970, after a major, unwelcome and damaging confrontation. Yet regain it he did, and in the process eliminated or neutralised all those who challenged his authority within Fianna Fail. He began the process of rebuilding the party's image. He brought about fundamental changes in public perceptions about unity and Northern Ireland. He went out of power, and yet retained the leadership. And he came back with the biggest majority in any Irish election.

To say that all, or any of this, sprang directly from foresight or judgments made at that fateful Government meeting is to suggest a visionary quality to Lynch's leadership that is difficult to prove. Nevertheless, of the many possible interpretations of the events between August 13, 1969 and May 1970, one at least must be based on the essential *quietism*, or passivity of mind, which is at the heart of Jack Lynch's political character. He recognised, during 1968 and 1969, the irredeemable elements of republicanism within his own party and Government, and when the circumstances so dictated, he allowed that faction to have its head. The men concerned, principally Haughey, Blaney and Boland, favoured, and helped to produce, a discreditable alternative policy which fortunately spent itself in indecision, suspicion and ineptitude at times edging towards outright chaos. By late April, 1970, some attempt was made by Jack Lynch to hold the whole crumbling edifice of Fianna Fail unity together. Unfortunately for him this was made impossible by Liam Cosgrave's knowledge of what was going on, and the humiliating crisis for Ireland of 1970 followed. Northern Ireland, and certain individuals representative of republican ideals, misguided but sincere, were the victims of politicians whose republicanism was aimed at a Republic of Ireland audience rather than at Northern Ireland. The real survivor was Jack Lynch himself. What can never be measured is the extent to which he foresaw himself rescuing more than survival out of the extraordinary events which grew out of the August 13, 1969, Government meeting.

Lynch's opponents would be united in rejecting this view in favour of the interpretation already suggested: that control within the Government passed out of Jack Lynch's hands. Yet they would then disagree about whose hands it passed into, just as they would also be at loggerheads over their views on what should be done, how it should be done, and why. Though publicly, when the crisis within the Government eventually came out into the open, they and others with similar views seemed to hold together, it was an apparent rather than an actual unity. The most they were united on was their disdain for Jack Lynch. They sought a hard-line, militant approach. They did not know what this meant, how it could be implemented, or where it would lead; but the sacred objectives of the Fianna Fail Party, if they were to be honoured, needed something more than pressure for reform, and against the backdrop of the riots in Derry and Belfast, in August 1969, it was possible for the old republican war cries about unity and the ending of partition to come strongly to the surface. After that relatively elementary point of accord, the three central hardline figures fell apart.

Neil Blaney was an outspoken republican of traditional views. He wanted the British out of Ireland, partition ended, and a single government in Dublin. He was most closely in touch with Northern groups, and was responsible for alerting the Department of Foreign Affairs and Government colleagues about first-hand reports from Derry which he received on the night of August 12. He was the most positive in identifying the practical demand for arms from elements within the minority community in Northern Ireland, both in Derry, and later in Belfast. He was genuinely and practically concerned about the plight of the North's Catholics, and consequently sympathetic to all those who, in his judgment, gave them *real* help, including the I.R.A. There was no clear or profound agreement between himself and Haughey on the North. More than ten years later, in Blaney's eyes, Haughey was still a compromiser.

Charles Haughey was in a permanent state of ambivalence, which was greatly aggravated by the secrecy he himself imposed over his own views, whatever the subject, but particularly about events in Northern Ireland. Indeed, the most outstanding fact to emerge about him during the course of the Arms Trials, which brought some of his attitudes into the open, was that, like the three wise monkeys rolled into one, he pleaded that he heard, saw and spoke no evil. He either denied knowledge, or denied comprehension, of most of what was going on around him, and in which he was directly involved; he passed on nothing to Government colleagues of what was told him as a member of the Government sub-committee about developments in Northern Ireland, and this even included other members of that sub-committee; he was similarly secretive in his dealings with people who were far more vulnerable, in many different ways, including being at risk physically and professionally in what they did. Not until 1980 did there emerge any picture of what Charles Haughey believed a Northern Ireland policy might be.

Boland played a different role and one that is not without honour. To some extent he demonstrates that, if the men in the Government who supported Jack Lynch were somewhat muddled and indecisive on Fianna Fail principles and policies toward Northern Ireland, those who were opposed to him, including Boland himself, were equally at odds in belief and motivation. Boland took a broadly historical view, based on principle. In his judgment there had been, within Fianna Fail, very substantial changes dividing the party in the ten years since Eamon de Valera had moved from its leadership to the presidential residence in Phoenix Park. A new generation, concerned with the country's economic progress, had been brought in under Sean Lemass. A new, pragmatic view of what power was for, in some cases a view of *whom* power was for, had prevailed, and was associated with a younger group of Government ministers who had never known Opposition.

Boland writes:

> After he [de Valera] became President for the first time there was something of an influx into Fianna Fail of people whose nature and tradition it was to be on the winning side, but who could not bring themselves to make the move while the hate figure was still there. Some of these had a kind of external association through the 'economic' ministers for a number of years. They moved in now, mainly through associate bodies...and some came via the fund-raising committees that preceded Taca.[1]

40

Boland was giving expression to the inherent dichotomy within Fianna Fail, which vacillated between the traditional republicanism of de Valera, based on an unreal dream of a Gaelic-speaking united Ireland, and the economic pragmatism of Lemass which had replaced dream with the reality of turning Ireland into a modern, competitive industrialised State.

In the end, isolated after his fashion and from his own lofty interpretation of ideology, Boland came to despise them all. He was close to total disillusionment at the time of the August 13, 1969, Government meeting. By then he had witnessed in Fianna Fail: the shift to a more capitalist, free enterprise and free trade economic stance; the abandonment of the 'pure' republicanism of Articles 2 and 3 of the Constitution;[2] a growing tolerance of corruption, deriving from the loss of idealism which Boland associated with de Valera; and the concern for power purely for its own sake.

Kevin Boland resigned verbally, at a Government meeting on Friday, August 15, and then left. He collected his personal belongings from the Custom House and went home. Blaney and Haughey tried to persuade him to change his mind. They engaged the assistance of a former Government Minister, Sean McEntee. All failed. Then the President contacted Boland and called him to a meeting. He explained that a constitutional crisis might be caused by Boland's resignation at that time, and that a Fine Gael Government would probably come to power. De Valera, according to Boland,[3] saw this as 'serious', while Boland himself saw it more specifically and more characteristically as 'a serious reverse for the national position'. He did have the good grace to add, however: 'In this I was wrong. A Fine Gael Government would probably have been as bad but it certainly couldn't have been worse.'[4] Boland reversed his decision, and undertook to attend the next Government meeting when it was called. He would do this to avoid the crisis outlined by de Valera, but would take no further part in Northern Ireland affairs.

The Irish people were almost totally unaware of what was going on in government at this time. Boland had preserved outward unity. Haughey's views were kept to himself. Other ministers were prepared to go along with events and any general consensus that emerged. Only Neil Blaney had any public profile as a 'rebel', and in the eyes of most people the degree to which he was at odds with his colleagues was not substantial.

5

The Blaney Factor

The events to which the Government in Dublin addressed itself during the nine months which followed the Derry and Belfast rioting were almost exclusively external: in other words, the objectives identified by Boland as central to Lynch's policy in fact prevailed — 'to preserve what we have down here and to restore normality up there'. The restoration of normality 'up there' was also the common objective of the vast majority of Catholics and Protestants in Northern Ireland, and of the British Government and people. It still is.

Security in Northern Ireland, following the week of rioting, was transferred to the British Army, under General Sir Ian Freeland. The R.U.C., and the B Specials, who were withdrawn from the cities, came under his control. The idea of a United Nations force was firmly rejected. Cathal Goulding, who was then Chief of Staff of the I.R.A., issued a statement on August 18 saying that the organisation was putting its men on full alert, and had already sent units into Northern Ireland. It warned British soldiers not to prejudice nationalists' defences against the R.U.C. or B Specials. This intervention by the I.R.A. was regretted by civil rights organisations, and Jack Lynch came out strongly against the I.R.A. usurping the authority of the Government 'freely elected by the people'. The U.N. Security Council postponed consideration of the Republic of Ireland's request for a peace-keeping force. While publicly the Government in Dublin declared against the deployment of British troops, it privately saw them as preferable to the R.U.C. and B Specials in sensitive areas.

The British Government issued on August 19, a 7-point Declaration re-affirming that Northern Ireland was a matter of 'domestic jurisdiction', and that 'the Border is not an issue'. The first paragraph of the Declaration re-affirmed the provisions of the Ireland Act of 1949, that Northern Ireland would remain part of the United Kingdom. The basic message was that reforms would continue and the troops be withdrawn only when law and order were restored.[1]

On August 21 the Government in Dublin issued a statement in reply to this, emphasising that the constitutional position of Northern Ireland had been changed by the transfer of responsibility for security from Stormont to Westminster. Its tone was similar to the statement which followed the August 13 Government meeting; only now the objectives were more political. In addition to asserting that the constitutional position had altered, it also repeated support for the United Nations peace-keeping approach to the North. But its real sting came at the end, in a direct challenge to the British claim that Northern Ireland was a 'domestic jurisdiction' matter:

> Finally, no Irish Government can, and never will [sic], accept the assertion... The Irish Government does not concede in any way, and never will, Britain's right to exercise jurisdiction over any part of Irish territory. As the Minister for External Affairs told the Security Council yesterday — the claim of the Irish nation to control the totality of Ireland has been asserted over centuries by successive generations of Irish men and women and it is one which will never be renounced.

These revolutionary echoes, and warlike tones, were wildly at odds with the realities behind the tense situation in Northern Ireland, and with the now swift and reasonably sensitive moves being made, including the important Hunt inquiry[2] into the R.U.C., which was to be followed shortly by the setting up of the Scarman Tribunal.[3] The Dublin statement can be regarded, perhaps cynically, as a political gamble. If, in the light of the rioting, things continued to go from bad to worse, then it represented the right militant stance in the event of a civil war in which many from the Republic would have been prepared to take part. Mercifully, events moved in the opposite direction, and for many the words quoted above were best forgotten.

More prudent, but still some way from his earlier stance, was Jack Lynch's statement of August 28, which was provoked by Britain's refusal to accept the Border as an issue:

> The Government reiterates its conviction that the unnatural and unjustifiable partition of Ireland is basic to the present unrest in the Six Counties and that no long-term, much less a permanent, solution can be contemplated without having full regard to its existence.
>
> The Government agrees that the Border cannot be changed by force; it is, and has been, its policy to seek the re-unification of the country by peaceful means.
>
> I am glad that the British Home Secretary has come to Ireland to see and hear for himself. It is of vital importance that present tensions be eased and solutions of the immediate problems be found.
>
> For one thing, the minority in the North cannot be expected to live with a police force which they distrust and even fear: therefore, no one will disagree with Mr Callaghan's contention that a police force that is respected and accepted is an essential element of a democratic society.
>
> Even if the Six County police force is to be re-organised and even if there is to be a marked acceleration in the pace of reforms, these would be interim solutions only.
>
> Nothing must be left undone to avoid a recurrence of the present troubles, whether in five or fifty years, but to continue to ignore the need for fundamental constitutional change, so clearly necessary, could only have such a tragic result.
>
> The time has come when everybody concerned must face up to the urgent necessity of finding an acceptable long-term solution. Already the presence of British troops and the placing of the existing police forces under the command of the British G.O.C. have wrought a fundamental change in the constitutional status of the Six Counties.
>
> There can be no return to the *status quo*. Distrust and fear must be banished and the barriers of suspicion and prejudice must be removed. That this is possible is illustrated by the fact that people of all religions can live as equals in peace and friendship with each other in this part of the country and that

the religious minority have no fears whatsoever of any discrimination against them.

I know that the ultimate solution that we seek will not easily or expeditiously come about but the Irish Government is prepared to explore every reasonable prospect. A solution along federal lines has been more than once suggested. My Government is ready and willing to discuss this possibility with the British Government. If this could be achieved only through intermediate stages — and such possibilities could well emerge in the course of objective examination and constructive discussion of the overall problem — we would be more than anxious to pursue them.

I recognise that there are social and economic problems involved as well but my Government does not regard these as insurmountable. We want to see all Irishmen living in peace and harmony together as one community and as one nation.

As in previous statements, Jack Lynch was concerned to represent two broad views of the Northern Ireland situation, the one favouring non-involvement, the other seeing all its ancient republican ideals being challenged by reality, and wishing to take some kind of action, no matter how foolhardy. Lip-service needed to be paid to this latter view, in the circumstances; but there was no doubt, then or later, about Lynch's own position, and his determination to keep the Republic of Ireland clear of any direct intervention. This is reflected obviously enough in the statement itself: the most hawkish demands are concerned with issues internal to the North — police reorganisation, reforms, and the irreversible nature of the change achieved by putting security under the British Army; more neutral is the tone of definition, about the Border and longer-term solutions; and when it comes to the potential actions by the Republic the mood shifts into the *subjunctive*.

Just as with Jack Lynch's essential political *quietism*, this use of contingent, hypothetical and prospective language is a fundamental aspect of his political character. In this instance it was a positive way of presenting a negative position: implicitly, he was indicating just how little had been done in the past to justify talk of unity, co-operation, and the two parts of Ireland joining together in an effort to solve the crisis; furthermore, it was clear to everyone that, with barricades up in the streets of Derry and Belfast, and with nightly rioting in different parts of Northern Ireland, it was hardly the time to open discussions with Britain about the process of constitutional change in the status of the Six Counties which Lynch was saying could not now be reversed. Nevertheless, it was politically necessary to *say* these things, just as it was politically necessary to *do* as little as possible.

Events came rapidly to a head during the ensuing weeks, not in favour of the 'Doomsday' situation predicted by the hardline element in Jack Lynch's Government, but in the opposite direction. James Callaghan, the British Home Secretary took a firm line on reforms and on law and order. An inquiry into the use of C.S. gas in Derry was set up, and the Cameron Committee's report, published on September 12, 1969, came out firmly with criticisms of the Stormont Government and of the R.U.C.[4] Agreement was reached on dismantling the barricades, first in Belfast and then in Derry. At the United Nations the Irish attempt to obtain a Security Council discussion leading to a peace-keeping force for the North was deferred and then dropped. This was followed by the proposal to hold a referendum on Article 44 in the Republic's Constitution, which recognised the 'special position' of the Catholic Church. There was a positive response from Stormont. Violence had given way to discussion again. This was emphasised by the continued success of Stormont–Westminster talks, leading to the acceptance by the Northern Ireland Government of the Hunt Report recommendations in early October.

But the language used remained somewhat ambiguous in the South. A key speech was delivered in Tralee on Saturday, September 20, 1969, by Jack Lynch in which he presented an outline of policy based on an aspiration for a united Ireland, but by peaceful means and in agreement.

> The unity we seek is not something forced but a free and genuine union of those living in Ireland based on mutual respect and tolerance and guaranteed by a form or forms of government authority in Ireland providing for progressive improvement of social, economic and cultural life in a just and peaceful environment.

Of its nature this policy — of seeking unity through agreement in Ireland between Irishmen — is a long-term one. It is no less, indeed it is even more, patriotic for that. Perseverance in winning the respect and confidence of those now opposed to unity must be sustained by goodwill, patience, understanding and, at times forbearance...

Every responsible person must hope that early and adequate reforms will bring peace and security to the people of the North of Ireland so that they may live together in neighbourliness without fear, sharing fairly in improving social and economic conditions, and with fading memories of past dissensions.

It will remain our most earnest aim and hope to win the consent of the majority of the people in the Six Counties to means by which North and South can come together in a re-united and sovereign Ireland earning international respect both for the fairness and efficiency with which it is administered and for its contribution to world peace and progress.

In part, at least, the Tralee speech was in response to one given the previous night in Dublin by Kevin Boland, Minister for Local Government, in which he had attacked forcefully the British Government and its claim that the Border was not an issue. The wrongs of history were trenchantly examined in this widely reported outburst:

If there is any desire to give justice to Ireland even at this late stage it must be obvious that it is time to agree to work towards the other and the only possible permanent solution — that is an eventual British withdrawal and a local government for an agreed area in an all-Ireland state or federation.

In their essential details these speeches represented the two elements so vigorously and bitterly polarising within Fianna Fail, and undermining the middle-ground.

Already, Kevin Boland, following his 24-hour resignation a month earlier, had given up putting forward his views in Government: 'I made a mental resolution that for the remainder of my time in the Government, I would speak no word about the Six County situation at Government meetings . . . I admit, however, that I often helped (or endeavoured to help) Blaney out with scribbled notes.' This did not, however, preclude Boland from public utterances such as the speech quoted above, although he believed, as a Government Minister, that he had to be 'ambiguous'. He felt quite strongly that a minority within the Government should not 'try to manipulate decisions so that factual policy would be contrary to the Taoiseach's wishes'.[5]

It is clear that, while Boland was certainly concerned to press hard, publicly, what he called the 'Republican approach', he was far from being party to the more vigorous efforts at manipulating decisions in order to change policy within the Government. Only Neil Blaney came out as publicly as Boland had done, when he made his controversial speech in Letterkenny on Monday, December 8, 1969. The occasion was the celebration of 21 years as a Dail deputy. Together with his father, whose death had caused the by-election which brought him into the Dail, the family had represented Fianna Fail interest in democratic politics for Donegal since the party first entered Leinster House in 1927. Blaney said:

> The Fianna Fail Party has never taken a decision to rule out the use of force if the circumstances in the Six Counties so demand. The situation last August in Derry and Belfast was such that, had the violence continued, the question of the use of force in defence of our own people under attack would have had to be urgently considered. If a situation were to arise in the Six Counties in which the people who do not subscribe to the Unionist regime were under sustained and murderous assault, then, as the Taoiseach said on August 13, we 'cannot stand idly by'.

The fault, he claimed, lay in partition, from which the violence derived. The 'grave responsibility' for that lay with Westminster, who were in error if they were relying on 'a rag-bag of reforms' to cover over the real problem. In doing this they were sowing the seeds of 'further violence and bloodshed for innocent people'.

Blaney used the phrase 'our people' throughout his speech to mean the Catholic minority in the North. Equally consistently he attacked the Unionist 'regime', 'junta', 'sham Government', 'sectarian extremists', 'set-up that stinks in the nostrils of all decent men', and invoked 'our past generations', 'our patriot dead and the future generations'.

It was the stuff of which dreams had been made in Ireland throughout its unhappy history. But it was the reference to force, and its possible use in the future, as well as its implicit consideration in the past, that caused acute embarrassment on both sides of the Border. Lest anyone should be in doubt, Neil Blaney was specific about the context of his remarks. Before the key sentences about Fianna Fail never having ruled out force, he cited the statement by Jack Lynch on the resumption of the Dail, on October 22, when the Taoiseach had said: 'The Government in this part of Ireland has no intention of mounting an armed invasion of the Six Counties.'

Jack Lynch's response the following day, was to reiterate more forcefully the 'peaceful means' by which unity would eventually be achieved, and cited his own various statements and speeches. Referring to Blaney's speech he said that while 'Mr Blaney's feelings on the partition issue are very deeply felt, and he occasionally finds it difficult not to give public expression to them, he knows and endorses Government policy.'

In Northern Ireland John Hume condemned Blaney's speech as 'totally irresponsible' and negative, offering no solution. 'It ill becomes Mr Blaney to be divisive.' Conor Cruise O'Brien, who was by then the Labour Party's most effective Northern Ireland spokesman, said that the continued presence of Blaney as a member of the Government completely destroyed the credibility of Jack Lynch's Tralee speech. What had been said at Letterkenny was 'the most irresponsible and demagogic statement made in recent times in this island with the sole exception of those by Mr Paisley.'

Yet still Jack Lynch waited. To use a phrase made famous in Ireland on a much later occasion, he was content to 'let the hare sit'. Truth to tell, there was more than one hare. The party faced its annual conference, the Ard Fheis, in January 1970. Whether the temperature was rising, as Neil Blaney clearly believed, or falling, as Jack Lynch more prudently sought, had to be ascertained.

As 1969 drew to a close, however, circumstances strongly

favoured Lynch rather than Blaney. Though not altogether easy to admit, the sombre truth was that the impotence of Irish republicanism in the face of economic and political reality had been clearly demonstrated. Lynch had recognised this, and acted accordingly; Blaney, Boland and others had tried to resurrect a form of 'Republicanism' which had laid for itself no foundations in reality, save in the reality of violence.

Virtually every policy initiative by the Dublin Government had failed. Its attempt to involve the United Nations had been dropped, under British pressure; its first aid stations along the Border at the times of worst crisis had remained virtually empty; its refugee camps had sheltered women and children from Belfast and Derry 'in hundreds' for a time, but they had returned soon enough to their homes; army activity had been fairly futile; army recruitment and the mobilising of the 'F.C.A.', an army reserve force, had provoked a good deal of interest, but had seemed mainly to be related to potential unrest within the Republic, activated by such events as the Ulster Volunteer Force's explosives attack on Wolfe Tone's grave, than to further unrest in Northern Ireland, which was increasingly under British Army control; finally, the propaganda campaign, which had involved withdrawing a number of public relations officers from State enterprises and sending them out to Irish diplomatic missions abroad to explain Irish policy, had proved to be of limited value.

The first important political event of 1970 was the party conference on January 17. Here the implications of Neil Blaney's speech in Letterkenny, together with Kevin Boland's earlier speech in Dublin, were examined by the Fianna Fail delegates. The trouble was that the traditional republicanism of the party was an inescapably prominent characteristic of the annual Ard Fheis, and delegates, therefore, provided no test at all of how serious republicanism was as a factor in Government policy.

Boland found this to his cost when, in his speech as one of the party's honorary secretaries, he 'paraphrased' Blaney's Letterkenny speech. To his amazement, the political correspondents' 'unanimous assessment was that I had deliberately and with considerable skill set out to defuse the situation of what they called "naked republicanism" engendered by the debate, and that I had done this in defence of the Taoiseach against a pro-

Blaney flood tide. They couldn't have been more wrong. I didn't set out to defuse the situation and my speech did not defuse it.' It did not ignite it, either; his use of a phrase about not conceding 'any legitimate British interest in any part of our country' passed over the heads of delegates, somewhat to Boland's own surprise. He was applauded for his speech; but Lynch was applauded even more. The delegates went home happy in the knowledge that the traditional but ill-defined republicanism which was the lifeblood of the Fianna Fail Party was still somehow safe in the hands of the equally ill-defined leadership of the party.

Lynch's speech to that January 1970 Ard Fheis, which, according to Boland, who was beside him, he amended heavily during the course of Boland's own completely misunderstood attack on Lynch, was a masterly piece of political rhetoric, paying heavy attention to partition, 'a deep, throbbing weal across the land, heart and soul of Ireland', while at the same time raising peace, goodwill, amity, persuasion, integration, to pride of place in dealing with Northern Ireland.

Lynch emphasised that the wishes of two-thirds of the population of Northern Ireland had to be respected; that the Republic did not have the capacity or desire to impose any solution; and that what he sought, and the way he sought it, shared common ground with Eamon de Valera and others, and, he indicated, also with the platform behind him.

Two critical challenges were contained in the interpolations which he had added to his prepared speech. 'We may feel with our hearts, but we must think with our heads, and when the heart rules the head the voice of wisdom goes unheard.' But used more directly as a challenge was the second: 'If anyone wants to change the policy that I have set out, this is the place to do it, and now is the time. If Fianna Fail want this traditional Fianna Fail policy to be pursued by me as leader of the Government and the party, now is the time to say it.'

It was, of course, not the time, or the place, to change policy; certainly not the time to oppose; but it was abundantly right, as an occasion, to get the traditional approach endorsed. And endorsed it was. Hugely. Neil Blaney stared up studiously at the proscenium. A group of delegates sat still during the standing ovation, and failed to applaud. But they were in a very small minority. Lynch had convincingly won a critical battle, establishing himself and his policies and strengthening himself for probable further trouble in the North during 1970.

It was far from being the end of the story. But in terms of the differences between Blaney and Lynch, the Saturday afternoon of that Ard Fheis was critical. It was a watershed based on policy that was to dictate events for the next ten years for Fianna Fail and for Jack Lynch.

6

'We Asked for Guns'

That most interesting of political questions, about what is *really* going on beneath the surface was never more appropriate than in the Irish Republic between August 13, 1969, and May 7, 1970. While the strange whiffs of discord within the Government were being given off by Boland and Blaney, as well as a host of lesser men who attested to tensions and arguments down through the party, a drama was being played out which would end in the sensational charges of conspiracy against two Government Ministers, and others, and the trial of one of these Government Ministers in the autumn of 1970.

Blaney was a central figure from the start. It was to him, because of his position, that many unofficial reports from Northern Ireland came in, following the riots. Specifically, it was to Blaney that Captain James Kelly, the Irish Army Intelligence Officer who was one of those accused of conspiracy, reported first on his own return to the Republic from Northern Ireland on September 14, 1969.

When I came back from Northern Ireland on the 14th of September or around that date, it came to my notice that a committee in the Government had been appointed, named to me as — rightly or wrongly, I don't know — but named to me as Mr Haughey, Mr Blaney, Mr Faulkner and Mr Brennan. And, in view of the information I had obtained, I decided that I should see some of these members of the Government, and I made arrangements to see Mr Blaney on a particular evening after my return. I went and did so, and told him the result of all the information I had gleaned in Northern Ireland. And, in effect, he was able to assist me also. I then went to see Mr Haughey ... So to say I was a liaison officer — it was a liaison officer on an *ad hoc* basis.[1]

This very peculiar situation, where 'it had come to' Captain James Kelly's notice that there was a Government sub-committee, and where he had 'made arrangements' to see one member, and then a second, represents the start of a process aimed at arming members of the Northern Ireland minority from the South. Captain Kelly should have liaised with neither of these men. His direct political superior, to whom he was answerable for all his actions as an intelligence officer, was Jim Gibbons, Minister for Defence. His self-appointed role as liaison officer to a Government sub-committee which did not meet was part of the process by which intended aid to the North broke down and deteriorated into something far more questionable.

James Kelly's main contact in Northern Ireland was John Kelly, no relation, the main organiser of the citizens' defence committees throughout the Six Counties, and a 'traditional republican'; in other words, a Belfast Catholic, educated by the Christian Brothers, apprenticed in marine engineering, and then active in the I.R.A. campaign in 1956. In 1957 he was arrested and charged with possession of arms and ammunition. He refused to recognise the court, and was sentenced to eight years in prison. He attempted to escape, lost remission, served six years and was released in 1963. He married in 1965, and his wife had a child in 1967. His involvement in citizens' defence began in August, 1969, in Belfast.

All of this he stated, not without pride, in court on Wednesday, October 14, 1970. It was evidence, enough and to spare, of the relationship between the defence committees and the militant republican tradition. As far as John Kelly was concerned the militant line in Northern Ireland was the correct one; arms had to be obtained for the defence of the minority communities, and the only source for such arms could be the South. Captain James Kelly, as a potential or actual liaison figure with the Southern Government, was an ideal link. He had already been approached by other representatives of the minority community in the North,[2] and had also received instructions from his superior, Colonel Michael Hefferon, Director of Irish Army

Intelligence, to develop further his Belfast and Derry contacts, when he met John Kelly on the evening of Saturday, September 13. 'In a calm and logical way he (John Kelly) explained the seriousness of the situation which he and the other minority representatives wanted to communicate to the Dublin Government — a government to whom he and the others felt they were entitled to look for assistance.'[3]

The kind of assistance being sought was specific:

I want to be very emphatic that we were coming from all parts of the Six Counties not to indulge in tea-parties, not to be entertained, but to elicit, in so far as we could, what was the opinion of this Government in relation to the Six Counties. We did not ask for blankets or feeding bottles, we asked for guns. And no one, from Taoiseach Lynch down, refused us that request or told us this was contrary to Government policy.[4]

As far as John Kelly was concerned, his involvement in North–South relations, and his involvement with Captain James Kelly, whom he believed from the start was an Irish Government liaison officer, had one purpose: to obtain arms.

On Saturday, October 4, 1969, John Kelly, together with other leaders of citizens' defence committees in Northern Ireland, came South of the Border to Bailieboro, in County Cavan, to meet Captain James Kelly, whose home town it was. Subsequently, the Head of Army Intelligence, Colonel Hefferon, was informed of details of the meeting, and he, in turn, told Jim Gibbons, his own Minister for Defence, 'about the meeting and what went on about the middle or more towards the end of October'.

On the day of the meeting two members of the Irish Special Branch, one of them its head, Chief Superintendent John Fleming, visited the Secretary of the Department of Justice, Peter Berry, in Mount Carmel private hospital in Dublin, where he was undergoing tests, to tell him of the Bailieboro meeting. The information which they gave to Berry suggested that 'subversive elements' from Northern Ireland, meaning members, past or present, of the then I.R.A. — this was before the split into 'Officials' and 'Provisionals' — were taking part in the meeting, and that Captain Kelly had been in touch with the Chief of

Staff of the I.R.A., Cathal Goulding. Peter Berry, whose over-riding interest was State Security, was already aware from earlier reports that Captain Kelly had given undertakings about money and arms to people from Northern Ireland who fell into the 'subversive' category.

Berry tried to contact his own Minister, Micheal O Morain, without success; then the Taoiseach, again without success; finally he did make contact, by telephone, that afternoon, with a former Justice Minister, Charles Haughey. Haughey visited Berry in the nursing home and was told about the Bailieboro meeting. Berry was asked about sources, indeed pressed for details, and gave some information. What Berry was not told in return, and was subsequently 'dismayed to learn',[5] was that Haughey had met James Kelly and Colonel Hefferon, the previous Thursday, October 2, at his home in Kinsealy, north of Dublin, had discussed there the Bailieboro meeting, and had arranged for £500 to be paid to Captain Kelly to cover the expenses of the meeting and for any subsequent payments connected with it. Colonel Hefferon was emphatic about this £500; Haughey denied any recollection of making this pro-vision for expenses.

On October 16, Superintendent Fleming visited Berry again, and gave him a full report of the Bailieboro meeting. Berry immediately contacted the Taoiseach who arranged to visit him the following morning. The meeting was handicapped by the fact that Berry was undergoing complicated medical tests. There were frequent interruptions by a nurse, and Lynch cut short the meeting. Nevertheless, Berry had given him an out-line of what was going on. How much Lynch was able to absorb of this disjointed information from a man who was known to be obsessed about security, was subsequently a matter for dispute. In effect, the Taoiseach told him that if anything illegal was happening the culprits were to be apprehended; Berry replied that this would expose secret Special Branch sources within the I.R.A. Subsequently, Lynch appears to have spoken of this additional information with Gibbons, the Minister for Defence, who had received a more formal report from Colonel Hefferon.

Captain James Kelly later asserted: 'What was of con-sequence was that in November 1969 the Taoiseach and his Minister for Defence were aware of a meeting which was the genesis of the later attempted importation of arms.'[6] While this itself is of limited significance, it is important that James Kelly in his book does *not* say anything about his, and Colonel Hefferon's visit to Abbeville, Haughey's home, two days before the Bailieboro meeting, in order to discuss it and the money for expenses. For £500 was a very large amount. The actual meeting, which involved overnight accommodation for the Northern Ireland citizens' defence committee delegates, cost a total of £35.

The £500, however, was a small sum compared with the £100,000 which was decided on by Haughey, following the Government decision of August 16, 1969, that 'a sum of money — the amount and the channel of the disbursement of which would be determined by the Minister for Finance — should be made available from the Exchequer to provide aid for the victims of the current unrest in the Six Counties.' This decision emerged the same day, though the amount involved was not mentioned. This remained uncertain, being paid out of a Department of Finance 'Suspense Account' in different amounts as required, and was only rounded out to the overall total by a Dail vote on March 18, 1970. In spite of an extensive Public Accounts Committee investigation which began in January, 1971, the details of what happened to the whole of the £100,000 have never been satisfactorily cleared up.

Initial payments went to citizens' defence committee representatives and were then paid in small amounts to men manning barricades and doing other defence work on behalf of the minority community in Belfast, Derry, and other locations. It relieved distress. Subsequently, it was channelled into I.R.A. hands, and could be said to have caused distress. Later still, substantial amounts were actually paid out for arms, Captain James Kelly stating that £32,500 went for arms purchase in Germany, £850 on a trip to the United States for the same purpose, and £1,600 on an abortive arms purchase in England.

The attempted arms purchases went on between the October meeting in Bailieboro and the spring of 1970. They involved Captain James Kelly and John Kelly throughout.

The early attempts to buy and import arms were illegal, and failed only through ineptitude. Neil Blaney, who was kept informed about them by Captain James Kelly, eventually took charge, and decided that the importations would be 'legal'; that is, he decided on a Department of Finance sanction for customs

clearance.[7] The arms were bought in Germany, the money paid
over in various amounts by John Kelly and Captain James
Kelly from the bank account funded out of the Government's
'aid for the victims of the current unrest in the Six Counties'. A
total of approximately £28,000 was paid to the German (Hamburg) arms dealer, Otto Schleuter. The attempt to bring the
cargo into Dublin on board the *City of Dublin* on March 25,
1970, was frustrated when Belgian customs officials stopped
the export because there was no licence. If the Hamburg consignment had arrived safely on the *City of Dublin*, it would have
been seized by members of the Provisional I.R.A.,[8] conveyed to
a convent outside Dublin, and then sent into Northern Ireland
in smaller consignments. Whether or not Captain James Kelly
knew this, as he waited in vain for the arms on the Wednesday
morning at Alexander Quay, the man with him, John Kelly,
did know. Differences of opinion between James Kelly, John
Kelly, and others, would undoubtedly have emerged, on the
quayside there and then, had the arms come into the country.
They did not, and once again there was a breathing space.

7

Arms and the Men

The attempted importation of arms in the early months of 1970 provoked the most serious political crisis of modern times in Ireland. Apart from the fact of charges for conspiracy and the dismissals of ministers, the repercussions of the events of 1970 permanently scarred Fianna Fail, and remain central to the party now. Given the political strength of the party, this means central to the country as well.

How much did Jack Lynch know of what was going on between the autumn of 1969 and May 1970? Allowing for the many permutations which could be offered, there are three broad interpretations of the facts. The first and most obvious is the 'official' version, that basically the head of the Government did not know what was going on until he was notified by the various sources which presented evidence in the trial, or before the Dail Committee set up to investigate the use of the £100,000, or in Dail debates. In other words, Jack Lynch first learned of the attempt to import arms in late April 1970.

The substantive outline of this version is as given by Jack Lynch to the Dail late on the night of Wednesday, May 6, 1970. According to his brief statement, the Taoiseach was informed on Monday, April 20 and Tuesday, April 21, by the security forces, of an attempt to import arms and of the involvement of two ministers. He told the Dail that he intended to interview both ministers the following day, Wednesday, April 22. But this was Budget Day, and one of the ministers, Charles Haughey, was responsible for presenting the Budget. To complicate matters further, Haughey had had an accident on the

Tuesday night, and was in hospital with severe enough concussion to prevent any interview until a week later. On Wednesday, April 29, Jack Lynch summoned Neil Blaney and requested his resignation, then went to the hospital to see Haughey and request his resignation. They asked for time to consider. The second request for resignation was made in the early hours of Wednesday, May 6. It provoked refusals in both cases, and Jack Lynch then applied to the President under Article 28.9.4., to dismiss the two men. The invoking of the constitutional provision for dismissal, and the involvement of President de Valera, followed later the same day. Still later that evening Lynch announced that Kevin Boland had resigned.

Two different versions were offered of the reasons for the dramatic departure of three senior ministers. At 2.55 a.m. on Wednesday, May 6, following a Government meeting, a statement about the resignations was issued. Jack Lynch said: 'I am satisfied that they do not subscribe fully to Government policy in relation to the present situation in the Six Counties.' Only much later the same day did the real reason emerge in Lynch's brief Dail statement, when he told the House that 'the security forces of the country at my disposal brought me information about an alleged attempt to unlawfully import arms from the continent. *Prima facie*, these reports involved two members of the Government.' The information came to Lynch on Monday and Tuesday, April 20–21. The probable explanation for the difference between the two statements made on Wednesday, May 6 is that, though Lynch had further details available to him on Tuesday night, they were not sufficiently substantiated for him to be in a position to make them public. It may have suited him for the impression to be created that Liam Cosgrave's acquisition of 'a document on official Garda notepaper' and his presentation of the information contained in this document to the Taoiseach, forced further revelations. Certainly this version of events was satisfactory from Cosgrave's point of view.

The second version, substantially researched and published by Vincent Browne,[1] argues that Jack Lynch knew from October 1969, of the Bailieboro meeting, which brought together members of the I.R.A. and Captain James Kelly, and also of a promise made by Captain Kelly at that meeting of £50,000 for the purchase of arms. No claim is made of knowledge by Lynch of the involvement of Haughey or Blaney at that stage. From he account given, the source for which was Berry, it seems that he fact that Haughey had been informed about the Bailieboro meeting was not passed on to Lynch. Nevertheless, technically he Taoiseach was aware, and by inference it is suggested that Lynch took further action to extend his own knowledge about what was going on, but no action to stop it.

Vincent Browne's judgment is that Jack Lynch was 'foolish' to give Charles Haughey a central role in handling the Northern Ireland situation, 'given that he had taken a line in Cabinet widely at variance with that of the Taoiseach', and that Jack Lynch did not really 'attain his real stature' until after the arms crisis. He argues that Lynch lacked authority:

> An inescapable conclusion from researching this article is that a great deal of blame for what happened lies with Jack Lynch, not because of any deviousness or duplicity on his part, as some of his enemies would like to allege, rather because of an indecisiveness and weakness which was responsible for a great deal of the chaos that ensued.[2]

It is a less benign version of events than that of the 'official' version, but almost certainly more accurate. However, it leaves important questions in the air, both broad ones about Lynch's political character, and specific ones about the inconsistencies between public and private events. In addition, there is that essential 'tiger' with which every political leader wrestles all the time: the aggregate of public, and perhaps even more, of party, feeling, support, and judgment of events. From October, 1969 to well after the crisis became common knowledge in May, 1970, the turmoil which is now history, but which at the time threatened the dissolution of the State and of law and order in Northern Ireland, swirled around Lynch's head, and presented him with the kinds of challenges with which few politicians ever have to contend. Could he move against an extremely powerful faction within his own party, at the head of which were at least three senior and respected members of his own Government? Perhaps even more important: if he did move, precisely on what evidence would he do so?

A third interpretation, then, is that Jack Lynch *was* broadly aware of what was going on, did fail to act, but had good reason for such an approach. He *was* more devious than is generally represented, but was so in the broad interests of not even the country alone, but of the island itself. He was prepared to sacrifice Fianna Fail, if necessary, power if it had to be so himself, almost without giving it a thought, and definitely the outworn republican ideals which, perhaps to his amazement were represented strongly around the Cabinet table. To do all this, however, he had to have the necessary support. His primary objective was to hold on to the centre. In the wake of the Derry and Belfast riots it was very difficult to know where that centre was eventually going to be. It was certain, however, that whatever happened in Northern Ireland, events in the South contained political dangers not necessarily related to reunification, or republicanism, or ideals of that kind, but rather to the direction of democratic government and the control of political power. In such circumstances, it was entirely consistent with Jack Lynch's political character to shift the onus of initiative on to the shoulders of those who opposed him and criticised him and let them either solve the insoluble, or founder in the attempt. The inherent absurdity of much that was being said both publicly and privately, by politicians such as Neil Blaney Kevin Boland, and much more circumspectly by Charles Haughey, while apparent to Jack Lynch, was far from being seen in these terms by the public. And, alone, of the three senior 'republicans' in the Cabinet, Charles Haughey recognised the political danger of adopting a public stance which would have allied him to the other two. Perhaps to Lynch's discomfiture Haughey never made speeches about the need for Britain to leave and partition to be ended. And when the crisis did break it was Haughey's involvement which astonished everyone, as did his defence, in the subsequent trials, that he knew no details.

Only in this context, and reading into Lynch's character that strange apparent inaction which is central to it, can one explain in terms that do not accuse him of irresponsibility, his truly extraordinary approach which led to the setting up of a Government sub-committee and its total lack of supervision, a fund which was unsupervised, and a general situation in which senior members of the administration continued to foment a highly dangerous level of antagonism in the Republic's ruling party at a time when lives were being lost regularly less than a hundred miles from the capital city.

Did Lynch envisage clearly where his *far niente* approach would lead? Even in late April 1970 he was unwilling to move against the ministers involved. As late as April 30 he had decided not to dismiss Blaney and Haughey. Again, this has been represented as weakness. Yet, as subsequent events were to show, and go on showing throughout the 1970s and 1980s, actions and attitudes that would be sufficient to terminate political careers elsewhere, serve in Ireland to do the opposite, so strong are the republican ideals and shibboleths, the tribal loyalties and emotions, and the curious political rules and standards which can emerge from this background. Lynch apparently contrived, in the first week in May, 1970, in a manner peculiarly fitting to his political character, that the pressures leading to the dismissal of Neil Blaney and Charles Haughey, and the resignation of Kevin Boland, appeared to come from outside his administration rather than from within it. An outraged Opposition, the forces of law and order, and a substantial majority of the Fianna Fail Party were lined up against the small republican faction within the Government which, after decades of verbal violence, seemed, in May of that year, to have been actually prepared to foment further physical violence by the provision of arms and ammunition to the minority, nationalist, Catholic, republican communities in Northern Ireland. It was illegal. It was against Government policy. It was being done behind the backs of most of the members of the Government. Reluctantly, in sadness rather than in anger, Jack Lynch allowed himself the ultimate privilege of power, to dismiss those closest of all to that power.

8

The Arms Crisis

Jack Lynch dismissed Charles Haughey and Neil Blaney from his Government on Wednesday, May 6, 1970, because they disagreed with Northern Ireland policy. The Taoiseach's statement, made public at 2.50 a.m. was as follows:

> I have requested the resignations as members of the Government of Mr Neil T. Blaney, Minister for Agriculture and Fisheries, and Mr Charles J. Haughey, Minister for Finance, because I am satisfied that they do not subscribe fully to Government policy in relation to the present situation in the Six Counties as stated by me at the Fianna Fail Ard Fheis in January last. Caoimhín O Beolain, Minister for Local Government and Social Welfare, has tendered his resignation as a member of the Government and I propose to advise the President to accept it. A special meeting of Fianna Fail deputies will take place at Leinster House at 6 p.m. today to consider the position that has arisen.

Jack Lynch explained that he had not received the resignations he had requested 'but the Constitutional position is that I am entitled to act on my request'. The House then adjourned at quarter to twelve until 10 p.m.

Paudge Brennan, Neil Blaney's parliamentary secretary, resigned at mid-day, bringing the political casualty list to five.[1] By then rumour had become widespread that the issue central to the crisis was not solely the internal difference of opinion about Northern Ireland, within the Government, but the involvement of the men concerned in an illegal attempt to import arms.

The Fianna Fail Parliamentary Party met at six o'clock. Jack Lynch gave a thirty minute speech and obtained a unanimous vote of confidence. A statement was issued:

> At the special meeting of the Fianna Fail Party, held at Leinster House, the party unanimously endorsed a motion by the Taoiseach that the party approves such nominations as he would make to replace the members of the Government whose appointments had been terminated. Each of the three former Ministers, deputies Neil Blaney, Kevin Boland and Charles J. Haughey, and the former Parliamentary Secretary, deputy Paudge Brennan, expressed unreservedly his loyalty to the Fianna Fail Party and the Taoiseach.

When the Dail then met, the two Opposition parties were uncertain about how to proceed, the Labour Party wanting to meet again the following day, and Fine Gael looking for a fuller debate on the Friday. Jack Lynch was prepared to accommodate either, or both, on condition that he would be able to move a motion of appointment to fill the vacancies in his Government. His insistence on this relatively minor point, in contrast with the evident disagreement and lack of planning on the opposite side of the House, demonstrated that, in an acute period of crisis, with himself at the centre, he was already planning an offensive designed to pre-empt any defeat. In spite of widespread speculation about a general election, the key question of Fianna Fail unanimity had already been decided. By insisting on a debate about the confirmation of appointments, rather than of confidence in the Government, he was moving forward towards a practical endorsement of party unity behind his own new appointments, a constitutional right with which even his most critical opponent could not argue.

Jack Lynch's own Dail statement was brief. Having dealt with the sackings and having referred also to Kevin Boland's resignation, he then carefully dissociated the fourth, Minister Micheal O Morain, from any involvement with 'the matter with which I now propose to deal.' O Morain cannot be so easily excluded. It was not just health grounds. He had, in addition, been derelict in his duties as Minister for Justice, deliberately ignoring what was going on around him and thus endangering the State's security which was his principal responsibility. On Wednesday, 29th April, Lynch saw both Blaney and Haughey.

> I told them both I had information which purported to connect them with an alleged attempt to unlawfully import arms, on the basis of which information I felt it was my duty to request their resignations as members of the Government. Each of them denied he instigated in any way the attempted importation of arms. They asked me for time to consider their position. I agreed to do so. In the meantime I authorised the continuation of investigations and I made personal investigations myself, following which I decided to approach the two ministers again and to repeat my request that they tender to me their resignations as members of the Government. I did so on the basis that I was convinced that not even the slightest suspicion should attach to any member of the Government in a matter of this nature. Having told the ministers that I wished to have their resignations forthwith, each of them told me he would not give me his resignation until this morning.

The Fine Gael leader, Liam Cosgrave, spoke immediately after Lynch, explained that he had been given information 'anonymously', linking the two dismissed ministers with the attempt to import arms. This information, said Cosgrave, was later confirmed, and he referred to 'a document on official Garda notepaper': 'A plot to bring in arms from the continent worth £80,000 under the guise of the Department of Defence has been discovered. Those involved are a Captain Kelly, the former Minister for Finance, the former Minister for Agriculture and two associates of the Ministers.'

The rest of Liam Cosgrave's speech underlined the essential crisis, suggested that there had been a failure to deal with it, and called for the Government's resignation.

The real story, somewhat more bizarre, was that Liam Cosgrave had been in possession of most, if not all, the facts about the attempted importation of arms, and the involvement of members of the Government, at least a week earlier, and had endeavoured to interest the political correspondent of the *Sunday Independent*, E. B. Murphy, in them. Murphy had written a story for his paper which was on the desk of his editor, Hector

66

Legge, on the night of Thursday, April 30. But Legge, under-standably cautious in the circumstances, and unable to confirm the sensational details, did not publish. The story then un-folded through the more orthodox channels of the Fine Gael leader taking his 'facts' to the Taoiseach, and 'forcing' the sequence of dismissals and resignations. One does not have to be excessively devious to see the deliberate leakage of informa-tion provoking the final unravelling of the drama.

Brendan Corish, leader of the Labour Party, expressed sup-port for the dismissals, but condemned Jack Lynch, Fianna Fail and the closing of party ranks in order to survive. He suggested that, far from being unanimous, the real situation at the Fianna Fail Parliamentary Party meeting had been 65 votes for Lynch, 10 against.

Other speeches raised other questions. Tom O'Higgins, the Fine Gael deputy leader, who later became Chief Justice, ex-amined the legal implications and the question of criminal charges. Richie Ryan questioned the role of the Defence Minis-ter, Jim Gibbons. Though many speakers referred to Northern Ireland, it was generally done in a cursory, superficial way, with the main emphasis on internal political issues and detail. In a very brief contribution, however, Conor Cruise O'Brien blamed Fianna Fail, and the dismissed ministers particularly, for contributing to the growing polarisation in Ireland, 'the growing strength of the Paisley movement of Protestant fanati-cism at one end of the island and at the other an irresponsible party and the I.R.A., all building up to the next July and August, towards a festival of destruction'.

It was clear from Jack Lynch's final speech in the debate that he was confident of survival and that there would be no ques-tion of an election. The division that night was carried by 72 votes to 65, after which the Dail adjourned.

On Thursday, May 7, Desmond O'Malley received his seal of office as Minister for Justice, and on Friday, May 8, the Dail reassembled, with three new members of the Government: Robert Molloy, Gerard Collins and Jeremiah Cronin. George Colley became Minister for Finance, and was replaced in In-dustry and Commerce by Paddy Lalor; James Gibbons moved to Agriculture from Defence; and Joseph Brennan took over the Department of Social Welfare in addition to that of Labour.

The thirty-five hours of continuous debate then began, but they added little information to what had already emerged They served as a political safety-valve of truly giant propor-tions, venting feelings generally, and, in more specific terms, allowing most of the central figures the opportunity to speak. Charles Haughey, who, since the Tuesday night, had been in the Mater Nursing Home with 'a fractured skull, a broken eardrum and an injured clavicle' issued a statement through his solicitor and election agent, P. J. O'Connor, on the morning of the debate.

I regret that on medical advice I cannot make a personal statement to Dail Eireann concerning the termination of my office as a member of the Government. Since becoming a Minister, I have endeavoured to the best of my ability to serve my country, Dail Eireann and the Government. I have never at any time acted in breach of the trust reposed in me, and I regret that I am now compelled to refer to the circum-stances which brought an end to my membership of the Government.

The Taoiseach informed the Dail that he requested my resignation on the grounds that he was convinced that not even the slightest suspicion should attach to any member of the Government. I fully subscribe to that view. So far as I have been able to gather, the Taoiseach received informa-tion of a nature which in his opinion cast some suspicion on me. I have not had the opportunity to examine or test such information or the quality of its source or sources.

In the meantime, however, I now categorically state that at no time have I taken part in any illegal importation or attempted importations of arms into this country. At present I do not propose to say anything further except that I have fully accepted the Taoiseach's decision as I believe that the unity of the Fianna Fail Party is of greater importance to the welfare of the nation than my political career.

Kevin Boland's speech came early in the two day debate, and dealt with five main issues: the Taoiseach's right to hire and fire, his own reasons for resigning, the questions of policy surrounding the use of force in Northern Ireland, the denial of policy disagreements, and his own disbelief that there could

1 and 2   Violence in Northern Ireland, from 1968, provoked political realism in the Republic and a fresh look at Southern values and safeguards. The process of change was slow. There was stubborn resistance to reconsidering old traditions about partition and unity. Yet changed attitudes represented the beginning of a new and different political era in the Republic.

4 and 5 John Hume (*above*) of the Social, Democratic and Labour Party, later its leader, and Ian Paisley (*below*) leader of the Democratic Unionist Party from 1971.

3 Captain Terence O'Neill, Northern Ireland Prime Minister, 1963–9. 'You either succeed or you fail. I failed.'

6, 7 and 8   Jack Lynch (*above*) with members of the Government and of Fianna Fail at the Dublin Airport press conference after the Arms Trial verdict. Micheal O Morain (*below left*) was his Minister for Justice; Jim Gibbons (*right*) was Minister for Defence, and a key trial witness.

9 and 10 Charles Haughey and Neil Blaney (*above left*) at the time of the Arms Trial. Kevin Boland (*right*) who resigned from the Government at the time of the arms crisis. On possible arms importation into Northern Ireland he said: 'It is not our business to interfere.'

11 and 12 Albert Luykx (*left*), a defendant in the Arms Trial. On the right are John Kelly (*left*) and Captain James Kelly, who were also defendants.

have been an attempt to import arms illegally. The disbelief was speculative, and qualified. While dismissing the newspaper stories of the previous day — 'I do not believe them for one moment' — and ignoring the more specific references relating his two former Government colleagues to the 'alleged attempt unlawfully to import arms', Boland went on to say that such 'importation into the part of the country in which the writ of this Government does not run is not illegal as far as I am concerned. It is our duty to advise against it but it is not our business to interfere, and any co-operation with the security forces of the country that continues to occupy six of our counties is, in my opinion, intolerable.' Earlier in his speech he had said: 'It would be unpardonable for us to take any action to frustrate the efforts of *our people* [my italics] in the Six Counties to protect their lives and property.' He repudiated force as a means of reunifying the country, and subscribed fully to Government policy, adding that he believed his colleagues did the same. He then went on to deny 'the right of any section of the Irish people to opt out of the Irish nation' and condemned the 'illegal' presence of the British 'aggressors'.

Kevin Boland's reasons for resigning, extensively dealt with in his speech, related to the methods used to find out what members of the Government were doing and the *lettre de cachet* basis for the dismissal of colleagues. This was 'highly objectionable not to mention undemocratic and a violation of human rights . . . intolerable . . . inconsistent with the dignity of a free man.'

Neil Blaney's reason for *not* resigning occupied less space in a speech of almost identical length:

> I refused to resign because I believed that, by so doing, in view of the extremely delicate situation in the Six Counties, I would be aiding, perhaps causing, something that would result in some explosion about which we might be very sorry in the future. If my judgment was wrong, I bow to those who would condemn me. This is why I did not resign at the time I was requested, and for no other reason.

Like Kevin Boland, Neil Blaney spelt out carefully his views on the use of force. Categorically, it was not to be used for re-unification, and he had never advocated this. He confined it to the defence of 'Nationalist people', 'our people' (both phrases are used in his speech) against 'murderous assault'. 'We in this part of Ireland cannot stand idly by in these circumstances.' Neil Blaney echoed Kevin Boland's criticisms of the 'root cause' of Ireland's problems, the British presence, dealt at length with the Fianna Fail Party, and his own upbringing in its traditions, and defended his colleagues, friends and brothers from Fine Gael and Labour attacks on them. He denied categorically that he had financed, paid for, procured, or 'run' any guns; and he denied 'that I have or had anything to do with subversive organisations *in so far as this country is concerned*' (my italics).

The principal purpose of this debate, well-judged by Lynch, was to resolve the week of crisis, to go through the politically cathartic process of unlimited discussion, before deputies dispersed to their constituencies, and to give the opportunity to the key figures to state their positions. With the exception of Charles Haughey, this they did. The real crisis had already been resolved, in the Fianna Fail Party meetings on the Wednesday evening. This does not mean that the debate was not important, only that it was not critical. The vote was there, and Lynch knew by six o'clock on the Friday evening, after Boland and Blaney had spoken, that he would win by the convincing margin of 73–66 when the division took place at eleven o'clock on Saturday night. Altogether there were 69 speakers, 53 of them from the Opposition parties. Most, one can safely ignore; the Opposition indulged itself, understandably enough, and during the long hours of the night there were frequent comments about repetition, as the supply of documents to quote from ran out.

Much, however, remained unresolved. Jack Lynch's own speech at the end of the debate left many questions unanswered; so did James Gibbons's. His pivotal role as Minister for Defence was recognised, but not clearly understood. Predictably, leading Opposition politicians recognised their opportunity, and pressed for a general election as the 'least dangerous' course of action for Ireland, in Conor Cruise O'Brien's words. But the prospect of this, and indeed the sense of it, receded steadily. On Sunday, May 10, Jack Lynch said that the papers on the attempted importation of arms had been handed over to the Attorney General.

Though the political difficulties facing Jack Lynch, and the dangers to the survival of his Government, had been successfully deflected, the legal processes set in train were to have continuing political repercussions for several years, and were to lead to the departure from Fianna Fail of Kevin Boland during 1970, and of Neil Blaney at the end of 1971.

More immediately, Lynch faced, the following week, a confidence debate in the Dail which he won comfortably. A week later Harold Wilson sought a dissolution at Westminster, with an election fixed for June 18, effectively ruling out any further constructive Anglo-Irish talks or Northern Ireland initiatives: not that either would have been well-judged. On Wednesday, May 27, Captain James Kelly, John Kelly and Albert Luykx[2] were arrested and charged with conspiracy to import arms. On May 28, Charles Haughey and Neil Blaney were similarly arrested and charged. Kevin Boland accused Jack Lynch of 'felon setting' and issued a demand for a special conference of the Fianna Fail Party with the express purpose of removing Jack Lynch from Party leadership, thereby removing him from leadership of the Government.

On Thursday, June 4, the Fianna Fail Parliamentary Party expelled Kevin Boland by a secret ballot, 60 votes to 11. One ballot paper was left blank. Those who voted for Kevin Boland are known to have included: Charles Haughey, Neil Blaney, Paudge Brennan, Des Foley, Sean Sherwin, Lorcan Allen and Flor Crowley.

On Monday, June 22, the Fianna Fail National Executive met, and 'in the interests of party unity', according to Tommy Mullins, its general secretary, Kevin Boland resigned. Neil Blaney, asked to comment, said, 'It isn't over yet'.

The next day, Kevin Boland's father, Gerry Boland, who had been a tough Justice Minister under de Valera, and was still a Vice-President and trustee of the Party, resigned all his posts. There was speculation that his son would also resign his Dail seat, but his decision was delayed until November.

On July 2 the charges against Neil Blaney were dropped, and he was carried shoulder-high from the Dublin District Court. The four other defendants were returned for trial.

It was clear that the arms crisis, in its first phase anyway, was over, and that it had done less damage than had been anticipated by the more alarmist members of the Opposition parties. There were few enough objective judgments to emerge about the main protagonists, in spite of the huge volume of words which the revelations of that first week in May had provoked. One such came from Senator Owen Sheehy Skeffington, an Independent member of the Second Chamber, representing Trinity College, and an outspoken critic of social injustice and religious prejudice. In an article in the *Irish Times* on May 11, under the title 'They'll none of them be missed . . .' he wrote about the two men who had been dismissed, and the two who had resigned:

> I have sometimes been asked which of the many Ministers who appear before us in the Senate I would think least worthy of public confidence and esteem. These are the four names I have always mentioned first; and in arriving at this opinion, I have always seen a clear gap between these four and their ministerial colleagues, not one of whom has their Messianic 'infallibility', their inflexibility, their arrogance, their ruthless pursuit of personal ambition, and their refusal to entertain even the possibility that they might ever be wrong.

Of O Morain he said 'He combines strength of character with futility of purpose'; of Boland that he was not 'overburdened with bothersome scruple' and 'quite unhampered by intellectual honesty in his juggling with figures to party advantage'. Neil Blaney's 'defect is that he has never been wrong about anything,' and on the North 'it is clear that his emotions are strong and his thinking weak.' He saved his judgment of Charles Haughey until the end:

> Intellectually, Mr Charles Haughey is the ablest of the four. His aesthetic sense is perceptibly greater than that of Mr Boland; the competition is not intense. He has an arrogance which beats the band, and he can be every bit as intellectually dishonest as Mr Boland; and there the competition *is* intense. He can be very charming, it is true, to those who flatter him, but a deep inner insecurity gives him a low temper-flashpoint, which renders him often petulant and sometimes absurd.

Mammon is an old business friend of his and an active supporter. If the present row has, in his case, anything to do with a high-principled concern about the situation in the North, I should be very much surprised. Mr Haughey has other things in mind; ambition to be the first Taoiseach of a 32-county Republic? Perhaps. Personally, I should prefer even Mr Micheal O Morain.

In his many years in the Senate, Owen Sheehy Skeffington had been the most outspoken critic of Fianna Fail hypocrisy in many areas of policy involving social and human rights, economic inequality and empty republicanism. His judgments were well-based; his observations prophetic. But the supreme irony lay in the title. With dogged persistence three of the four men remained in the political arena; two are still there. Unfortunately, Skeffington had written his last article about Fianna Fail. He died in early June, and in a subsequent by-election his Trinity University seat was taken by Mary Robinson, who has since assumed, in part, her predecessor's radical mantle.

9

The Arms Trials

The Arms Trial opened in Dublin on Tuesday, September 22, 1970. The four defendants were charged with conspiracy to import illegally, on different dates between March 1 and April 24 of that year, arms consisting of 500 pistols and approximately 180,000 rounds of ammunition. On the sixth day of the trial, September 29, at the end of the morning, Peter Berry, Secretary of the Department of Justice was called. Having given critical evidence in respect of the telephone conversation between himself and Charles Haughey on Saturday, April 18, he was cross-examined by Ernest Woods, counsel for Albert Luykx, particularly about a Department of Justice letter confirming that Luykx had neither offended against the law, nor been engaged in subversive activity. Though this was sufficient for Luykx's counsel, Peter Berry volunteered further information by way of background, and Ernest Woods took grave exception: 'Why Mr Luykx's personal affairs should be bandied around the court I don't know. I don't know what they are but I strongly suspect that your lordship thinks they might hurt Mr Luykx in some way. It is only illustrative of the rather unfair tone in which your lordship sometimes has conducted this trial.' Mr Justice Andreas O'Keeffe, the trial judge and president of the High Court took even graver exception; he first adjourned, and then resumed to discharge the jury, ordering a new trial. The second Arms Trial began before Mr Justice Henchy on Tuesday, October 6. It lasted fourteen days.

The defence of three of the four defendants, Captain James

74

Kelly, John Kelly and Albert Luykx, was to admit that they attempted to import arms, believing that what they did was legal because it had the sanction of the Minister for Defence, James Gibbons. The fourth defendant, Charles Haughey, adopted a different approach: to deny that he had any knowledge of the attempt to import arms, and that he played no part in the operation.

Politically, the central confrontation was between two former colleagues in Government, Haughey and Gibbons. The key evidence in the trial, given by Gibbons, was that he requested a meeting with Haughey, either on April 17 or April 20, 1970, and that this meeting took place. At it, he told the Minister for Finance that his own Department of Defence had received a telephone call from Dublin airport asking if the Army expected delivery of arms and ammunition. There had also been other calls from the Department of Transport and Power. In summary, Gibbons claimed that Haughey used the phrase, 'The dogs in the street are barking it', referring to the escalating knowledge about the importation of arms. Gibbons then asked Haughey to stop it. 'I'll stop it for a month.' 'For God's sake, stop it altogether.'

While not denying the meeting in his office, in spite of considerable efforts by the defence counsel to raise doubts about how it came about and when, Charles Haughey denied the conversation. The decision, corroborated by another witness, Anthony Fagan, a civil servant who had, as Haughey's press officer in the Department of Finance, 'to call off the importation of a certain consignment' was made without knowing what the consignment was. The whole conversation, which involved the potential confrontation between the Special Branch and the Army, was held without knowledge of what it was the two men were discussing. In his summing up, the trial judge, Mr Justice Henchy, said:

> It seemed to me, and you are free to dismiss my opinion, either Mr Gibbons has concocted this, and has come to court and perjured himself, or it happened. If there is another explanation, please act on it. There does not seem to be any way of avoiding the total conflict on this issue between Mr Haughey and Mr Gibbons.

Amazing though it must have been to his co-defendants, to hear Haughey resolutely denying knowledge of information which at least one of them, Captain James Kelly, had equally firmly said he gave him, it was the only possible or logical defence for a senior Government Minister who had no legal role to play in an operation of the kind which had been undertaken. From as far back as August 1969, the direct involvement of Haughey, Blaney and Gibbons, in Government work related to Northern Ireland, to security, to the Army's role, to defence plans for the minority community, had run contemporaneously with attempts to buy arms which could not be traced to Irish Government sources, and supply them to organisations in Northern Ireland. Some of those engaged in the attempted purchase and attempted importation believed they were acting for the Government, as represented by the same ministers. While there is no suggestion that Peter Berry ever told Jack Lynch of ministerial involvement with Captain James Kelly in the autumn of 1969, following the Bailieboro meeting, it is clear that some indication of what was going on was given on October 17, 1969, in the meeting to which reference has already been made. Yet for six months different Government ministers and private individuals skirmished, negotiated, gave undertakings, paid out substantial sums of money, and eventually found themselves embroiled in the greatest political crisis in the Republic of Ireland this century.

On Friday, October 23, all four defendants were found Not Guilty. The unprecedented scenes of jubilation in the Four Courts were followed, within an hour, by a press conference given by Haughey in which he challenged Lynch: 'Those responsible for the debacle have no option but to take the honourable course open to them.' He saw fundamental differences of political philosophy between himself and Lynch, and suggested that the Taoiseach's speech, given at the United Nations on Thursday, October 22, did not represent Fianna Fail policy. 'I think there is some dissatisfaction about the leadership at the moment. The Taoiseach's position is something that will be decided by the parliamentary party. I confine myself to that at this time.' But he went on to describe as 'the most satisfactory aspect of the affair, apart from the verdict,' the extent of his support within the parliamentary party and round the country. What support in the party would he have, he was asked? 'I don't believe in counting heads. Since this whole affair happened I have been surprised at the enormous reaction and support I have received personally from my own, and from people in politics and outside it.'

He was also questioned about arms, about the verdict and about Northern Ireland. On whether arms should be sent to the North, he said that it would be a matter for serious discussion by the Government. Personally, he would help the people there in every way he could, and he went on: 'In all my time in politics and in public life I have never met a finer person than John Kelly.' Boland, O Morain and Blaney all echoed Haughey's view that Lynch should resign.

Jack Lynch was in New York. He issued a statement there in which he said he was confident of the outcome in the event of any leadership challenge, and that he stood by his actions and had made the right decisions in initiating the legal moves which had led to the trial. He followed this with a Saturday morning press conference at which he re-asserted that there had been an attempt to import arms illegally, and confirmed, 'Blaney was involved too.'

He returned to Dublin on the Monday morning to a reception by the whole of the Government except two ministers, Paddy Hillery, who was in New York, and Sean Flanagan, who was in London. Altogether some fifty Fianna Fail deputies and twenty senators were there, and the Fianna Fail 'old guard' was represented by former Foreign Minister, Frank Aiken,[1] and former Tanaiste, Sean McEntee. It was a carefully orchestrated show of strength, with Lynch handling the lengthy press conference confidently. He made considerable capital out of the inquiries which had been carried out, and would be intensified, into the sources for the funds used to purchase arms. There was a justified fear, he said, that public monies had been misappropriated.

At a meeting of the Fianna Fail Parliamentary Party the following day, Tuesday, October 27, 1970, the frailty of the challenge against him became clearly apparent, and, with it, the major errors of judgment made by Charles Haughey in the aftermath of the Arms Trial acquittal. That 'most satisfactory aspect of the whole affair', the 'tremendous support' from around the country, was represented within Fianna Fail, in the end, by five members of the parliamentary party, including

77

himself and Neil Blaney. Even this situation, which was potentially disastrous, given the narrow Dail majority Lynch enjoyed, turned into something of a farce, when, in the parliamentary party discussions, both former ministers pledged that they would vote with the Fianna Fail Party in the 'no confidence' debate fixed for the following week. They did so only after a 'roll-call' vote in which 68 Dail deputies stood up to pledge support for Taoiseach and Government in the forthcoming 'no confidence' debate. It seemed incidental, but at the same meeting the party pledged unanimous support for the wage and price control measures being introduced by George Colley which Charles Haughey had criticised at his press conference as having not been approved by the parliamentary party.

Immediately afterwards an emergency meeting of the Government was held, followed by a press conference at 1 a.m. attended by all ministers, at which Lynch said he was reserving his position, as far as calling a general election went, until after the Dail debate on the 'no confidence' motion.

On Wednesday, November 4, 1970, at the end of his speech in the Dail debate, Jack Lynch warned deputies, 'I do not want any deputy to go into the lobby with me to buy time, because I am not in the market for the buying or selling of time.' The Ceann Comhairle (Speaker of Dail) then announced that Kevin Boland had resigned his Dail seat. In response to Opposition demands for the by-election to be held as soon as possible, Jack Lynch moved the writ immediately, and then went on to the division. It was won comfortably by the Government, 74 votes to 67. In the general mêlée of the division, Kevin Boland slipped away quietly, his political career at an end, his honour more or less intact, his perverse sense of principle maintained.

10

The Aftermath

In 1970, the arms crisis year, there were 20 violent deaths in Northern Ireland. In 1971 there were 172, and in 1972, 467. It was the blackest of all the chronologies. On becoming Prime Minister in the summer of 1970, Edward Heath had promoted Reginald Maudling as Home Secretary, with collateral responsibilities for Northern Ireland. Maudling detested the North, and visited it infrequently with ill-concealed distaste.

Edward Heath's victory had been greeted with widespread dismay in Dublin. The Conservative Party was seen as the natural ally of the Northern Ireland Unionists, with whom the Conservatives had been direct political allies at Westminster for more than half a century, and it was to be quite some time before a different perception emerged. For the present, the gloomy predictions which heralded the change of government in London seemed to be confirmed by the swift escalation of brutal deaths in the North. Additional troops were sent to Belfast in February, 1971, coinciding with the retirement of the G.O.C., General Sir Ian Freeland, and his replacement by General Erskine Crum. And in March a further 1,300 troops were flown to the province. Lord Carrington, who was Defence Secretary, paid several visits in an endeavour to explain British Government security policy, while the Home Secretary, Maudling, did the same. Then, on March 20, James Chichester-Clark resigned as Prime Minister. The succession was between William Craig and Brian Faulkner. By 26 votes to 4, Faulkner became Unionist leader and Prime Minister on March 23.

It was clear from the increasing violence that the new Northern Ireland Prime Minister faced growing security problems, particularly with the approach of August, and the traditional marches of Protestant and Orange Order fraternities. More troops were brought in bringing the total to 11,900. On August 7 rioting broke out in Belfast after a van driver whose van backfired was shot dead by troops. Two days later, in dawn raids by the British Army, 300 I.R.A. suspects were arrested and internment without trial was introduced by Brian Faulkner under the Special Powers Act. Twelve people were killed in riots which followed that day, a further five the next day, and six more in street gun battles on August 11.

It was by far the blackest week in Northern Ireland. Widespread condemnation of internment was followed by protest marches and passive resistance; this, in turn, by arrests. The Government in Dublin re-opened the Army refugee camps along the Border, and some 6,000 people fled to them at the height of the violence. Jack Lynch called for the abolition of the 'Stormont Regime'. He also held a meeting with the Fine Gael leader, Liam Cosgrave, and with Brendan Corish, leader of the Labour Party.

Brian Faulkner's meeting with Edward Heath at Chequers, following the introduction of internment, was then followed by a meeting between Edward Heath and Jack Lynch, also at Chequers, on September 6–7, at which tripartite talks were announced. Initially, the Social Democratic and Labour Party in Northern Ireland declined to accept Jack Lynch as representing them at the talks, so that when they actually took place, on September 27–28, the primary objective, as far as Lynch was concerned, was to find a formula involving the Northern Ireland minority, a prelude to the idea of power-sharing.

Lynch already had the backing of the Opposition for power-sharing overtures. If anything, the Conservative Government led by Heath had an even more willing Opposition, led by Harold Wilson, who had announced a 12-point plan for Northern Ireland which also included a proposal for an 'all-Ireland Council'. Wilson then followed this plan with a visit to both Belfast and Dublin after which he proposed an inter-parliamentary commission – Dublin, Belfast and London – to debate Irish reunification, with the Republic of Ireland seeking readmission to the British Commonwealth.[1] Maudling, speaking for the British Government, responded favourably to this proposal, and in December both the Dail and Stormont agreed to inter-parliamentary talks. The most significant veto came from Gerry Fitt. Not so long as there was internment would the S.D.L.P. take part in such talks.

Nevertheless, the contrast in attitudes which prevailed at the end of 1971 was truly remarkable: the gap between the realities of violence and the stated objectives of the politicians was very wide indeed. On the one hand there had been an appalling escalation in violence. Brian Faulkner's first five months in power had seen bomb explosions in the North at an average rate of two a day. Regular increases in the strength of the British Army had brought it close to 15,000 men by the end of the year, and Maudling had ended a Belfast visit, on December 15, with his now celebrated apothegm about the I.R.A., that they would 'not be defeated, nor completely eliminated, but have their violence reduced to an acceptable level.' At the same time, politicians in London, Belfast and Dublin were contemplating a curiously unreal programme of talks embracing reunification, a council of Ireland and a new constitution.

All of this collapsed swiftly and decisively on Bloody Sunday, January 30, 1972. British paratroops, confronting a banned civil rights march in Derry, shot and killed thirteen people. On February 2 the British Embassy in Dublin was burnt down following massive demonstrations to coincide with the funeral of the victims, attended by five ministers from Dublin as well as a representative of President de Valera. More troops were sent to Northern Ireland, and Brian Faulkner, under growing pressure from the Unionist Right Wing, notably William Craig and the Ulster Vanguard Movement, had further talks with Edward Heath and other senior ministers. While talk of direct rule was discounted, its growing imminence was real enough. 'Exceptional and radical' initiatives were called for by Lynch in appeals to the British Government, and to the S.D.L.P., in early March. A 'political' cease fire followed on March 10, with the Provisional I.R.A. demanding troop withdrawal, first from the streets then from Northern Ireland altogether, coupled with a complete amnesty for political prisoners and the abolition of Stormont.

On March 24 the British Government prorogued Stormont and introduced direct rule. William Whitelaw was appointed

Secretary of State for Northern Ireland. A further 4,000 troops were mobilised in Britain for movement to Northern Ireland in the event of an escalation of violence, and the formation of a replacement government for the one led by Brian Faulkner began with the appointments of Paul Channon and Lord Windlesham as Northern Ireland Ministers of State.

William Whitelaw began the process of 'normalising' security in Northern Ireland by an amnesty of people convicted of organising or taking part in illegal processions, and by the phased release of internees. By June he had set free 470. At the same time he initiated talks with political leaders, decided on the use of proportional representation for Northern Ireland local elections, and fixed a constitutional conference on the North's future to be held in Darlington in the early autumn. The Provisional I.R.A., anxious to be part of the political process, sought a meeting on the basis of their 'peace proposal', which involved British withdrawal commitments and self-determination by the Irish people. They had already contributed to the abolition of Stormont, and, in part, to their second objective of a general amnesty. William Whitelaw publicly rejected the Provisional I.R.A. overtures on June 13. But on July 7 he secretly met Gerry Adams, Martin Bell, Martin McGuinness, Daithi O'Connell, Seamus Twomey and Sean MacStiofan for talks. Two days later he announced the meeting, but did not reveal the names until July 18, on which day the British Opposition leader, Harold Wilson, also had talks with the Provisional I.R.A. leadership in London. Jack Lynch was excluded from the Northern Ireland conference as such, but was invited by Edward Heath to a meeting which would follow immediately afterwards.

The S.D.L.P., in anticipation of the Darlington conference, adopted a condominium approach to Northern Ireland in a policy document called 'Towards a New Ireland'. Its central proposal was joint sovereignty over Northern Ireland by the British and Irish Governments. The Alliance Party put forward proposals for a regional assembly for the North, operating a committee system, and would not accept devolved security powers. The position adopted by the Official Unionist Party, and explained in a policy document called 'Towards the Future', was that the North should get back an enlarged, single-chamber parliament, to which all powers, including security, would be restored. The conference took place. Of the seven political groupings invited only these three attended, and they came out with their views about the future much the same as they had been when they went in.

Both the proposed Border referendum and the local government elections, using proportional representation, were postponed by William Whitelaw in October, and the British Government published instead its Northern Ireland 'Green Paper'.[2]

Lynch weathered the storms both north and south of the Border, and at the end of 1972 was politically stronger than he had been at any time in his career. He had repeatedly taken on and defeated the dissidents within his own party without undermining his Dail majority. He had taken a tough line against the men of violence, and had initiated and sustained a programme of anti-terrorist legislation of quite extreme proportions.[3] There had been no major reforms in any area of social or economic legislation. The single most significant event between 1970 and the end of 1972 was the country's decision, by referendum, to enter the E.E.C. At the end of August in that year a by-election in Mid-Cork gave Fianna Fail 53 per cent support. It was not unreasonable to anticipate, in the autumn of 1972, the quite extraordinary possibility that Fianna Fail, under Jack Lynch', after all the party confrontations and expulsions, would win the general election which, though constitutionally not required before the summer of 1974, was expected some time in 1973.

The Fine Gael and Labour Opposition, at the end of 1970, had done all it reasonably could to dislodge a divided administration. It failed repeatedly on numerical grounds. While the threatened or actual defections from Fianna Fail seemed serious enough at the time, there was never any danger of their being of benefit to Fine Gael or to Labour. In the spectrum of views represented by democratically elected politicians, Jack Lynch, supported by the vast majority of his own party, stood firmly *between* the Opposition and his own rebels. Their departure, if and when it came, was, democratically and politically speaking, into outer darkness. And, realistically, this was the fate of both Kevin Boland and Neil Blaney, as well as of lesser men such as Des Foley and Sean Sherwin. The instability was not of a comparable kind to that which, in history, has seen public representatives crossing the floors of parliaments to change the balance of power and threaten the survival of governments.

Within reason, Jack Lynch could afford to shed a small number of his own party and still survive. And this he did in the eighteen months or so which followed the arms crisis. Once the Dail had gone through the major test which followed the Arms Trial verdict, and which saw the promised support for a challenge by Charles Haughey evaporate almost completely, so that the challenger himself was forced to vote for his opponent, the two Opposition parties were left to make the most of a situation which was likely, if not certain, to remain stable until Jack Lynch chose to dissolve. They did make the most of it, in a variety of ways. Tyro politicians such as Conor Cruise O'Brien, Garret FitzGerald, Justin Keating, David Thornley, Michael O'Leary, Richie Ryan and others made political reputations for themselves by means of indefatigable debating marathons and, perhaps more seriously, by addressing themselves to major social, economic and human rights inequalities in Irish − that is, Republic of Ireland − society.

The effect of events in 1970 was to quicken considerably a process which had begun after the 1969 general election: essentially, it was realised that after twelve years of opposition, any alternative government to the 'natural party of power', Fianna Fail, would require a careful and professional balance of power between the partners in a coalition. Agreement would have to be reached which would enable forces to coalesce under proportional representation, and would produce policies which answered the real needs of the country. This was by no means an easy set of objectives. Yet arguably a more talented team than ever before was now involved in working out the details.

The most basic lesson of all to have emerged from the 1969 general election was that the kind of idealism which had led the Labour Party to adopt a Left-wing, go-it-alone stance simply would not produce power. Much is made of the fact that the 1969 Labour performance produced the highest vote in the party's history, 17·02 per cent, resulting in 18 seats out of an assembly of 144. What is conveniently forgotten is that four years later, when the votes dropped to 13·67 per cent of the total the number of seats, again in a 144-seat assembly, went *up* to 19, proving the point that absolute achievements under proportional representation matter less than relative ones, and that the success in 1973 was more firmly linked to the practicality of offering the Irish electorate a coalition alternative, than in offering it a package of ideologically laundered ideas.

In pragmatic terms Fine Gael and Labour had failed to judge accurately the mood in 1969. They had offered the wrong remedies for a *laissez-faire* administration in which the divisions about Northern Ireland between Jack Lynch and Neil Blaney, and the divisions on economic policy between Jack Lynch and Charles Haughey, were indicative of their arrogance.

The burden of action rested primarily with the Labour Party. At their 1970 annual conference, in Cork in mid-December, the party decided to allow negotiations on a coalition to be undertaken by the parliamentary party, in conjunction with the administrative council. About 150 delegates, led by Noel Browne, walked out before the vote on the key resolution.

The events of 1970 more than the election result of 1969 dictated the shift vital to any future partnership, which was itself seen as a basic prerequisite to power. But the conference decision was also indicative of a shift within Labour itself. Rural Labour deputies were, on the whole, predisposed in favour of coalition. It had been the urban deputies, notably Dublin ones, who had advocated a Left-wing doctrinaire militancy which had been successfully seized on and exploited against Labour by Fianna Fail. In the 1969 general election new Labour deputies in Dublin included Barry Desmond, Justin Keating, Conor Cruise O'Brien and David Thornley, and they were determined to concentrate more on electoral strategy than on socialist ideology. They did so with a reluctant leader, Brendan Corish, who believed, quite correctly, that the Labour Party, unique among the three parties in the Dail, derived maximum support from its policy. Corish had been equivocally anti-coalition before the 1969 election when he had eventually rejected an approach made by the Fine Gael leader, Liam Cosgrave, in early 1968, with a view to merging the two parties; later moves towards establishing a pre-election coalition pact failed also. The election result had shown that Corish was right about the appeal of policy in getting votes, wrong if he believed that votes alone resulted in seats. A more subtle formula had to be applied, and its implementation presented problems. Brendan Corish had actually given an unwise pledge on the issue in January, 1969: if annual conference changed its mind on coalition 'I will, as I have consistently done since I became a member of the parliamentary Labour Party 24 years ago, accept that decision. But the party must appreciate that to me this is a matter of conscience, and that in such an eventuality, my continued support for socialism will be from the back benches.'[4]

Liam Cosgrave, the Fine Gael leader, had not taken kindly to the Labour leader's rebuff before the 1969 general election, and had decided to make no more overtures. If Labour wanted a coalition arrangement next time round, they could come to him. The reality, however, was that Cosgrave was by no means secure enough at the head of his party to indulge in the luxury of waiting for such overtures. If there were to be a coalition deal, and if Liam Cosgrave were to lead it, then he would need to declare his intentions and strike whatever bargain was required in a response to Brendan Corish. Otherwise, he would be in danger of being overtaken within his own party by men who were less than satisfied with his leadership.

Cosgrave had not been very successful. A marginal increase in electoral support between the 1965 and the 1969 general elections, the period during which he had led the party, had been accompanied by policy work based on the 'Towards a Just Society' document produced in 1965 by the Fine Gael Party and principally the work of Declan Costello. But the reality behind this document was neither flattering to Liam Cosgrave, nor even conducive to his peace of mind. It represented a movement within Fine Gael which, however necessary in making the party more relevant and more effective, had little to do with Cosgrave's own political ideals.

Essentially, these were of a law-and-order variety. An undoubted high point in Cosgrave's political career had been the part he had played in exposing the plot to import arms. The Garda letter was regarded by many people as the evidence which had set in train the dismissals and resignations. The residual credit was sufficient to spill over at the Fine Gael Party's annual conference for 1970, on May 16–17, when Cosgrave made capital of his own leadership and probity, and that of his Front Bench colleagues, stressing party unity and readiness to take over government in defence of democracy.

Jack Lynch continued to play a careful and cautious political hand following the challenge for leadership by Charles

Haughey which came immediately after the Arms Trial. He gave deliberate 'hostages' to the Opposition parties, that winter. One of these was the Dail Committee of Public Accounts set up at the beginning of December 1970, to investigate the dispensing of the funds provided by the Government for the relief of Northern Ireland distress in 1969. This committee then asked the Dail to pass legislation conferring on it powers comparable to those enjoyed by the High Court: that witnesses could be compelled to appear, and held to be in contempt if they did not. The legislation went through all stages in the Dail in the space of half an hour. This raised serious constitutional questions about the justification for giving unique powers of this kind to an all-party committee of politicians, thereby transferring the judicial function to the legislature, and doing so in dramatic circumstances. Moreover, it was clear to everyone involved that police investigations, which had gone on for eight months, would, if they had come up with any evidence justifying charges, have resulted in such charges. Nothing that the committee, with its extraordinary powers, might discover would be likely to result in anything more than the further verbal arraignment of men who had already been through the courts on conspiracy charges. Finally, there was the question of timing. On two previous occasions, in May by Brendan Corish, in late October by Liam Cosgrave, the Opposition had pressed for an investigation into the uses to which the £100,000 for relief of Northern Ireland distress had been put. This pressure was resisted by the Government because of 'other inquiries' until December, which meant that the investigation by the committee would go on during the two months leading up to the Fianna Fail Party's annual conference in February, the first such annual conference since the dismissals, and the final major hurdle to be faced by Jack Lynch within his own party organisation.

This, in fact, is what happened. On the Wednesday of the week of the Ard Fheis, Padraig Haughey, Charles Haughey's brother, refused to answer questions put to him. As a result he was cited for contempt. He was subsequently given a six month sentence, which was suspended pending appeal. The Ard Fheis itself was lively enough, involving some fisticuffs, and provoking vituperative speeches. But, predictably, Jack Lynch triumphed.

On April 21, 1971 the Committee of Public Accounts heard evidence from James Gibbons, now Minister for Agriculture but formerly Minister for Defence, that he had known from Captain Kelly on April 30, 1970, that the funds used for arms had come from the Dail money voted for distress relief in Northern Ireland. Jack Lynch, a fortnight after this date, had told the Dail the opposite: that no money from the fund had gone to buy arms. When asked why he had not passed on the information gleaned from Captain Kelly, James Gibbons replied: 'The Taoiseach did not ask me that question.'

This particular revelation, making visible fundamental cracks in the constitutional doctrine of collective Government responsibility, did not bear political fruit until the following November 10, 1971, when a Dail debate on a motion of no confidence in the Minister for Agriculture was defeated by the Government by only three votes. Charles Haughey voted with the party; Neil Blaney and Paudge Brennan abstained, and were expelled from Fianna Fail exactly one week later.

This was really the culmination of the arms crisis traumas, and emphasised that Jack Lynch had finally survived them. From his stormy Ard Fheis in February onwards, he was faced with continuing difficulties. On April 17, both Neil Blaney and Paudge Brennan attacked his Northern Ireland policy, Blaney claiming that he knew the names of 25 deputies and senators who had supplied guns to Northern Ireland in August 1969. Later in the same month, in a vote on the dole cut by the Government, a Fianna Fail backbencher voted against the measure and was expelled. At the beginning of May Kevin Boland resigned from Fianna Fail in order to start another political party, called Aontacht Eireann. In mid-September another Fianna Fail deputy, Sean Sherwin, also resigned to join him, and when the party held its inaugural meeting there were, among those attending, the former army intelligence officer and Arms Trial defendant, Captain James Kelly, and his former boss and head of Army Intelligence, Colonel Michael Hefferon.

Jack Lynch put his Northern Ireland policy before his party in September, and won endorsement for it, and in October the Dail resumed for a two-day debate on the North which revealed widespread consensus in favour of Lynch's policy; and this in the closing stages of a year in which the number of deaths had substantially increased. One further Fianna Fail backbencher

Des Foley, attacked Lynch's leadership on October 29, and then resigned on November 4. The purge was virtually over.

It was perhaps symptomatic both of the domestic situation faced by Jack Lynch, and of the increasingly serious developments in Northern Ireland, that the main legislative initiatives between 1970 and the end of 1972 were concerned with security and law and order. The major exception to this was Ireland's E.E.C. entry. The Taoiseach and Foreign Minister, Patrick Hillery, signed the Treaty of Accession on January 22, 1972. On May 11 a constitutional referendum was held resulting in an overwhelming national endorsement of entry: 1,041,890 in favour, 211,891 against. Hillery was subsequently appointed Ireland's first commissioner.

The controversial security legislation grew out of Government claims on December 4, 1970, that 'a secret armed conspiracy exists in the country to kidnap one or more prominent persons. Connected with this conspiracy are plans to carry out armed bank robberies which the police believe may involve murders or attempted murders.' In the Government briefing which followed the statement, political correspondents were told that detention centres were being prepared, and that the relevant section of the 1940 Offences Against the State Act, bringing in internment without trial, might be invoked. This announcement, despite its seriousness, was made apparently without any full Government discussion, since several ministers were concluding their by-election campaigning in Donegal–Leitrim. It was followed, on December 8, by the announcement of the retirement of the Secretary of the Department of Justice, Peter Berry, to take effect in late January, and this was read, with some accuracy, as a mark of dissociation by Berry from an alarmist Government response to a threatened situation which did not materialise. Many people took it in the context of the setting up of the Dail Public Accounts committee and the impending Fianna Fail Ard Fheis, and it was not until the following May that legislative action was actually taken. This consisted of an Emergency Prisons Bill, authorising the Minister for Justice to transfer republican prisoners from civil to military custody, and the activation of section five of the Offences Against the State Act, setting up a 'special criminal court' to which three judges were then appointed. The court went into action in June and republican prisoners were moved to the Curragh, amid protests which culminated in a hunger strike starting there at the end of the month.

The most serious legislative change proposed by the Government came before the Dail in November in the form of an amendment to the Offences Against the State Act, allowing for the indictment of 'a suspected member of an illegal organisation' on the suspicion of a police officer not below the rank of chief superintendent. The debate was controversial; a defeat for the Government was expected, with a general election before Christmas. The tensions surrounding the Bill had the additional impact of dividing the Fine Gael Party, with growing pressures against Liam Cosgrave, whose law-and-order approach had persuaded him to support a measure seen as draconian by many others in Fine Gael, and by members of the Labour Party.

Then, on December 1, two bombs exploded in the centre of Dublin, one outside Liberty Hall, one in Marlborough Street. Two people were killed and 127 injured. Fine Gael withdrew its opposition to the Bill, and it was carried by 70 votes to 23. Liam Cosgrave recovered control over his party. The Opposition were divided and in disarray.[5]

Jack Lynch had completed another difficult year. His continued survival was his greatest achievement. But he had also negotiated Ireland's entry into the E.E.C. and had successfully protected the country from the escalation of Northern Ireland violence. A great deal of Dail time had been given over to security legislation, and to debates arising directly or indirectly from the arms crisis. The economy had suffered from several damaging strikes, the most notable being the lengthy one by bank employees and the cement-makers' strike.

In December 1972 a second, double referendum was held, with a more than five-to-one vote in favour of both deleting from the Constitution the special position accorded there to the Roman Catholic Church, and reducing the voting age from 21 to 18.

In terms of his public political image Jack Lynch's reputation could hardly have stood higher. All the challenges which he had withstood within his own party had derived from an extreme republican source which he had repeatedly shown to lack support. He had also repeatedly beaten off Opposition challenges to his power. He had maintained an even and well-judged demeanour towards the increasing violence in Northern Ireland, and in his many meetings with Edward Heath, and with Harold Wilson before that, had judged with equal skill the mixture of conciliation and firmness appropriate to the insoluble, complex problems of Northern Ireland.

In none of these areas had he overtly demonstrated toughness or stubborn intractability. If anything, quite the reverse. His image with commentators was much as it had been more than six years before, when he first became leader of his party and of the country: the reluctant man of power, doing the minimum, and delaying it for as long as possible. He was the classic Irish leader, passive, seeking consensus, pushed towards firmness and action by others, more in sorrow than in anger. Because of this, and in spite of the unprecedented vicissitudes through which he had passed, and the negligible social or economic reforms achieved, as well as the fairly draconian measures taken or contemplated against the real or supposed enemies of the State, he was indisputably in control of his party, and more than likely to win a general election on the strength of E.E.C. entry. This position was confirmed by the disarray of the Opposition at the beginning of December over the Offences Against the State Amendment Act, and had he sought a dissolution then he would have won a clear mandate. It was in fact the Government's intention to dissolve and go to the country precisely on the amendment to that Act, and it was only when Fine Gael's opposition collapsed following the bombs that it was judged more prudent to delay, since only a genuine confrontation over a key issue could justify a December campaign leading to a poll just before Christmas Day. Once Fine Gael withdrew its opposition, the confrontation argument was replaced by one based on opportunism at the expense of divisions between Fine Gael and Labour on law and order. The resultant delays allowed the Opposition to regroup, and make at least some preparations for a joint coalition package against Fianna Fail. Even then, the 14-Point Programme with which Labour and Fine Gael fought the election in February 1973, was a brief and rushed package. It just did the trick. The real surprise of that election was not that the Coalition won, but that Jack Lynch lost.

I I

Cosgrave's Men

In the February 1973 general election the Fianna Fail Party increased its overall vote by just over half a percentage point, and went out of power. Even without the arms crisis and the debilitating wrangles which stemmed from the Arms Trials and the investigation into the missing £100,000, it was an honourable defeat; with these factors taken into account, Lynch's electoral performance in 1973 was remarkable. He regarded it himself as his greatest electoral achievement, outclassing the twenty-seat majority achieved in 1977.

The two Opposition parties came into power by virtue of one key factor: the effective transfer of votes, under proportional representation, from the candidates of one party to those of the other. This was in marked contrast to what had happened in 1969.[1]

The Fine Gael–Labour campaign had been based on a simple '14-Point Programme' for government which placed the greater part of its emphasis on economic issues, particularly housing and unemployment. The initial character of the administration, not necessarily borne out by events or by performance, is best presented in the context of individuals rather than of the Programme. Effective as this had been against a party which had made no elaborate preparation for the campaign, it did not display any clear political character, but expressed instead widely felt frustrations, and a general desire for change. This now having taken place, its instrument, the Coalition Government, was a mixture of talent and conservatism within both parties.[2] Within individual members could be found radicalism on social issues, conservatism on moral ones, as well as radicalism on economic issues coupled with conservative thinking on security, law and order and Northern Ireland. Only a visionary sense of purpose, design, pace and direction in a leader could effectively harness and use what was available. Would Liam Cosgrave be able to meet this challenge?

The deal with Labour allowed that party five of the fifteen Government seats and two junior ministers. Liam Cosgrave exercised no veto over the Labour members of Government. Brendan Corish, overcoming his scruples about watching a coalition administration from a principled position on the backbenches, became Tanaiste. He brought James Tully, Michael O'Leary, Justin Keating and Conor Cruise O'Brien in as his nominees for membership of the Government.

Cosgrave disposed of the ten appointments under his own control with political skill though without necessarily using talent to best effect. The men closest to him were Richie Ryan, Mark Clinton, Richard Burke, Tom O'Donnell and Paddy Donegan. They were characterised, above all, by firm loyalty to their leader. A more liberal faction, including Garret FitzGerald, Tom Fitzpatrick, Peter Barry and Declan Costello — who was made Attorney General — had portfolios which gave them no direct involvement in either the economic or social sphere.

Garret FitzGerald's Foreign Affairs responsibilities, at a time when Ireland had just become part of the E.E.C., necessitated many trips abroad. The last to be given Government office was Patrick Cooney, whose post was offered by Cosgrave on the way into the Dail Chamber, possibly to emphasise the fact that he was the 'tail-ender' as far as his party leader was concerned. The two men were very much at odds as a result of the part Cooney had played in the December 1972 attempt to remove Cosgrave from the Fine Gael leadership. It was a cool and deliberate act on Cosgrave's part, placing Cooney in the sensitive Department of Justice, and the repercussions were to prove interesting.

Jim Tully, the Labour deputy leader, fitted in well with Cosgrave's own views on politics, and, more important, shared his political astuteness on constituency matters, a necessary qualification for steering through the electoral legislation

which was due. Justin Keating was one of the complex intellectuals who had come late to politics as part of Labour's new
guard in 1969. His substantial responsibilities ultimately
placed him at the centre of highly controversial legislative
moves. But in the early stages he was regarded as a solid,
central figure in the Labour Party, and one of the more talented
members of the administration.

Talent and flair were the hallmarks of the youngest member
of the Government, Labour's Michael O'Leary, who was 36
when appointed Minister for Labour. Last, but anything but
least was Conor Cruise O'Brien. He was the Government's
only first-class brain. His chequered career had led him, by
way of the Irish Foreign Service, to work for the United
Nations, and eventually to the Congo where he became a
central figure in the controversy over its attempted partition,
after which he resigned from both the United Nations and the
Irish Foreign Service. He pursued an academic career until
1968 when he joined the Labour Party, winning a seat in 1969,
and then playing a major part in Dail debates, particularly
after the arms crisis of May 1970. Persuaded, as Lynch was, of
the need for reforms in Northern Ireland to meet the justified
civil rights demands, O'Brien moved much further and more
swiftly away from any belief at all in unity as a solution. This, in
turn, made him a strongly outspoken critic of I.R.A. violence,
and of any politicians who compromised about aims and
methods of achieving the supposed nationalist or republican
'ideals'. Inevitably this brought him into fierce conflict with
elements in Fianna Fail, and he became the central figure in the
unending debate about Northern Ireland, and North–South
relations, which began in renewed earnest in the second half of
1968, and has gone on ever since. On this issue he came to the
conclusion that Irish unity was not a sensible, still less an
attainable, objective for a southern Government, and that
politicians in the South did harm by expressing it as such. On
one occasion Liam Cosgrave referred to him, in the Dail, as 'a
stimulating debater'; in a sense this was his principal role in the
1973–7 administration. As Minister for Posts and Telegraphs
he had, in addition, responsibility for R.T.E. broadcasting, and
therefore for the controversial Section 31 of the Broadcasting
Act, which precluded members of the Provisional I.R.A. and
Provisional Sinn Fein from being interviewed on radio or
television.

94

No woman was appointed to office in the Cosgrave administration. There were only four women deputies, none of them active in the women's movement in Ireland, which at that stage was passing through an initial militant phase with only the earliest indications of an awareness of the political potential of feminist issues. In general, the new administration was seen in a benign light. The change after sixteen years of Fianna Fail rule was welcomed on all sides. Expectation was high. The talent available within the Government was widely recognised and extolled.

The character of the new coalition Government was not as clearly reflected in the character of its leader as the previous administration had been. Liam Cosgrave's political character was complicated by a certain inscrutability. He was 'his own man'; he was firm on 'the institutions of the State'; on law-and-order; on the traditions of Fine Gael; on the teachings of the Catholic Church. He neither liked, nor was good with, the press. His political speeches were frequently punctuated by extremely witty and telling asides, delivered in an exaggeratedly flat, Dublin accent; but the body of his texts, almost always prepared by other hands, were generally tedious homilies, in keeping with detailed party policy in which he took only a superficial interest. Where issues related to party politics, and in respect of policy as a means of obtaining and keeping power, it was a different matter. He could deliver off-the-cuff speeches which were only rivalled in their verbal dexterity, their occasionally brilliant apophthegms, and their pointed sarcasm, by another member of his party whom he appointed Government Chief Whip, John Kelly.

This emphasis on his parliamentary and speechmaking performance is in keeping with Liam Cosgrave's political philosophy, which was limited in its vision and cautious in its execution. In Opposition he had often been content to leave press conferences, briefings, and announcements about policy to other members of the party. He adopted a similar approach to many issues while in power, and gave considerable freedom to individual ministers to get on with their jobs.

When Cosgrave became Taoiseach, on 14 March, 1973, he was a month away from his 53rd birthday. He had been a Dail deputy for thirty years, and had served as a junior minister in the first Inter-Party Government (1948–51) and as Minister for

External Affairs in the second (1954–7) in which portfolio he had led the first Irish delegation to the United Nations, in 1956. Though leader of the Fine Gael Party, and therefore Opposition leader, only since 1965, his experience of both the Dail, and Irish politics generally, was immense. It had made him sceptical, not just about the achievement of change and reform, but even about attempting it. In a sense this reluctance had made him the butt of antagonism from the growing band of liberals within his party, particularly between 1969 and 1973. His cautious leadership, which had drawn heavily upon two quite different sources within Fine Gael, had been uninspiring, and there had been several ineffective attempts to replace him.

By the autumn and winter of 1972 antagonism towards Cosgrave was quite pronounced, and the divisions within Fine Gael were well defined. Saved, as it were, by the bombs in Dublin in December 1972, Cosgrave was nevertheless in the position when he came to power of having done so by the skin of his teeth. He was therefore determined to head off any possibility of internal challenge. To some extent this explains the appointment of Garret FitzGerald to Foreign Affairs, and of Declan Costello as Attorney General. On his record, Costello might have been expected to win a senior Cabinet appointment, while FitzGerald saw himself, and was widely seen by others, as an ideal Finance Minister. But Cosgrave saw neither of them as central to his administration. Declan Costello was typical of the traditional Fine Gael politician; combining a legal career with politics was part of this equation; more central to it was the curious amalgamation of economic radicalism with moral conservatism. He was opposed, for example, when legalising contraception came up in the Dail, to the provision being extended to all adults, preferring that the facility should be limited to married couples.

The contraception issue was an interesting one, politically, as well as being central to human rights and constitutional issues. It gave also, when it arose in the legislature, an interesting insight on Cosgrave's mind and his handling of a difficult problem. In 1973 the Supreme Court had judged in the McGee case that the State had no right to intervene in marital privacy, including the question of a couple's right to choose artificial means of contraception. The effect of the judgment was to allow the unrestricted *importation* of contraceptives. Legislative controls, taking cognisance of the Supreme Court judgment, were introduced by the Minister for Justice, Patrick Cooney, in a *Government* Bill in July 1974. Without giving any warning to his colleagues the Taoiseach, Liam Cosgrave, then voted *against* the second stage of the Bill, supported by another Minister, Richard Burke, and two backbenchers, Oliver J. Flanagan and Tom Enright. The effect was the defeat of the measure and unrestricted access by everyone to artificial contraceptives! Fianna Fail adopted a curious dog-in-the-manger approach, rejecting the idea of actually legislating, by amendment, and voting *en bloc* against the measure. They promised their own Bill, which Charles Haughey introduced in 1978. It created an equally nonsensical situation, was described by its promoter as 'an Irish solution to an Irish problem', but did reach the Statute Book.

Others were totally opposed to the provision of artificial methods of contraception.[3] These included Mark Clinton within the Government, as well as Richard Burke, Minister for Education, who were *ultramontanes* on moral issues as well as being among the politicians closest to the party leader. This same closeness was true of Tom O'Donnell (Gaeltacht), and also of Paddy Donegan, the Minister for Defence, though in his case the political make-up was interestingly different. He had been a deputy since 1954, with a break between 1957 and 1961, and was a wealthy and successful businessman with decidedly Right-wing economic views and a trenchantly dismissive attitude about the intrusion of moral issues into politics. Strongly law-and-order in his views, and intensely loyal both to the Fine Gael party and its leader, he was the right kind of no-nonsense Minister for Defence needed in the tense atmosphere that prevailed as a result of the Arms Trial.

He shared his security responsibilities with Paddy Cooney, Minister for Justice, whose position in the National Coalition Government was perhaps to prove the least happy of all. Cooney had been a so-called Fine Gael 'young tiger' in the mid-1960s, a liberal, and the party's Justice spokesman from 1972, only two years after his election to the Dail. He had opposed the Offences Against the State (Amendment) Bill in December 1972, describing it in withering terms as an unnecessarily draconian measure and one more suited to South Africa than Ireland. He had been active with Garret FitzGerald at the same time in trying to oust Liam Cosgrave. His appointment as Minister for Justice was variously seen as a concession to liberalism and as an acceptable continuation of his responsibilities when in Opposition. In reality it turned out to be a punishing job, and the party leader must have had a fair idea that the appointment, at best, only attracts little credit, and at worst can be identified with repressive actions. Given the potential for I.R.A. violence in early 1973, the latter of these two possibilities was the more likely.

I 2

The Economy

Liam Cosgrave's appointment of Richie Ryan as Minister for Finance was a surprising choice. Cosgrave had chosen him for the most powerful position in the Government because of his unquestioning loyalty rather than because of his potential economic wizardry. Nevertheless Ryan's reputation stands up reasonably well when compared with subsequent holders of the office. His principal fault was a certain inflexibility. As the basic instrument of Government policy, he reflected, to a heightened degree, the solid virtue of reliability upon which the Taoiseach placed a high premium. This meant that economic policy, once decided, would be firmly sustained; commitments would be honoured, the books would balance, greater equity would be introduced, and the overall controls would be clearly and firmly emphasised. Had circumstances been as stable as Ryan was, this might well have worked. But quite different economic weather was on the way.

The first oil crisis occurred in the winter of 1973–4. The Dail Chamber was illuminated on one occasion by candles in bottles. Long queues formed at petrol stations, and provision was made for the introduction of petrol rationing. Though not directly the responsibility of Richie Ryan, this shock to an economic system which had enjoyed growth and expansion throughout more than a decade, necessarily restrained the new administration. But this sudden sharp shock by no means represented the whole story, economically speaking. At the same time the public and the unions still nurtured high expectations of continued growth, especially on the wages front. This illusion should have been dispelled and the pressure resisted. Instead, in his first year in office, Ryan presided over the negotiation of a national wages agreement which resulted in an overall pay award of around 15–16 per cent in a single year. This highly inflationary level of pay was itself the result of the boom years spilling over from the 1960s. Ryan was faced with a crisis over energy, clear indicators of economic instability in the future, excessive wage demands from the unions, a balance of payments problem, high domestic consumption unmatched by exports, an unfamiliarity with the workings of the E.E.C. coupled with a sense of optimism about the Community's ability and willingness to transform Ireland's economy for her, and a high degree of self-confidence within the coalition itself. At the same time, the new administration was awkwardly caught. Having come to power on the basis of undertakings about housing and other elements in the public capital programme, the political reality was that the coalition had to sustain a certain level of expansion when it ought economically to be cutting back. During its first year in power a 27 per cent increase in the public capital programme saw large sums of money pumped into housing, education, industrial and agricultural development by way of grants, while at the same time the feeling grew that austerity was inevitably on the way.

In such circumstances the underlying certitude of the man in charge becomes a key factor. Ryan, superficially confident, bouncy, sharp and reactive in debate, plucky and aggressive in political confrontation, failed nevertheless to spread the more profound confidence which private investment needed. After sixteen unbroken years under Fianna Fail *laissez-faire* politics, the pragmatism of which had managed, superficially, to satisfy the wealthy and the poor, the country was now having to come to terms with an ostensible partnership between capital and labour, between economic conservatism and socialism. Such sleight-of-hand was, politically speaking, infinitely more difficult for a Fine Gael–Labour alliance, the supporters of which, on both sides of the traditional economic divide, would demand realism rather than illusion.

By the end of the first year in office, certain cracks were becoming apparent in the underlying economic confidence which is essential to any administration, but is particularly so with one that jointly represents the Left and the Right, and which has also declared an intention to reform. This declaration, in favour of a capital taxation package, had been repeatedly confirmed, by Ryan among other members of the Government in the autumn of 1973, and was further developed in 1974, with a capital taxation White Paper, followed by the introduction of capital gains and capital acquisition taxes. The package was not completed until the spring of 1975, with the introduction of wealth tax, the most controversial of all the measures. But well before that date a clear picture of the intended reforms had emerged; and the reactions, predictably enough, were strong.

In principle, the reforms were logical in both political and economic terms; in practice, their introduction was clumsy and uncertain, first creating doubt over what was actually intended, and then very substantial opposition. The groundswell of bewilderment and suspicion was undoubtedly fomented by the Opposition, and exploited by the wealthy. But the initial errors were those made by the Government and the Minister for Finance in the presentation of the package to a public still dominated by rural, peasant standards on property and wealth, rather than by urban and bourgeois ideals, and still not acclimatised to the supposed threats of a socialist party dominated by intellectuals sharing power with the more traditional Fine Gael of Liam Cosgrave.

The oil crisis had prejudiced the prospects created by the E.E.C. entry at the beginning of 1973. The election promises had led to budgetary action which was overheating the economy at the tail-end of a boom, the ending of which was already being foreshadowed in larger economies. Ireland's nearest neighbour, Britain, under Edward Heath, was going through a period of acute industrial strife in which the corrective measures, while sensible in theory, were not working in practice; the comparative peace in Ireland had the unfortunate effect of encouraging complacency and over-confidence. Yet more than anything else it was the uncertain fumbling that damaged credibility rather than the justice of what was being attempted. At the time of Ireland's capital taxation White Paper the country had only one form of capital tax in the form of estate duty. Of Ireland's eight other E.E.C. partners, all had capital gains tax in addition to some form of inheritance tax or death duty; six of Ireland's partners had a gift tax, and four — Holland, Luxembourg, Germany, Denmark — had wealth tax. Every other country in Europe had death, gift and capital gains taxes; and Sweden, Norway, Iceland, Finland and Austria had wealth tax as well. The not unreasonable recognition was abroad in the country that greater equity in taxation was legitimate and wise; it was the form, degree, extent and phasing that was of paramount importance.

It was this which went awry in 1974. The combined impact of the April Budget and the capital taxation White Paper gained for Richie Ryan a standing ovation from the Labour Party in the Dail, and the tag 'Red' Richie in the country. On the 'Right' of the Fine Gael Party warning bells began to ring, and it became apparent to the Government as a whole that politically some curtailment of the taxation legislation was needed. It was precisely at this point, however, that a certain stubborn streak in Ryan's character emerged. At the conclusion of the Budget debate, in mid-May, he reiterated that the Coalition had 'the will and the courage to effect real reforms'. But as he spoke, in the Dail, Paddy Donegan, the Defence Minister, and an outspoken critic of wealth tax, came pointedly into the Chamber and took a backbench seat. This provoked Opposition derision about growing Government uncertainty over measures which had been set in motion well before the oil crisis, and which were increasingly seen as less appropriate in the less optimistic mood of mid-1974. The irony lay in the fact that capital taxation, as such, was not a prerequisite of the partnership between Labour and Fine Gael. Nevertheless, once the course had been embarked upon, the motivating forces for Opposition were provided, and the seeds of economic instability sown.

The economy performed reasonably well under Ryan's guidance, during 1974 and 1975, his doctrinaire inflexibility favouring the input of the officials in the Department of Finance in a way that met with Liam Cosgrave's approval, itself based on a relatively conservative view about the part played by the politician in running the State's finances.

During 1975 the transition from a financial year, April-to-April, to a common Budget and calendar year came into effect, and the figures for that year became those for nine months. This condensed its impact within the time-scale of the

Coalition's four-and-a-half years in power. There was an additional June Budget, however, from which dated the reflation and recovery programme brought in by the Coalition to counter the impact of the oil crisis. Even so, for Richie Ryan, by the time he came to present his Budget for 1976 in January, the Coalition's economic strategy had still not gathered any steam, and the credibility of its architect was substantially undermined. The overriding problems were constant: the need to reduce inflation, to protect employment and create jobs, and to control public expenditure.

By any standards, the first of these problems was acute. Inflation was running at around 30 per cent. Unemployment was higher than when the second Inter-Party Government went out of power in 1957. This fact was significant for Liam Cosgrave, in whose hands rested the main political decision at the end of three years in power: the timing of the next general election. Altogether, in those three years, Richie Ryan had coped, in his resilient fashion, and had produced five Budgets. It would have been cruel to replace him; and yet, politically, it would have been wise. In any assessment of the mistakes made by the National Coalition, most of which were not directly related to the economy, arguably the most serious was an act of omission: that of not reshuffling the Government in the first half of 1976, and expressly in not moving Ryan out of Finance and replacing him by Garret FitzGerald. A change seemed desirable.

Garret FitzGerald's reputation was high as a result both of a convincing performance at Foreign Affairs, with widely respected work within the E.E.C., and also because his duties had kept him largely out of the various political wrangles at home, including those directly related to economic policy. In reality, he had played a full part in Government decision-making on economic and particularly taxation strategy, and shared with Ryan a radical approach not fully supported by other Government colleagues. Even so, his appointment to Finance would have given a fresh image and a fresh impetus in what was becoming the run-up period to a general election.

Cosgrave, however, to whom political loyalty was a fundamental principle, and who feared the rivalry of Fitzgerald, made no change. He stuck with Ryan as he stuck with the basic composition of his Government, with two exceptions,[1] and the economic strategy of the partnership continued throughout 1976, and on into the run-up to the general election. By then, the political character of the administration had been given substantial shape and colouring by forces other than economic ones; notably by security and law-and-order.

13

Sunningdale

The formation of the National Coalition Government, in March 1973, coincided with the British Government White Paper, 'Northern Ireland Constitutional Proposals'. At that stage Edward Heath's Conservative Government had been in power for almost three years and was facing economic stress and strain. But in Northern Ireland William Whitelaw had made an impact as Secretary of State, and in terms of combining understanding with careful but positive action had done substantially better than any other British politician in the period since the Northern Ireland troubles had started. Together with James Prior, who came to the post much later, he demonstrates the essentially more effective performance on Northern Ireland of the Conservative Party when compared to Labour.

Whitelaw's proposals, published on March 20, 1973, six days after the setting up of the Cosgrave Government, were for elections in Northern Ireland, by proportional representation, to an 80-seat assembly, to which would then be devolved executive powers so long as these were shared between representatives of the two communities. Control of law enforcement and justice would remain with Westminster for the time being, and the emergency powers, including internment, would remain in force. There was provision also for a Council of Ireland, involving Dublin.

The following day Unionist organisations led by William Craig and Ian Paisley rejected the proposals. They represented the major loyalist bodies outside the Unionist party. Brian

Faulkner, the former premier, and leader of the Unionist Party, accepted the proposals with the grudging backing of the party. The S.D.L.P. pronounced in favour. The ground was laid for the conference at Sunningdale, outside London.

The Assembly elections were held on June 28, and resulted in Brian Faulkner's Official Unionist Party winning 23 seats, the S.D.L.P. 19 and Alliance 8. This gave a majority to those in favour of power-sharing. Of those opposed to the idea of a power-sharing executive, Unionists of various colouring won 10 seats, Ian Paisley's Democratic Unionist Party 9, Vanguard 6 and West Belfast Loyalists 2.

It was an unstable result. The committed opponents to the proposed sharing of power had a limited, but single-minded objective: to defeat the Westminster solution. The combined commitment to this simple end included William Craig of the Vanguard Movement, John Taylor, who led a group of un-pledged Unionists, and Ian Paisley, whose political star had risen steadily since the late 1960s. Both Lynch and Cosgrave declared their support in the Dail for the Northern Ireland Assembly, and said they would do all they could to make it work.

The burden of doing this lay with Brian Faulkner. But the motives for seeing it successfully achieved were shared by both Lynch and Cosgrave as well. From Lynch's point of view the successful creation of a government in Northern Ireland in which Unionists and Nationalists shared power would vindi-cate all he had stood for, and justify much of what he had gone through between 1968 and going out of power in March 1973. In addition, it would strengthen his hand in Opposition, when all the traditional temptations for Fianna Fail were to move towards a more hard-line republican standpoint.

The claim has frequently been made that the de-stabilising of the whole 'Loyalist Front' in Northern Ireland, arguably an essential prerequisite to the unprecedented joining of hands between Unionists and Nationalists, was the work of the National Coalition. Yet, in reality, Lynch's judgment and tact, following the arms crisis, had largely brought this about, and, as we have seen in an earlier chapter, the general predisposition towards power-sharing which had been created in Northern Ireland by the end of 1972 was in part due to him. Correspon-dingly, he had a serious political interest in continued progress.

Moreover, Lynch had already achieved a not inconsiderable movement in Edward Heath's thinking, before the change of Government in March 1973. When the preparations for an Irish involvement in the four-party conference were going on in the summer of 1973, and Edward Heath came over to Dublin for talks with Liam Cosgrave at Baldonnel Airport in September 1973, Lynch asked for a meeting with Heath. This was arranged, and it contributed to the optimism with which the approaching conference was viewed by the two sovereign governments.

For Liam Cosgrave, Northern Ireland had not been, nor was, a central political issue. His belief in unity as an attainable ideal was perfunctory, and his thoughts, either on how it might be attained, or on what might be done in preparation within the Republic, were severely limited by the prior claims of preserving the institutions of the State. This not only meant the institutions dealing with law and order, and security, but also the Catholic Church, to which his devotion acted as a barometer in respect of what was acceptable legislative, constitutional, social or ideological change. The prospect of a form of government being restored to Northern Ireland which appeared to offer the stability and fairness of Unionists working with the Alliance Party and the S.D.L.P. was enormously attractive. It gave him bi-partisanship without the bother of negotiating with Jack Lynch. It satisfied the minority within his own administration who believed in action on Northern Ireland, and it reflected primarily upon him as the leader responsible for achieving the breakthrough. Cosgrave was representative of the vast majority of deputies in the Dail, and of those who had elected them, of all parties, in wanting some kind of Northern Ireland settlement which would not cost too much in time, money, violence or death; which would not challenge too deeply the fundamental structure of the State in the southern half of the island; and which would permit the Government to continue to steer the economy and to enjoy the active, inter-party political life which was really the Taoiseach's primary interest.

He stood at a pivotal point, politically. He had come to power in the South when political life in Northern Ireland was at a deeply traumatic phase. Between 1968 and 1972 the fundamental reforms in an essentially corrupt State had been forced through, ending sourly, however, in the confrontation between Stormont and Westminster over Brian Faulkner's decision to bring in internment. Though this was done by Faulkner in consultation with the British Government, the initiative was his. Internment was offered as a solution to an impasse in which I.R.A. violence was continuing in spite of the implementation of the reform programme, tighter security measures, and ever-increasing troop strengths in Northern Ireland. It proved regressive. Nationalists had already pulled out of Stormont; violence was continuing; and then the British Government took over responsibility for law and order, forcing the resignation of Brian Faulkner and his Government.

Now, in 1973, there was no question initially of this control of law and order being restored under the power-sharing proposals, and therefore, if Brian Faulkner were to return to Stormont as Unionist leader, his new beginning would be several rungs down the ladder from his position in March 1972. Whatever the implications for Unionists, and for Faulkner himself, to all political parties in the South this altered plane on which the political process would be reactivated was acceptable.

Agreement was reached on November 21, 1973, after six weeks of talks that there would be an eleven-member Executive (Cabinet) drawn from a fifteen-member Administration (Government) the constitution of each to be as follows: Executive to consist of 6 Unionists, 4 S.D.L.P. and 1 Alliance member, with Brian Faulkner as Chief Executive and the S.D.L.P. Leader, Gerry Fitt, as his deputy; Administration to consist of 7 Unionists, 6 S.D.L.P., and 2 Alliance. The detailed breakdown, in terms of portfolios was also agreed on party lines. It was a genuine share-out of power, an historic moment, and warmly endorsed as such by Liam Cosgrave in the Dail the following day. It involved two other elements, however: a tripartite conference to set up a Council of Ireland, and a British commitment to bring internment to an end. Liam Cosgrave's judgment, which includes the degree to which he accepted the judgment of key colleagues in Government, was critical in one area: that of the proposed Council of Ireland.

In his statement to the Dail, on November 22, he outlined the objectives. The Council would be confined to Northern Ireland and Republic of Ireland elected representatives on a two-tier basis, with executive functions confined to those drawn either from the Executive in the North, or from the Government in the South, and with advisory or consultative functions coming from the remaining members. Overall, it would have both an executive and a consultative role, but would operate on the basis of unanimity. Initially, according to Cosgrave's statement, it was envisaged that the Council would address itself to 'a common law enforcement area, the question of extradition processes, human rights, and what role a Council might play in the law and order field'. This was the background to the Sunningdale Conference of December 6–9, 1973.

Liam Cosgrave handled well the whole procedure leading up to the conference at Sunningdale, imposing careful restraint on himself and others, emphasising the risks and the delicate balance that would have to be struck between the twin objectives of the political settlement: power-sharing, which it was hoped would gain widespread support in Northern Ireland, and a Council of Ireland which would endeavour to bring 'growing harmony and common benefit' to Northern Ireland and the Republic. On the eve of his departure he said:

> The Irish public should not pin exaggerated hopes on what these talks can produce in the immediate future. I have to tell you, and it is important that you remember, that these talks are essentially about men's lives and there is no guarantee that peace will return in the immediate wake of the talks . . . The danger of further serious violence is not to be excluded. We will deal firmly with such activities here.

It was Cosgrave's stated belief that the Anglo-Irish proposals would further isolate the men of violence, and add to the community pressures on them to abandon terrorism. He took with him to Sunningdale a strong Government team.[1]

The Conference opened with a plenary session at which it was agreed that all sides would emerge *only* with an agreed package, and that there would be total confidentiality until that stage was reached. The essential problems were that the S.D.L.P. would enter a Northern Ireland Executive only when there was a Council while the Unionists said there would not be a Council until there was an Executive. There were additional obstacles, including security and the transfer of policing to the Executive. The position of each of the four parties to the conference may be summarised thus: The S.D.L.P. did not want the restoration of policing to the Executive, but were looking instead towards an all-Ireland police force. They wanted also the abolition of internment.

The Faulkner Unionists wanted recognition of Northern Ireland by the Republic. Faulkner was distinctly worried about the Council of Ireland, and certainly wanted it postponed until after the Executive had started to function. He regarded the restoration of police powers as vital to the self-confidence of the new administration. He looked also for extradition from the Republic, but settled for the Criminal Law (Jurisdiction) proposals which formed part of the Republic's position.

The British Government's primary objective was to get Faulkner and the S.D.L.P. working together, and then operating the Executive together. Heath, subsequent to advice from both Liam Cosgrave and Jack Lynch, recognised the political rawness of the material out of which an administration had to be forged. At the same time the British were reticent over security and policing, wishing to postpone the restoration of powers in that area for the present; they were also anxious to persuade the Irish Government to drop its Strasbourg case on R.U.C. torture,[2] a change which the Dublin Government rejected.

The Irish Government wanted the establishment of the Council of Ireland as a key part of the agreement; this was vital for the S.D.L.P. as well as politically at home. As far as the recognition of Northern Ireland was concerned, the importance of this to Faulkner and to the British was fully recognised, and conceded in principle; the difficulty arose when a verbal formula was sought, and there were over forty draft versions of what was eventually to prove a controversial and damaging element in the communiqué. The request for extradition was refused, but the Dublin Government agreed to the setting up of a Commission which would lead to common jurisdiction legislation.

In a private conversation before the end of the Conference, with only Irish Government representatives present, it was suggested that each man present should award marks out of ten to each of the four main participating groups — leaving out

Alliance — in terms of what each had obtained from the Conference. The aggregate came out with a result which placed the British and Irish Governments best equal, the S.D.L.P. next, and Faulkner undoubtedly the worst off. There was no jubilation about this. At least one of those present was distinctly gloomy at the way things had turned out.

The Conference ended with agreement, in which 'none had compromised ... in relation to basic aspirations'. The Irish Government made a solemn declaration, as part of the agreed communiqué, 'that there could be no change in the status of Northern Ireland until a majority of the people of Northern Ireland desired a change in that status', and the British Government reaffirmed Northern Ireland as part of the United Kingdom, support for the wishes of the majority, and support also 'if in the future the majority of the people of Northern Ireland should indicate a wish to become part of a united Ireland'.

A considerable part of the communiqué was given over to details about the Council of Ireland, how it would be constituted, what issues it would consider, and what the timetable would be for setting it up. The approach was not precipitate. Before the Council's implementation there were to be the equivalent of 'joint studies'. Also included was a detailed assessment of security, and in particular a common law enforcement area with an all-Ireland court, extradition legislation, and the extension of the jurisdiction of domestic courts. The need for some expression, in both parts of Ireland, of the European Convention on Human Rights — in other words, a Bill of Rights — was agreed, and it would be handed over to the Council of Ireland to consider in due course. Policing was reviewed, as was the eventual devolution of authority over this, and, fairly rapidly, over everything else as well. This was the message of the penultimate, paragraph 19 of the joint communiqué:

> The British Government stated that, in the light of the decisions reached at the Conference, they would now seek the authority of Parliament to devolve full powers to the Northern Ireland Executive and Northern Ireland Assembly as soon as possible. The formal appointment of the Northern Ireland Executive would then be made.

As already suggested, the crowded stage, on which all sorts of leading lights were performing, had left one vital figure in the drama arguably upstaged, if not at times pushed into the wings altogether. This was Brian Faulkner. A tough political survivor, and confident within the positive accord engendered by the British and Irish Governments, as well as the apparent support of Jack Lynch and Fianna Fail, the putative head of the Northern Ireland Executive had overlooked certain vital facts. The most important of these was that the basis on which he had gone into negotiations on devolution had been quite different from the deal with which he came away from Sunningdale. The Unionists had fought the assembly elections on a relatively clear distinction between a committee-based Administration involving power-sharing, but a one-party, Unionist Executive, or 'Cabinet' drawn from that Administration, or 'Government'. This had also been the basic position of the Unionist document at the Darlington conference in the autumn of 1972.[3] Yet it never really emerged at all during the Sunningdale Conference itself, that Faulkner, in agreeing to S.D.L.P. and other participation in the Northern Ireland Executive, was surrendering a key aspect of the Unionist position.

The defections from 'Official' Unionism, substantial enough before Darlington, and in the aftermath of the elections to the Assembly in June 1973, grew rapidly as the accelerating pace of Sunningdale added what was seen as the massive dimension of a Council of Ireland.

Then came the backlash. On January 4, 1974, after five hours of bitter debate, the Ulster Unionist Council rejected the Sunningdale Agreement. On Monday, January 7, Brian Faulkner resigned as leader of the Unionist Party, though not, of course, as chief executive in the new Administration. The first full meeting of his Administration took place the following day, on which there were further resignations from the Unionist Party and growing speculation about the setting up of a new, middle-of-the-road political organisation. The backlash was not confined to Northern Ireland. Kevin Boland, whose Aontacht Eireann Party had been conspicuously unsuccessful in the general election of the previous year, was nevertheless still active. On January 11 he started a High Court action in Dublin against the Irish Government seeking a declaration that the Sunningdale Agreement, specifically in the clause which 'accepted and solemnly declared' no change without majority wish, was unconstitutional, and ran counter to Articles 2 and 3.[4]

It was a legitimate, indeed stimulating point of law, and the action was consistent with Kevin Boland's political character. But it had to be defended, and this was where the Government was forced to spell out in detail exactly those aspects of Sunningdale which it would have preferred to keep vague, for the sake of the power-sharing Executive in Northern Ireland. In its defence of the action, the Attorney General's interpretation was that the Sunningdale 'communiqué' did not constitute an 'agreement' either to the fact that Northern Ireland was part of the United Kingdom, or that Northern Ireland's reintegration 'into the national territory' would have to depend on the agreement of a majority within Northern Ireland. Technically correct, in distinguishing between an agreement and a declaration, and successful as a defence when the action came to be dismissed, first in the High Court in January, and then in the Supreme Court on appeal, on March 1, 1974, the damage was nevertheless quite serious in political terms. As *The Times* in London put it, the Irish Government's interpretation 'has brought a yelp from Mr Faulkner – and no wonder.' There were phone calls between Faulkner and Cosgrave 'clarifying' the situation, and a visit by the Chief Executive to Dublin, after which he said he was 'now much happier about the situation'. Growing numbers of Unionists were not, and noisy opposition at the first meeting of the Northern Ireland Assembly led to the forcible removal of Ian Paisley. Other Unionists withdrew formally in protest at the formation of the Executive. Then, on February 7, Edward Heath sought a dissolution of the Westminster Parliament followed by a general election on February 28. The return of Harold Wilson, notwithstanding his slender majority, should have represented no great threat to the Sunningdale package. The Irish Government, in spite of disruptive tactics by Neil Blaney in a Dail debate at the end of February, maintained its supportive stance, and, in a statement in the Dail on March 13, welcomed by George Colley on behalf of Fianna Fail, gave *de facto* recognition to Northern Ireland.

After a one-day visit to Northern Ireland, on April 18, the new British Prime Minister, Harold Wilson, said that the Labour Government was not prepared to accept an alternative to the power-sharing Executive. In the Assembly, on May 14, power-sharing survived an anti-Sunningdale motion and this was the signal for the Ulster Workers' Council to declare a general strike in Northern Ireland. The strike became widely effective, and by May 23 both the Northern Ireland Executive and the Dublin Government were calling on Wilson to break it. Instead, he made an inconclusive radio and television broadcast about the Loyalist thugs and bullies who were 'sponging on British democracy'. The S.D.L.P. threat to pull out of the Executive on May 27 forced the deployment of British troops in oil depots and filling stations as a partial move against the anti-Sunningdale U.W.C. strike, but the Executive's position, dependent on vacillations by Wilson and by his Secretary for Northern Ireland, Merlyn Rees, had become untenable, and the following day Faulkner and five of his fellow Unionist ministers resigned. On May 29 the Northern Ireland Assembly was prorogued. The Sunningdale experiment had been deliberately defeated.

Sunningdale was an honourable and determined effort by the Irish Government, working closely with the British Government, to bring a political 'solution' to Northern Ireland based on power-sharing. Equally honourably supported by Lynch, whose own handling of the North had contributed substantially to making Sunningdale possible, it was sustained as far as was possible by him in Opposition. Its collapse had a number of different causes, including, at the centre, the lamentable loss of nerve by Harold Wilson, itself a by-product of the unfortunate changeover of power at Westminster. Had Heath survived, he would almost certainly have taken on the U.W.C. and the course of events might have been different. Brian Faulkner also failed to carry with him, into undoubtedly altered political conditions, the body of Unionism, relying, as such political survivalists do, on an ability to survive against mounting odds. Arguably he would have done this with adequate Westminster support. Certainly he had the necessary support from the South, in spite of the best efforts of Kevin Boland and Neil Blaney to sink Sunningdale.

The main argument against the Sunningdale Agreement has always been that it placed too much emphasis on the Irish dimension, and that the detailed proposals for a Council of Ireland represented the breaking point. There were in fact many breaking points, many errors of judgment, some bad luck, and some treachery. Brian Faulkner, far from being out-talked or out-voted, was himself over-confident at the Sunningdale talks in believing that he could make the package work. On the Republic of Ireland side, Conor Cruise O'Brien was certainly the most cautious, having a finely-tuned ear to Protestant, Unionist and Loyalist sticking points. He was listened to with insufficient care. Edward Heath led a British team which, although incomparably better than any group that had previously been got together over Northern Ireland, was still dealing with a highly evolutionary phase in Northern terrorism, and political change within the Unionist monolith. Liam Cosgrave himself contributed to the instability when, in the course of an R.T.E. interview, he answered that he thought Sunningdale would lead to a united Ireland.

The Boland factor was unfortunate, to say the least, in that it raised obvious anomalies the settling of which, by the Irish Attorney General in his defence of the Sunningdale Agreement, increased Unionist fears about movement towards unity. If ever there was a time when the failure to implement the unanimous proposal by the all-Party Constitutional Reform Committee of 1967 to re-write Articles 2 and 3 of the 1937 Constitution was seen to be damaging, the immediate aftermath of the Sunningdale Conference was that time.

Finally, there was Harold Wilson. The miners, in defeating Heath, defeated Sunningdale as well. The fact that Northern Ireland hardly rated a mention in the general election of February 1974 was an endorsement of bi-partisanship, and of the effectiveness of the British public servants responsible for Northern Ireland. But bi-partisanship needs to be a positive, as well as a negative force. And when the going got tough over power-sharing, and the Ulster Workers' Council challenged the British Army, Wilson effectively reneged on the work of more than a year. Questions remain unanswered about the attitude of the Army to the issue of taking on the loyalists, and it is clear that Wilson was not happy about this, having faced similar problems during his previous administration in the context of Rhodesia. Nevertheless, he must shoulder a substantial part of the blame. Anyone who in Ireland sat through the crucial broadcast of May 25, 1974, was given a bland taste of Albion's perfidy, hard to stomach.[5]

It was in Liam Cosgrave's political character to register Sunningdale as an honourable defeat, put away his Northern Ireland files, and call it a day. In spite of its failure, Sunningdale had been enormously beneficial in bringing a new realism to thinking in the South about Northern Ireland. It continued and developed the careful and conscientious leadership of Jack Lynch in eviscerating the mindless republicanism which had found periodic expression at particular moments such as the aftermath of the Arms Trial, and the burning of the British Embassy following Bloody Sunday. And from Sunningdale on, men like Conor Cruise O'Brien and Garret FitzGerald within the Government, sustained the educative process. But in policy terms the Republic learned caution and restraint.

14

Security

The Republic of Ireland learned some painful security lessons under the National Coalition, but none as painful as the events of May 17, 1974, in the middle of the Ulster Workers' Council Strike which brought down the Northern Ireland power-sharing Executive. On that day, in the country's capital, and in the Border town of Monaghan, bombs went off killing 23 people in Dublin, two in Monaghan, and injuring over 100, many seriously. Initially, Cosgrave responded with a proposal for an auxiliary force of reserve security personnel in every city and town in Ireland, to offer protection against car-bombers. The idea was not pursued. But it was indicative of the under-lying law-and-order approach which became a dominant factor of the National Coalition, and a form of substitute policy for Northern Ireland initiatives.

The Coalition's security performance had been mixed. Within a month of coming to power there had been the arrest of the *Claudia*, a Cypriot motor vessel, off the South coast, with a 5-ton cargo of arms on board. In September and October 1973, pressure, including a hunger strike, by Republican prisoners in Mountjoy prison for political status provoked from the Minister for Justice the threat of movement to alternative detention. The protest ended when concessions were made which the prisoners claimed were equivalent to political status, a claim denied by Cooney. More colourful breaches of security occurred during 1974. The Provisional I.R.A. hi-jacked a heli-copter on January 24 and carried out an unsuccessful bombing raid, with explosives packed into milk churns, on the Strabane

R.U.C.–Army barracks. The Littlejohn brothers[1] escaped from Mountjoy, only one being recaptured. Senator Fox[2] was murdered in March 1974, and in April and May the robbery and recovery of the Vermeer and other paintings owned by Sir Alfred Beit took place, with Bridget Rose Dugdale being found guilty and then going on hunger strike. In August nineteen republican prisoners escaped from the top security prison at Portlaoise.

No legislative response was called for; none would have been desirable. Most of the events were indicative of security failures of one kind or another which could be remedied, and were remedied by administrative and technical tightening of procedures. Consequently, when in March 1975 a major breakout was again attempted at Portlaoise, it failed, and a prisoner was shot dead, the first such death in the Republic since 1940.

Out of Sunningdale, however, there did emerge the Criminal Law Jurisdiction Bill, published in mid-April 1975, just a fortnight before the Northern Ireland convention elections. The Bill was debated first in the Senate, and did not come to the Dail until the autumn. In the light of the Loyalist victory in the elections, the solitary survival of this single practical vestige of Sunningdale was both bleak and controversial. The Bill made terrorist offences committed in Northern Ireland subject to trial in the Republic.

In the Senate, in April, the main challenge to it was on constitutional grounds, with Mary Robinson setting out extensive arguments against the admissibility of the proposed legislation, and, as in the case of the Kevin Boland Court challenge to Sunningdale, underlining the inflexibility of the basic law to the kind of practical co-operation between Northern Ireland and the Republic which had emerged as the only possible way forward.

When the Bill came to the Dail it had acquired for the Fianna Fail leader, Jack Lynch, an importance which took it into the broad policy area. That importance was not unconnected with Lynch's own position at that time. He had reshuffled his Front Bench at the beginning of 1975, bringing back on to it as Health and Social Welfare Spokesman, Charles Haughey. It was an act of reconciliation, of the binding together of factions within his own party, but it was widely interpreted as a response to pressures. Lynch was at that stage two-and-a-half years into his eriod in Opposition, and had witnessed the most notable Republic of Ireland initiative, at Sunningdale, of any attempted either until then or afterwards. Though the elements of success in that Sunningdale initiative would not have been possible without much of the work achieved by Lynch between the arms crisis and his general election defeat, few people were prepared to give him credit of this kind. Electorally, he was gearing himself for a confrontation in which he had long since decided he would lead Fianna Fail. And he had made a number of judgments about the Coalition which now dictated the playing of his hand. Two misjudgments on the Government's part were now relevant: the first of these was a growing emphasis on law-and-order solutions to security problems, prison unrest and North–South tension; the second was a strong predilection on the part of the politically more active ministers in the Government, notably Conor Cruise O'Brien, to attack both Lynch and Fianna Fail as leading and being a divided house, unsure and unsafe on the much-debated, ill-defined 'national question'. Whether justified or not, and much was yet to come, both in draconian legislation and in evidence of two distinct facets of nationalism in Fianna Fail, the reality was that a Government which was presiding over a multitude of quite massive economic problems, seemed over-obsessed with security and the political need to defeat Fianna Fail a second time, at the next general election.

It was in this curious wasteland atmosphere for an Opposition leader that Jack Lynch rose to speak in the second stage debate on the Criminal Law (Jurisdiction) Bill on September 10, 1975, and made a speech which, in its elusive subtlety, had the effect of leaving his listeners with the distinct impression that the legislation was of questionable relevance, and even more questionable motive. It was the only shred of Northern Ireland policy left in the Government's policy locker, he said, and it would do nothing for reconciliation, nothing to bring peace or stability in the North, and nothing to advance eventual unity. In addition, the proposed Bill was constitutionally and legally unsound and would prove unworkable, playing into the hands of the men of violence. Setting it in the context of Sunningdale, and of Fianna Fail's support in principle for the objectives of the Sunningdale Agreement, Lynch pointed out that not only had every other shred of Sunningdale's respect for

the principle of reconciliation, represented by power-sharing
and of the Irish dimension, represented by the proposals for
Council of Ireland, been swept away, but that, in addition, th
basic message now coming from the Northern Ireland Con
vention was the Unionist majority one of a return to Stormon
In such circumstances the Criminal Law (Jurisdiction) Bi
was unacceptable.

The Bill was eventually passed by 65 votes to 61, but no
until March 1976, a full year after its introduction as a Sena
Bill in 1975.

As a watershed for Lynch, and in the context of Norther
Ireland policy, there are a few more things to be said about i
Jack Lynch was under pressure from within his own party t
adopt a more 'republican' approach on Northern Ireland. I
came, indirectly, from Charles Haughey, and from the residua
elements of the pro-Blaney faction. In more open form, it cam
also from the newly-appointed Foreign Affairs spokesman
Michael O'Kennedy.

Electorally, Lynch's position was finely balanced. In March
1975, Fianna Fail had won two by-elections, in Galway Nort
East and Galway West. While the former was a convincing
enough result, the latter recorded a combined Fine Gael
Labour vote which was within a half percentage point o
Fianna Fail, with an additional Sinn Fein and Independen
vote which was considerable enough to present problems fo
the future. On September 25, 1975, Henry Kenny, a popula
Fine Gael parliamentary secretary from West Mayo, died. O
October 29, 1975, mid-way through the by-election for the sea
Fianna Fail published a distinctly more hawkish policy docu
ment on Northern Ireland in which it called on the Britis
Government 'to declare Britain's commitment to implement a
ordered withdrawal from her involvement in the Six Countie
of Northern Ireland'. On November 12, 1975, Fianna Fail wer
resoundingly beaten in the by-election by Henry Kenny's sor
Enda, in a traditionally 'republican' west of Ireland constitu
ency, in the third year of an administration grappling wit
huge economic difficulties, and imposing severe law-and-orde
measures which Liam Cosgrave quite clearly emphasised in th
campaign. On one occasion, in Louisburg, County Mayo, o
November 1, he devoted the whole of a long speech to the singl
issue of security of the State, and the danger that 'violenc
threatens to spill over into our territory all the time'.

There was an additional factor. Several weeks earlier, a
Dutch businessman, Tiede Herrema, had been kidnapped, and
then held in a house in Monasterevin, a small midland town, by
Eddie Gallagher and Marian Coyle. His release, negotiated on
the basis of a secret deal giving both kidnappers guarantees
about reduced sentences, took place the day before polling, and
played a significant part in the opinion of many in swinging
support behind the Cosgrave Government. Details of the 'deal'
only came to light later. It was an arrangement endorsed by the
Government but subsequently breached by Gallagher and
Coyle, and therefore rendered void.

Whether or not Liam Cosgrave believed that his 'law-and-
order' image had partly won the by-election, Jack Lynch was
convinced that his party's arguably intentional lurch into an
unconvincing 'republicanism' had been in part responsible for
the loss, and that the burden had to be carried by those who
had pressed for the Northern Ireland policy shift, with Michael
O'Kennedy carrying the main onus. Perhaps not surprisingly,
Lynch himself came out of the whole episode strengthened.

Security misfortunes continued to dog the Coalition. On July
3, 1976, the newly-appointed British Ambassador to Ireland,
Christopher Ewart-Biggs, was killed by a bomb exploded in a
culvert under the road leading from the Embassy residence,
Glencairn, in Sandyford. It was detonated from a field over-
looking the road.

On August 31, the Dail resumed for a special emergency
sitting. Liam Cosgrave placed before the legislature three
measures: a motion invoking a national emergency, the Criminal Law Bill, 1976, and the Emergency Powers Bill, 1976.

The first of these measures involved revoking a State of
Emergency which, technically, had been in existence since
1939, and had been invoked then because of the Second World
War, in which Ireland had remained neutral. There were,
therefore, two parts to Liam Cosgrave's motion, one claiming
that the 1939 national emergency had 'ceased to exist', the
other claiming that 'arising out of the armed conflict now
taking place in Northern Ireland, a national emergency exists
affecting the vital interests of the State' and should be resolved
on by the Dail under Article 28.3.3. of the Constitution.

The principal difference between 1939 and 1976 was one of
consent. Eamon de Valera had the support of all sides in Dail

Eireann against a perceived and sinister threat to the State from the Axis Powers (a parallel threat was perceived by some from the Allied Powers), including naval and submarine interest in Irish waters. Liam Cosgrave was invoking an emergency without even attempting to ascertain the views of the Opposition. Jack Lynch was not consulted, and at least three members of the Government gave conflicting views of the situation, none of them adequate enough to meet the gravity and purpose of the constitutional provision. Paddy Cooney described it as an emergency with a small 'e'; Conor Cruise O'Brien said that it was a form of exhortation and assurance for the citizens of the Republic and of Northern Ireland; and Liam Cosgrave himself said it was an expression of the 'Government's view of the gravity of the situation'.

It was a largely cosmetic response to a single shocking act of terrorism which had not fundamentally changed the level or degree of security threat in the country. Politically, it represented an opportunity to wrong-foot the Opposition. A law-and-order election would then be on the cards, with the real emergency, the economic one, left on the sidelines.

It did not work. Jack Lynch made a speech in the Dail in which he supported all the normal security measures which were in force against a situation which had been in existence for six or seven years, but claimed that the current security threat to the country was not so great or so serious as to warrant the suspension of constitutional safeguards.

His attitude was the same towards the Emergency Powers Bill, introduced by Paddy Cooney the next day, September 1, with its principal provision of extending to seven days the period during which a person 'suspected in connection with offences under the Offences Against the State Act' could be held in custody. It very soon transpired that there was confusion about the wording of the Bill's 'Long Title', and that it was equally unclear whether the seven days' detention was to be added to the 48 hours for which there was already provision in other legislation, making nine days in all, or not. In addition, there was no effective time limit on the Bill, and there were no adequate safeguards about its renewal by the Dail. It was simply covered by Government Order. Fianna Fail opposed it both on constitutional grounds and in the light of these apparent anomalies. Because of the tense atmosphere which had

'esulted from the British Ambassador's death and the early
'ecall of the Dail in the summer, there was no Government
willingness to compromise.

The third measure, the Criminal Law Bill, sought to tighten
up controls on a wide range of issues, from the provision for
road blocks to the maximum sentence for membership of an
llegal organisation, which was raised from two to seven years.
Fianna Fail accepted the principle of such amendment, and
then argued the detail.

The whole emergency package was pushed swiftly through
the Dail and Senate during September. The Emergency Powers
Bill completed its passage, unamended, on September 16, and
on September 17 President O Dalaigh called a meeting of the
Council of State[3] to seek advice on the constitutionality of the
Bill, and whether he should refer it to the Supreme Court. He
did the same on September 20 with the Criminal Law Bill. The
Council of State met on September 23. The following day
O Dalaigh signed the Criminal Law Bill but sent the Emergency Powers Bill to the Supreme Court. As he later made
clear, O Dalaigh was distinguishing between the former piece
of legislation, which was open to normal constitutional challenge, and the latter Bill, which had a special protection under
Article 28.3.3. It was the constitutional legitimacy of this protection which O Dalaigh wanted the Supreme Court to
consider.

On Friday, October 15, the Supreme Court judged in favour
of the Bill's constitutionality, but with important reservations
about the Emergency itself, and they endorsed the legitimacy of
the President's decision to refer the legislation in the first place.
It was an exercise of his presidential function to protect the
interests of the people, whose 'mastery is maintained during the
period from election to election through the President, who has
been chosen definitely to safeguard their interests, to see that
nothing they have not in a general way given approval of is
passed by the small majority which used to be threatened here
as a danger to the country as a whole... in exercising these
powers he is acting on behalf of the people who have put him
there for that special purpose. He is there to guard the people's
rights and mainly to guard the constitution.'[4]

Some thought otherwise. The Minister for Defence, Paddy
Donegan, opening a new cookhouse and dining hall at Columb
Barracks in Mullingar on Monday, October 18, departed

from his scripted speech to describe President O Dalaigh, with additional expletives, as 'a thundering disgrace' for having referred the Emergency Powers Bill to the Supreme Court. Though a gauche and embarrassing blunder, few saw it leading to a constitutional crisis. Donegan issued a statement on the Monday evening regretting what he had said, and indicating that he would be seeing the President the following day to offer his personal apologies. He also privately offered to resign from the Government.

O Dalaigh refused to see him. The clear implications were constitutional rather than personal. The Minister for Defence is specifically answerable to the President, who is head of the armed forces, in addition to his normal Government obligations, and he had, in the presence of senior army officers, rejected a key presidential and constitutional function. President O Dalaigh made no statement. The Government issued a statement to the effect that there would be no question of Donegan resigning. There was no clear constitutional precedent for what had happened, but there was a constitutional responsibility on Cosgrave to 'keep the President generally informed on matters of domestic and international policy', and clearly, if reluctantly, a new policy departure was visible in relations between Government and Head of State. In the impasse the onus was on Cosgrave to go to O Dalaigh and apologise on his own and on his Minister's behalf. If, at that stage, O Dalaigh requested Donegan's resignation, it is difficult to see how Cosgrave could have refused, or, if he did, how his refusal would have produced less than O Dalaigh's resignation.

It did not work out like that. Cosgrave was in communication with the President only twice during the week of October 18–23, both times by telephone. He did not attempt to see the President. He did not apologise, either on his own, his Government's, or his Defence Minister's behalf. The two phone calls were on the Monday night and the Tuesday afternoon. On both occasions O Dalaigh indicated his willingness to see the Taoiseach but declined to discuss the affair on the telephone. In addition, and in the Tuesday conversation, O Dalaigh told Cosgrave that 'he had already taken certain preliminary decisions, the nature of which he did not disclose to me'. In the circumstances only one 'decision' was open to the President: resignation. In the Dail debate, on Thursday, October 21, in which the Opposition called for Donegan's resignation, the Taoiseach referred repeatedly to 'adequate', 'full', 'sincere', and 'unreserved' apologies. The motion was defeated. Donegan stayed on. The following day President O Dalaigh resigned, and published the exchange of letters between himself and the Minister for Defence. Donegan's letter, while containing a 'sincere and humble apology', also qualified the strictures on O Dalaigh with references to the non-referral of the Criminal Law Bill. To this the President had replied with a long and peppery lesson in constitutional and legal niceties which firmly rejected the attempts to gloss over the constitutional affront, and equally firmly established the seriousness of O Dalaigh's views about the presidential office.

It was blatantly clear that neither Donegan nor Cosgrave had treated the issue with any serious understanding of the legal, constitutional, political, or even personal implications. Having reached all-party agreement on the appointment of Cearbhaill O Dalaigh on December 19, 1974, after the sudden death of the previous President, Erskine Childers, on November 17, 1974, Cosgrave had consistently failed to honour his limited constitutional obligations to the presidential office, and had seriously underestimated the interpretations which O Dalaigh, an eminent constitutional lawyer, had made of his duties and responsibilities.[5] It was a damaging under-estimation, in every sense, and the 'thundering disgrace' remark, with the constitutional crisis which followed, clung like some malodorous marsh gas to the remaining days of Coalition rule.

15

The Opposition

It was clear that the 'thundering disgrace' fiasco had ruled out any possibility of an election in the autumn of 1976 on the issue of State security. It was equally clear, as the Coalition Government approached the end of its fourth year, that the political temperature was rising in anticipation of the increasingly imminent general election.

Within the arena of Leinster House, the vigour and the urge to return to power did manifest themselves, but were largely misread or underestimated. Dogged legislative performance by an opposition never commands great attention, and yet is often critical to recovery and return to power. This was the case with Fianna Fail, and the recovery was led by George Colley.

In 1976 George Colley had been fifteen years a Dail deputy, eight of them a Minister, and three of them deputy leader of party and Government. He had challenged Lynch for the leadership in 1966, which had greatly annoyed certain sections in Fianna Fail but had in no sense alienated Lynch, who relied heavily on Colley, and was happy to hand over to him responsibility for the economy. Since, in the end, politics and elections almost invariably come down to economic issues, Colley's responsibilities were critical within the party. And throughout this period he performed the comparatively thankless task of opposing Budgets, Finance Bills, capital taxation legislation, and did much related economic and industrial relations work. He was helped principally by Desmond O'Malley; but in addition a small group of Fianna Fail politicians, among them Eamon de Valera's son, Vivion, Tom Fitzpatrick and Ruairi Brugha, came together and worked consistently as a back-up team.

During 1976 the Government had largely taken the right measures, and the worst aspects of high inflation were being weathered. There was a reasonable expectation of growth during 1977 which would have allowed for a favourable election climate in the autumn, well within the full time-span of the Twentieth Dail. But in politics perceptions of future events count more with voters than past performance. The perceptions in late 1976, early 1977, were that the country faced an inflation crisis, unacceptably high unemployment, a weak pound, the absence of any overall economic plan, and the prospect of an election Budget which would set out to solve none of these difficulties, but instead would increase the deficit, leaving the country even more vulnerable internationally.

A less direct economic issue had emerged, however, which was to play a significant part in the closing stages of the Twentieth Dail. On January 25, 1977, the Government published its Bula Limited (Acquisition of Shares) Bill. The Bill proposed that the State should acquire a minority holding of 49 per cent in this mining company for a sum not exceeding £9·54 million. The deal was based on an 'Agreement' the terms of which were not divulged, and it brought to a head a specific sequence of events which went back to 1971, but which raised more generally question about mineral rights and the constitutionality of State intervention in their exploitation. This went, in turn, to the heart of the peculiarly Irish issue of land, its ownership and its uses. At the centre of what was to become a major storm was Justin Keating, Minister for Industry and Commerce, one of the newer and more radical men in the Labour Party.

Bula had been set up in March 1971 to take over land and mineral rights at Nevinstown, near Navan, in County Meath, which held the largest zinc orebody in Europe, subsequently estimated at 21·6 million tons. An agreement was struck between Bula and the State for joint involvement. On December 12, 1975, the substantive agreement between the Irish Government and Bula was signed, giving the State 25 per cent of the company 'free' and 24 per cent for the sum of £9·54 million, the agreement itself remaining confidential. Most of 1976 was spent in planning applications, arbitration talks and feasibility studies, concluding with an overall valuation of £39·75 million out of which the figure to be paid by the Government was derived.

The Minister, Keating, brought before the Dail a simple, two-page Bill which implemented an agreement which itself was to remain secret.[1] The central political fact was that the State was acquiring a minority, non-controlling share in a company which owned certain Navan fields which might one day become a zinc mine. The money paid for the shares was to go to private individuals, not the company, leaving un-capitalised and unplanned the whole enterprise. The deal, in other words, was with a property company.

The Opposition handled the debate extraordinarily well. Though he remained a key figure in the different stages of the Bill, George Colley gave way to Desmond O'Malley, who, in turn, used Bula to establish quite firmly his own formidable skills in debate. Again, a small team of Opposition deputies, among them Sylvester Barrett, kept up a sustained attack on the secrecy, on the prodigality of the £9·54 million going into private hands, on the ill-defined future for mining generally, and they substantially undermined the National Coalition's credibility.

In spite of this, the National Coalition in the early summer felt over-confident and sure of victory. Within the Government certain cautious voices advised Liam Cosgrave to hold on until the expansionist moves in the Budget had neutralised the effects of the 1975–6 economic turbulence. And this advice was redoubled after the annual conference of Fine Gael, on May 21, at which Liam Cosgrave made what appeared to be a minor if characteristic gaffe; he attacked an unnamed political journal-ist, describing him as a 'blow-in', and told him during an unscripted aside in his main conference speech 'to either blow up, or blow out'. The remark was widely applauded in the hall, but was received with deep gloom privately by the Fine Gael Party, and exploited significantly in the country by Fianna Fail, both immediately afterwards and during the election. This was called by Liam Cosgrave in the week following the Fine Gael Ard Fheis, and June 16 was fixed as polling day.

The National Coalition ran on a joint Fine Gael–Labour platform based on the Budget and their performance in office. Fianna Fail produced its first ever general election manifesto, offering a strategy for recovery and placing the main emphasis on the creation of jobs. It offered other things besides, including the abolition of rates on houses and of car tax. The manifesto had been carefully prepared, in secret, by Jack Lynch's closest adviser, Martin O'Donoghue, together with the party's general secretary, Seamus Brennan, and with additional contributions from Desmond O'Malley and George Colley.

The main electoral focus, however, was on the party leaders, and this was where Jack Lynch easily and immediately swept into a convincing lead which was never seriously challenged. He toured the country in a seemingly tireless exposition of his own unique brand of Fianna Fail politics, winning hearts and minds more or less effortlessly. Liam Cosgrave, in contrast, was slow to set off in a meet-the-people tour, and then gave up midway through the election with a 'sore throat'.

For all three parties June 1977 was a watershed. Fianna Fail won its biggest share of the vote since the 1938 general election, and returned to power with a twenty-seat majority.[2] Three members of the outgoing Government, Paddy Cooney, Conor Cruise O'Brien and Justin Keating, lost their seats. Liam Cosgrave resigned as leader of Fine Gael, and was succeeded by Garret FitzGerald. Brendan Corish resigned the Labour Party leadership which was subsequently contested, with Frank Cluskey beating Michael O'Leary by one vote.

16

Commitments

In order to win the 1977 general election, Jack Lynch had made very substantial promises. His manifesto, 'Action Plan for National Reconstruction', involved tax cuts amounting to £160 million and an ambitious job-creation programme costing £100 million. It set a target on jobs, of 80,000 between 1977 and 1980, and was supported by a specific pre-judgment on Lynch's part that any government in Ireland allowing unemployment to rise above 100,000 deserved to be rejected by the people.

The plan contained a high level of risk. The job-creation programme involved an initial increase in foreign borrowing. Under the Coalition, in 1977, this stood at 11 per cent of G.N.P. Fianna Fail proposed raising this in 1978 to 13 per cent, bringing it down in 1979 to 10·5 per cent, and then to 8 per cent in 1980. Coupled with this broad economic strategy were exceedingly generous tax cuts. Having assumed power, Fianna Fail went ahead with the abolition of rates on all private dwellings, the abolition of road tax on cars up to 16 h.p., the reduction of the social welfare stamp for low wage earners, and certain increases in personal tax allowances. It was, according to Jack Lynch, 'a responsible and realistic programme'. It was anything but; from it stemmed a growing tide of problems.

Its implementation was placed in the hands of an inner 'cabinet' consisting of Martin O'Donoghue, George Colley and Desmond O'Malley. Under the Irish Constitution there is no provision for 'cabinet' government in the accepted sense of the word. Executive power is vested in a Government of no more than fifteen members, and that is the position.[1]

The relevance of this grouping went beyond the economy. It was not unreasonable to anticipate, after Fianna Fail came back to power in 1977, that Jack Lynch would relinquish the leadership at some stage before the next general election. He had been Taoiseach during the extremely difficult period from 1966 to 1973. He had held the party together in Opposition, bringing it back to power with dramatic success in 1977. He had always seemed a reluctant 'Chief', and he was already on record as saying that it would be his intention, if standing down, to leave sufficient time for his successor to establish a fresh power-base for himself before the obligation to go to the country came round again. With a 20-seat majority this could be deliberately planned, and it was anticipated widely that Lynch would hand it over in the post-1977 period of government. It was therefore important who effectively governed the country, and how successful they were.

By exactly the same token, however, the exclusive approach which arrogated to a small group of men the ultimate control of the administration had built-in dangers for the very people whose ends were being served. The privilege enjoyed by Colley, as Finance Minister, and by O'Donoghue as principal economic strategist, would pay off handsomely if they were seen to be successful, but would represent a handicap if their plans went awry, or were seen in adverse circumstances not necessarily connected directly with the success of the economy.

This Government structure, most dangerously of all, left Charles Haughey relatively isolated in Health and Social Welfare, though with two distinct advantages: in Health he was in direct contact with deputies through medical card and other problem areas, while in Social Welfare he was responsible for the main hand-out of benefits, and was directly associated with the Social Welfare awards in conjunction with each of the Budgets.

The economy was, in fact, on an expansion course already, without the additional input which had been guaranteed to fulfil the job-creation targets for 1977–80 which had been spelt out in detail in the manifesto. The theory adopted by Martin O'Donoghue was simple enough: the country was looking at a domestic growth rate in 1977 of 6 per cent, likely to be sustained in 1978; this would combine with a modest acceleration in world trade, and Ireland would take advantage of it, cutting inflation, and becoming more competitive; cutting interest rates and taxation, thereby encouraging investment, would create more employment; tax cuts and tax incentives would be part of an overall wages deal which would result in an agreed wages ceiling; this would add competitiveness and the country's ability to attract foreign investment, something which had been elusive in the past because of unstable industrial relations in the country.

It was good, in theory; and Martin O'Donoghue was a confident and assured exponent. He spoke at length in the Dail, dealing with many economic complexities; he was also a frequent public speaker, and appeared often on television. Yet the difficulties which O'Donoghue faced were enormous.

O'Donoghue's Government position, without real departmental power, had the effect of turning his statements and proposals into 'options' which were increasingly at odds with economic realities such as real wage demands substantially higher than those allowed for in the economic plans which began in earnest with the publication, towards the end of 1977, of the Government White Paper, 'National Development 1977–80'. This offered to the 'social partners', the employers and trade unions, economic recovery and social advance in exchange for moderation in wage demands. And such moderation, spelt out in the post-election period, meant an annual wage round target of less than 5 per cent. This was too ambitious a target from the Government's point of view. Organised labour would not be responsive to a wages deal which represented a halving of their previous pay round award.

Moderation of wage demands was critical to Lynch's administration. Its whole economic strategy depended on this. Regularly, since 1970, there had been national wages agreements of varying duration and complexity.[2] The 1977 agreement, negotiated under the National Coalition, was ratified in February and covered 14 months, 3 months of which was a wages freeze. But the increase for the 11 months was 9·4 per cent, which presented a somewhat threatening background against which the new Fianna Fail Government was required, by its overall economic package, to impose wages restraint.

In his 1978 Budget speech, George Colley said: 'Our target for pay increases is about 5 per cent.' The agreement, ratified seven weeks later, March 23, 1978, awarded 8 per cent for the

13 Liam Cosgrave, who became Taoiseach at the head of the National Coalition Government in 1973. A former Army captain, he favoured a law-and-order image, and appointed a close political associate, Paddy Donegan, as Minister for Defence, ultimately with unwelcome results.

14 and 15   The Sunningdale Conference of 1973, leading to the establishment of a power-sharing executive in Northern Ireland, was a major joint achievement. *Above, from left*, four of the principal participants from Northern Ireland: Brian Faulkner, Gerry Fitt, John Hume and Paddy Devlin. *Below, left*, Liam Cosgrave with Edward Heath.

16, 17, 18 and 19   Four of the five Labour Party ministers in the National Coalition Government: *above left*, Michael O'Leary, *above right*, Justin Keating, *below left*, Brendan Corish, *below right*, Conor Cruise O'Brien. Keating and O'Brien lost their seats in 1977. Corish resigned the Party leadership at that time, and left the Dail in 1982. O'Leary joined Fine Gael.

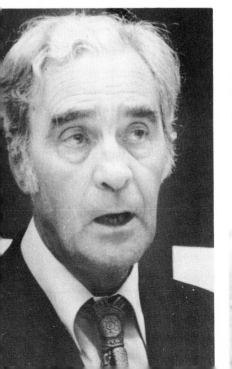

20 and 21   Senator Mary Robinson, who ran unsuccessfully for Labour in the 1977 election, with the outgoing Coalition Finance Minister, Richie Ryan, and Garret FitzGerald, who was to become Fine Gael leader. *Below*: the wreckage of the car in which the British Ambassador, Christopher Ewart-Biggs, died on July 21, 1976.

first twelve months of a 15-month period. On top of this comparatively modest gap between target and agreement, the Budget of January 1978 had also to implement the balance of election promises made by Fianna Fail the previous June and it was inescapably generous when the economy positively needed the opposite of the demand being generated. It was the beginning of a process whereby the carefully laid theories on which Martin O'Donoghue had based his economic strategy since well before the general election of 1977 began to come unstuck. At a time when Ireland's closest competitors in Europe, including Britain, were containing wage demands reasonably successfully, Ireland herself followed the excessive 1978 settlement with a more generous one in 1979. In his Budget speech George Colley was looking for the same moderation on which O'Donoghue's economic strategy was based: 'The increase in average earnings per worker in 1978 worked out at over 16 per cent... real earnings rose by about 8 per cent... this should be followed by a year of pay moderation.' The actual deal, ratified in July 1979, represented 13·7 per cent average wage increase.

By European standards some economic indicators were very healthy indeed, and had been during the latter part of the Coalition's period in power. Since late 1975 there had been a recovery; in 1976 growth in industrial output and exports had led to a real G.N.P. increase of 3 per cent; in 1976 this had risen to 5 per cent; in straightforward comparison terms the National Coalition had produced better economic growth than Fianna Fail had done between 1968–73, and on going out of office in 1977 they had left behind an economy in no need whatever of the pump-priming interventions which were both implicit and explicit in the election manifesto. Whatever may have been the political needs of Jack Lynch – and in 1976–7 they looked fairly desperate – the economic needs of the country were not best served by the additional stimulus which was offered in fairly emotive language to counter Richie Ryan's policies, which had lost credibility and damaged confidence for reasons quite different from those which could be remedied by the job creation platform at the centre of the Fianna Fail election campaign. Admittedly, unemployment was unacceptably high. At the time of the general election, Fianna Fail talked of the 'real unemployment level' standing at 160,000 when the 'live register' showed 110,000. But it was far from clear that the correct remedies were contained in the manifesto or in the budgetary or general economic policy which followed. The manifesto had promised that Fianna Fail would reduce unemployment. It later shifted ground on this, and promised it would create jobs. And it did. Only the equation went wrong. Committed overall to a reduction in borrowing, the pump-priming budgetary exercises of 1977–8, which were designed to shift the job-creation burden to the private sector at a relatively early stage, required one element above all the others: moderation in wage demands. Without it, the necessary competitiveness of Irish industry would be further undermined and the burden of job-creation, instead of reflecting true buoyancy, would remain a public sector burden, bringing disrepute upon the Colley–O'Donoghue strategy.

The result of having a population liberated from rates on their houses, and taxes on their cars, as well as enjoying better personal tax reliefs, and then demanding more in their pay packets, was Swiftian in its caustic logic.

In the autumn of 1978 a new economic problem presented itself: the creation of the European Monetary System. Entry was arguably the most significant fiscal decision faced by an Irish Government since the foundation of the State, irrespective of what Britain decided to do. With Britain likely to remain outside the 'snake', Ireland was faced with a break with sterling, and either a revaluation or a devaluation. So 'bullish' were many politicians that a revaluation was talked of more frequently than a devaluation.

There was also grand talk about how much Europe would pay to Ireland to help the country over the transition stage. A figure of £650 million was judged by Opposition deputies as inadequate in the E.M.S. debate in the Dail in November 1978 (in the event the country received much less, and it was spread over five years, and divided into a combination of loans and grants). Nevertheless, the deal was generally welcomed, and the huge public emphasis placed on it, part of which interpreted the arrangements as offering a new start, and a further set of economic aides and incentives to the country, justified Jack Lynch saying in the adjournment debate on December 14, 1978: 'When the House rises at the conclusion of this debate, it will do so at the end of one of the most successful periods on record for the Irish economy.' Had he picked that occasion to resign, power would have undoubtedly passed to George Colley, and the continuity, within Fianna Fail, of Lynch's economic and Northern Ireland policies would have been assured.

Instead, Lynch led his administration forward into 1979, a year that was to be filled with disasters. The first of these came in early spring, with a postal strike which also increasingly affected telephone services except those which were automatic. It was the second such dispute, there having been a less serious postal strike in February 1978. The 1979 dispute was bitter and long. It was in part a recalcitrant expression of the basic demands which Fianna Fail policies of expansion had created. But it was also indicative of poor industrial relations in the public sector, and of an absence of the reforms and streamlining of the system which had been long overdue in the telephone service particularly. Posts and Telegraphs was the largest single sector of public service employment, and the Government stood firm against the pay demands of the unions involved, and won. After five months the unions climbed down. But the damage, real or imagined — and both matter in politics — had been considerable. Among other things, the Government had failed lamentably to convince workers of its own case. The Minister responsible, Padraig Faulkner, had acted courageously and with patience in the face of a fair degree of political opportunism at his and the Government's expense, some of it deriving from within Fianna Fail. But he had never successfully argued the importance of an unfamiliar Government strategy, that of confrontation.

The postal strike was credited with more damage than it in fact inflicted; nevertheless, it did undermine confidence in an administration which had come to power on a Macmillan-like message to the Irish people, that they had never had it so good. And it set in train a sequence of political setbacks which reflected growing uncertainty about the direction which the economy was taking.

There was a crisis in agriculture. It was aggravated in early 1979 by a Government decision in the Budget to introduce a 2 per cent levy on farmers' turnover. The levy was a substitute for the fact that no serious attempt had been made to tackle the tax position of farmers. In terms of sectoral envy, the country as a whole began to pay the price for the absence of reforms in taxation and other related areas. The levy was a small element in this, but it induced a rural backlash of considerable importance politically. What should have been a bearable 'option' in Martin O'Donoghue's view of the economy — wages moderation on the one hand and agricultural levy on the other — and in return the growth and job-creation that was judged by everyone to be desirable so long as it was paid for by someone else, created instead a mood of disaffection and envy. And it was thus that the country faced European and Local elections.

They were held in June. The turnout, on the European elections, at 64 per cent, was low. The result, for Fianna Fail, was something of a disaster. With 34·68 per cent of the vote (compared with 50·63 per cent in the general election of 1977) Fianna Fail won five of the fifteen seats; four each went to Labour and Fine Gael, and there were two Independents, Neil Blaney and T. J. Maher.

In the local elections the fact that domestic rates had been abolished removed a very real power base from local government, and rendered the objectives for the candidates much more circumscribed. Nevertheless, the result also reflected disillusionment with the Government, and its decline in credibility. Lynch's administration seemed to be running out of steam.

17

Changing the Pilot

Disillusionment and electoral fears were rife within the Fianna Fail Party from the early summer of 1979 on. Yet the post-mortem meeting of the Parliamentary Party attributed the dual defeat in the E.E.C. and local elections to a number of setbacks, including the postal strike, the agricultural levy scheme, and the not abnormal mid-term disenchantment that a government might expect to face. This did not satisfy many members of the party. It provoked a growing round of private discussions, and the emergence of a small group of backbench deputies determined to take positive action. Five men met on the night of the parliamentary party meeting and continued the discussions which had been terminated earlier to the general dissatisfaction of a much wider group of backbench deputies. The five were Albert Reynolds, Thomas McEllistrom, Jack Fahey, Sean Doherty and Mark Killilea. They organised then the basic strategy for what was to be an attempted backbench revolt against the party leadership. They were closely associated, in the early stages of their planning, with a further group which included two Fianna Fail senators, Flor Crowley and Bernard McGlinchey, and the only office-holder in the administration who was directly involved in the attempt to topple Jack Lynch, Ray McSharry, who had been appointed a junior minister in George Colley's Department of Finance.

It was recognised from the start that any overt leadership challenge by a group favouring Charles Haughey over Jack Lynch would inevitably fail. What was needed was the removal of Lynch on grounds of general dissatisfaction about policy and the direction in which the party was going. Only then, and very much as phase two in an orchestrated plan, would there emerge any strong pro-Haughey campaign. It was judged, correctly, that while Lynch could not be defeated in a direct leadership contest, the succession was much more open. This small meeting of the 'gang of five', as they came to be called, led in turn to the famous 'caucus meeting' within Fianna Fail, which took place the following Tuesday, July 3, 1979.

It was essential that the caucus meeting should not openly discuss the leadership of the party. Instead, the emphasis had to be on policy and general 'direction'. In fact, an attempt to raise the issue of Jack Lynch's leadership, made by Paddy Power, was ruled out by the 'chairman', Jackie Fahey, in favour of the general discussion he and others in the 'gang of five' wished to promote, on agricultural, economic and social policy, and, much more marginally, on the party's republican image and the apparent stalemate on Northern Ireland to which the Republic of Ireland seemed merely to be contributing close security co-operation. It was a lively and vigorous encounter, quite different from the ponderous atmosphere which had come to characterise normal parliamentary party meetings which were subject to the autocratic approach of a small group of senior men surrounding Jack Lynch. It was clear to the five men responsible for the meeting that there was serious unrest in Fianna Fail, and potentially sound support for a radical change in party leadership rather than a dutiful succession which might, and probably would, leave general party policy unchanged. It was equally clear, from the subsequent parliamentary party meeting at which Jack Lynch angrily and unsuccessfully sought the names of those who had attended the caucus meeting, that such an open and unofficial debate could not be repeated.[1] Instead, the 'gang of five' set in train a series of private approaches to individual deputies which were designed to build up support for change and, more covertly, support for Charles Haughey.

What followed was a summer of discontent, with issues of policy unchanged, those of party morale unresolved, and no clear indication from Jack Lynch of what his position would be over the leadership of Fianna Fail and the next election. It was an ill-judged return to quietism at a time of noisy unrest.

Increasingly the focus for discontent was Northern Ireland, and the apparent loss of republican determination in the South. In common with other issues, and as a reflection of the closeness of Martin O'Donoghue to Jack Lynch, policy on the North had taken on an economic cast.

Then, with the murder of Lord Mountbatten in August, 1979, while he was on holiday in Sligo, there came a more specific testing of Lynch's position, between the distinct poles of republicanism and reconciliation. Though repeatedly advised by Irish security, because of his close family ties with the British Royal Family, not to holiday in Classiebawn Castle, Mountbatten had persistently visited the West Coast of Ireland where he adopted a fairly cavalier approach to his own personal safety. The tragedy coincided with Lynch himself being on holiday in Portugal. Before leaving, he had undertaken to return in two circumstances: an E.M.S. crisis or a security crisis. Neither had arisen, though the enormity of Mountbatten's assassination was quite naturally exaggerated by virtue of his rank, and not diminished, as it should have been, by virtue of his stubborn disregard for the risks he had repeatedly taken in regularly visiting Ireland when, like other British public figures, he should have gone elsewhere. Lynch was aware of the parallels between the murder of Ewart-Biggs, which had provoked an unjustified and damaging security crisis under Liam Cosgrave, and the killing of Mountbatten, and he was at pains not to give to the terrorists responsible for the latter death the credit for provoking a security crisis at will.

This defence, if such it needed to be, was largely ignored in the emotional atmosphere which followed the killing and the subsequent pageantry of the funeral in London. In the public mind Lynch seemed to be under attack from two sides diametrically opposed to each other, the republican voice in his own party calling for a tougher, if ill-defined stand on the North, and a broad body of opinion which seemed to detect in Lynch's coolness over the Mountbatten affair a coolness towards Anglo–Irish relations carried to unacceptable extremes.

Attack on Lynch from the republican wing of his own party came from an unpredictable but emotive source. That September, in Fermoy, Sile de Valera, the grand-daughter of

Eamon de Valera, made an outspoken republican speech, the underlying message of which seemed to be that Fianna Fail had abandoned the republican ideals of her grandfather. Had her grandfather been alive he would probably have contradicted her; but he was, conveniently, a dead hero. It was a policy challenge to the leader of the party. Vague and emotional as the speech itself had been, its impact seemed to throw everyone into confusion, from the party leader downwards.

Where was Fianna Fail going? Secretly, within the party, the question was being asked. Sile de Valera was giving public expression to a general atmosphere of unrest which she herself cast in the mould of her own interpretation of the party's republican ideals, but which many others in Fianna Fail saw in terms of broader economic and social dissatisfaction which was threatening the party's future fortunes at the polls. This was given precise and devastating proof in the autumn.

On November 7, 1979, Fianna Fail lost equally disastrously in two by-elections, in Jack Lynch's own constituency of Cork City, and in North East Cork. Jack Lynch had had enough. On Wednesday, December 5, 1979, he told the meeting of the Fianna Fail Parliamentary Party, 'I have decided to resign as Taoiseach'. He had already informed members of the Government, and he went on to explain that he had fixed on this course of action well before the 1977 general election, irrespective of the result. He was aware of party unrest. He was also conscious of public uncertainty about his intentions, which was not good for the country. A new approach, and fresh thinking, were needed. He asked for an early meeting of the party to elect his successor, and this was arranged for the Friday morning, two days later. The struggle for the future control of the largest political party in Ireland was on.

It was a remarkable occasion in Irish politics. In far from auspicious circumstances for those who had stood closest by him in the party, Lynch was plunging Fianna Fail into a leadership struggle which was essentially divisive because it raised the key question of alternatives both of policy and personnel. Economic strategy, social thinking, agricultural policy, commitment to Europe, republicanism, Northern Ireland, were all arguably open to change because of the lamentable electoral performance of Fianna Fail throughout 1979. The ingredients which might have offered a smooth succession to one of the closest heirs apparent, George Colley or Desmond O'Malley, were absent. The unrest which favoured a radical shift in emphasis, and a backbench revolt against a collective leadership which had failed to sustain the party on the lines established during the triumphant 1977 general election, was firmly manifest in just one man: Charles Haughey. Even the contrast between Haughey's singleness of purpose, and the uncertainty about whether or not Colley and O'Malley would stand against each other was significant. And when O'Malley declined to let his name go forward it served as a further handicap. In addition, the handling of George Colley's canvas for support during the crucial two days of December 5–7 was primarily in the hands of a political novice in such things, Martin O'Donoghue, while that of Charles Haughey was organised by the determined group of back-benchers who had been working towards this objective since mid-summer, and whose motives were clear-cut and absolute.

The issues were hotly debated. Leinster House became a maelstrom of arguments and meetings, of lists and lies, of fundamental divisions within Fianna Fail about a single basic question: was the party to continue with its existing policies, or was there to be a new departure? On the Friday morning at 11 a.m. the parliamentary party meeting took place. Just over an hour later the vote was announced: Charles Haughey 44, George Colley 38. The new Taoiseach-elect went directly into a press conference to tell journalists that he was 'more over-whelmed by the responsibility than anything else', and that 'two wonderful things have happened': these were that he had been assured of George Colley's 'total and fullest co-operation in my new task, and I have been assured by Jack Lynch that all his vast reservoirs and experience as Taoiseach will be totally at my disposal in my new position'. In the event, the vast reservoirs were never tapped, and Colley publicly denied not long afterwards that he had said anything of the sort. But it was a jubilant press conference, and the more optimistic Fianna Fail Party view was voiced in emphatic terms by the party's youngest member, Sile de Valera: 'I am absolutely delighted. We've got what we needed, a strong man, able to handle the political and economic challenges now facing the country. The whole party will be united behind Mr Haughey. They've al-ready made that clear.'

Opposition reaction was less encouraging. The leader of the Labour Party, Frank Cluskey, made a statement expressing 'deep concern' about Charles Haughey's views on Northern Ireland. They were expressive, he said, of a fundamentally unacceptable interpretation of Irish society and departed from the policy of peace and reconciliation which had guided his predecessor. The Workers' Party leader, Tomas MacGiolla, also attacked the decision: 'It can only be deplored by all progressive elements in the country, North and South.'

Worse was to follow. On Tuesday, December 11, 1979, Charles Haughey's nomination as Taoiseach was confirmed in the Dail, and he announced his new Government, from which four ministers were dropped, Martin O'Donoghue, Robert Molloy, Jim Gibbons and Denis Gallagher.[2] In the debate on the new ministerial appointments, the Fine Gael leader, Garret FitzGerald, launched a bitter attack on Charles Haughey, which included ambiguous references to his 'flawed pedigree', as well as a stern indictment of his 'overweaning ambition', his ambivalence about the I.R.A. and his potential divergence from the broad agreement that had existed in the past over Northern Ireland policy. Both FitzGerald and Frank Cluskey questioned the Fianna Fail leader's fitness to be Taoiseach. No Fianna Fail deputy spoke in the debate. Government benches remained vacant, except for Charles Haughey himself, who sat alone through six hours of relentless attack, having told members of his party their presence would be unwelcome until the division was called. He was watched during this ordeal from the public gallery by his wife, his mother and other relations. In spite of anticipated defections, the vote, when it came, endorsed the new Government by 82 votes to 62. Nevertheless, all was far from united within Fianna Fail. The following week, on December 20, Haughey's deputy leader, George Colley, qualified his support for the Taoiseach in words which were openly divisive. Referring to the undermining of Jack Lynch's leadership during the summer and autumn of 1979 as a change in the basic rules within Fianna Fail about 'full loyalty and support to the elected leader', George Colley pledged his own support to the Taoiseach only 'in all his efforts in the national interest'. As far as party loyalty went, that was a different matter. It was there that the rules had been changed, and, as far as Colley was concerned, they remained changed: 'We are in a new ball game...The possibility of change at another time is always there.' It also emerged that Colley had exercised a triple veto in Government appointments. It had been conditional on his serving as a member of Charles Haughey's Government that he should be Tanaiste, and that he should have a say in two other appointments connected with State security, those of the Ministers for Justice and Defence.

It is hard to imagine a more inauspicious start for a new leader. Yet Charles Haughey deserved much that was said of him then, and bore out subsequently in his actions many of the gloomy and threatening predictions which were made. He had changed fundamentally; from being the suave, financially sophisticated peer of the new Irish business élite, he had reverted to being a more open republican, glib about the economy, and courting outdated nationalist feeling in the rural west; he was also using as his closest lieutenants men of a suitably ambivalent disposition. He had come to power as a result of a conspiracy which had split Fianna Fail more or less permanently. He was, and had been, at odds with the party on Northern Ireland policy, and his views, in so far as they were known or could be adequately interpreted, were regarded in Northern Ireland and elsewhere as threatening. His reputation, in the economic and financial field, related to an earlier decade. His basic political philosophy, not without a good deal of justification, had been warped by the setbacks and obstructions in his political career from the time of the arms crisis almost ten years earlier.

In the stormy changeover Jack Lynch seemed to slip quietly and swiftly out of the public eye. He had been leader of Fianna Fail for thirteen years, and they had been among the most turbulent years the State had experienced since independence. He had imposed upon the party, and the country, the Arms Trial crisis of 1970, on the one hand, and on the other had given Fianna Fail the greatest electoral triumph in its history. He had undoubtedly established himself as the country's best-loved leader. He had deployed judgment and skill of a high order, and as a leader had used his very substantial intellectual and emotional resources. He has been referred to in these pages as of a 'quietist' disposition; this should not be taken to mean passivity. In terms of real achievement he is to be credited with substantial change of heart and mind in Ireland on the

143

country's economic future, and on its relationship with Northern Ireland and Britain. In his own political career he regarded the successful conclusion of the negotiation for Ireland's E.E.C. entry as a major achievement, and one on which, as Minister and Taoiseach, he spent more time than anyone else. He always appreciated the economic centre of gravity in Irish political life, recognising the complex urban-rural mixture involved, and catering for it with the country's limited resources. It was an imperfect performance: the resources were never enough. And in the latter period in power he indulged in a prodigality which was damaging. But overall, the economic balance for which he was largely responsible during two decades, was the best available.

He referred to Northern Ireland as his major preoccupation as Taoiseach. His essential policy approach was established in Sean Lemass's footsteps, well before the troubles began in 1968, and was based on reconciliation rather than confrontation. It was at least two-way reconciliation: North–South, as well as Nationalist–Unionist within Northern Ireland. It embraced also a calmer and more positive approach to Anglo–Irish relations.

Lynch achieved a genuine change of attitude in the South on what is euphemistically called the 'national question', and he did so without losing broad support. This was clear in the election of both 1973 and 1977. But he did it at enormous personal and party cost. Of the two elections he regarded the 1973 defeat as his party's greatest electoral achievement:

> In the event we lost by a mere handful of votes. Had about 2,000 votes spread throughout key constituencies swung to us then we would have ended up with the two-seat majority instead of a two-seat minority. In the event I think that 1973 election result was probably Fianna Fail's greatest electoral achievement with me as leader, although the party was the loser.

The subsequent tributes to Lynch from within Fianna Fail were predictably lukewarm. By the following April the party's new Chief Whip, Sean Moore, *could not remember* whether there had been any formal presentation to the man who had led the party for thirteen years.[3] Having checked, he discovered that there had been no such presentation. A trifling matter, and one which would have been embarrassing to both Lynch and Haughey had it been otherwise, it nevertheless indicated the degree of change, and the deplorably short and ungenerous memories of the human moths who flutter round the candles of power.

18

Charles Haughey

On Wednesday, January 9, 1980, Charles Haughey went on television to address the nation about the economy. The essential message was the need for rectitude. The country was living beyond its means. The gap between production in goods and services and the actual level of national consumption was being filled at an accelerating rate by foreign and domestic borrowing which in 1979 had reached one-seventh of total national output. The remedy was to cut Government spending, since the tax burden on the individual was already too high. At the same time greater emphasis was to be placed on better industrial relations, and Haughey appealed for 'a universal commitment to peace in industrial relations in 1980'. While legislative remedies in the industrial relations field were alluded to, the tone was soft and ameliorative, and any such legislation 'would not be directed against trade unions'. There was no mention of the job-creation programme which had been the cornerstone of Martin O'Donoghue's economic planning.

A month later, on Saturday, February 16, 1980, Charles Haughey addressed his first annual party conference as leader in the Royal Dublin Society, Ballsbridge. It was a broad, substantive statement of overall party policy, and thoughtfully prepared. In it he reiterated the basic economic message that the country was living beyond its means. But when it came to the remedies, the simple, harsh prescription of the January television address was somewhat modified; it was *either* cutting down Government spending, *or* increasing tax revenue, *or* a combination. 'Hard decisions are called for, but because it is our duty to protect and sustain the economy, and not to damage it, these decisions will be taken on the basis of sound judgment and common sense.' In reality this meant that the period before a general election, even if that were still two-and-a-half years away was not the time for public expenditure cuts. And as far as taxation was concerned, although Haughey made clear his appreciation of the widespread concern in the country over the unfair distribution of the tax burden, the remedy offered was 'a high-level Commission which will have full powers to carry out a major inquiry into every aspect of the taxation system and which will make recommendations for the modern equitable system we clearly need.'

In other words, the radical change of direction on the economy, which would be tough, and would bring it under control, and for which there had been an agonising and diverse backbench revolt within Fianna Fail, was to be abandoned, and with the existing course would be followed with only minor modifications.

In sharp contrast, the sections of the speech dealing with Northern Ireland did represent a substantial shift, and one that was to be more permanent. Northern Ireland, he said, as a political entity had failed. A new beginning was needed. This was to be provided by the two sovereign governments of Dublin and London coming together 'to find a formula and lift the situation on to a new plane, that will bring permanent peace and stability to the people of these islands'. The problems, admittedly, were massive financial, security and constitutional ones, but as a start, Charles Haughey recommended, 'a declaration by the British Government of their interest in encouraging the unity of Ireland, by agreement and in peace'.

It was pointed out swiftly enough by the two leaders of the Opposition parties that the new London–Dublin axis proposed by Haughey, together with the dismissal of Northern Ireland as 'a failed political entity', was a not unpredictable result of the limited trust with which the Taoiseach was regarded, by Northern Protestants in particular, whose collective memory was long enough to embrace things said and done ten years earlier. Yet the basic prescription formed the policy stance with which Charles Haughey went to London in May for his first meeting with Margaret Thatcher, who was still in her first year as British Prime Minister. It was Haughey's obvious wish to make Northern Ireland the centre of debate. But it did not work out that way. He came away with considerable admiration for Mrs Thatcher, privately describing her as 'a tough lady'; and he also felt relief at the positive and friendly atmosphere in which the talks had been held. But he was puzzled as well. Mrs Thatcher had declined to reveal her intentions on Northern Ireland and had more or less excluded the future of the Six Counties from their detailed discussions, which she had shifted towards international questions, including Europe and defence.

In the press conference given in London immediately after the talks he put a more positive gloss on the encounter. He made clear that, as far as the Dublin Government was concerned, he was prepared to go to very considerable lengths indeed to gain a 'solution', the prospects for which had not actually been discussed. Ruling out Ireland's re-entry to the British Commonwealth, Haughey was nevertheless favourably disposed to the idea of an Irish NATO commitment, or to some other kind of defence pact which might lead to the abandonment of neutrality, and he was also positive about constitutional and other changes. To some members of Fianna Fail the positive responses seemed to go too far.

Skilful though it was, in political terms, it left unanswered several key questions. The shift to a Dublin–London axis left open the question of an Irish guarantee to the Northern majority which had been at the root of previous policy positions under both Lynch and Cosgrave. Coolness about any interim solution within Northern Ireland aggravated the absence of a clear guarantee; Haughey went so far, in his press conference, as to say that he would be unable to support 'anything entirely within the Northern Ireland context'.

The broad impact in the country of the first Haughey–Thatcher summit had been positive and had made considerably easier and more attractive the prospect of a second in the autumn or winter.

Or it seemed so, for the semblance of things rather than their actuality was an important characteristic of Charles Haughey's first administration. He had come to power in place of an administration which had not set in train any sizable, positive legislative programme. For a man who had aimed for the leadership of his party all his political life, and who had actively worked for it during most of the previous decade, Charles Haughey seemed to have very little idea of what he wanted to do with it. Lynch had left him with two and a half years to run with an unchallengeable majority in the Dail; yet in the eighteen months which he then chose to use of that allowance, and having done an about-face on economic policy and wrapped Northern Ireland policy up in the secrecy of a joint Haughey–Thatcher solution, the rest of the programme was remarkably empty, and consequently dependent on appearances. The Taoiseach had *appeared* to wrestle with the economy; yet between January and February the essential focus on rectitude became blurred, and the Budget of 1980, which should have been clear and determined above all else, was curiously ambivalent: not quite an election budget, it straddled two opposing requirements — the need to get things right, and the need to be popular.

By June 1980 there were growing numbers of concessions visible to all: the resources tax hanging over the farmers was to be abandoned, foreign borrowing was to be increased by a further £100 million to be split equally between industry and agriculture, inflationary settlements of wage claims in the public sector were agreed, and job-creation, the justification for prodigality which had been dropped at the beginning of 1980, crept back now as an escape clause. Not surprisingly, the Opposition descended heavily upon the vacillations and uncertainties. Both Garret FitzGerald and Frank Cluskey had adjusted fully by the midsummer to the new style of politics pursued by Charles Haughey, and were, to an impressive degree, mutually complementary. Cluskey's gutsy expressions and flat Dublin accent brought more than a touch of the shop-floor — both trade union and butcher's[1] — to the Dail Chamber, while Garret FitzGerald's comprehensive grasp of economics and voluminous use of statistics never totally obscured the essential and consistent political message which he had been pounding out since 1977, that the overall economic strategy pursued by Fianna Fail was running the country steadily, and at an accelerating rate, into impossibly excessive debt. Into the bargain, Michael O'Kennedy, appointed as Minister for Finance to replace George Colley, was handicapped by the intrusive approach of his leader and by the magnitude of the problems. Less able than Colley, he needed clear policy lines on

which to work. Instead, he was reliant upon an economi
strategy which had already gone through a complete U-turn i
the space of six months.

Some embarrassment was caused to Charles Haughey by th
publication, in the May, June and July issues of the monthl
magazine, *Magill*, of an extensive re-examination of the arm
crisis and the Arms Trials of 1970. Based on the private paper
of Peter Berry, who had been secretary in the Department c
Justice at the time, and was now dead, they contained furthe
revelations about Haughey's knowledge of the attempted im
portation of arms for the I.R.A. in Northern Ireland. Coinci
dental with the *Magill* articles was a growing mood c
dissatisfaction within Fianna Fail about its leader. As the Dai
went into recess, a bare seven months after Charles Haughe
became leader, it was clear that the magic for which backbenc
deputies had been searching when they elected him was no
forthcoming. And because of the nature of the man, and hi
conspiratorial methods, the normal reserves of the party wer
not available to its leader.

His preferred approach, wherever possible, was a silent one
Throughout the ten years which had elapsed since the arm
crisis, Charles Haughey had remained silent on it and al
related issues. His policy towards Northern Ireland, his atti
tude on republicanism, his judgment on the I.R.A., his mind o
a host of specific issues and events, were all subject to a rigorou
self-censorship. He had been silent throughout the cauterisin
debate which ended in his nomination for Taoiseach, on De
cember 11, 1979. And this imposition of profound verbal re
straint became a characteristic, a hallmark even.

He gave virtually no interviews, and held only carefull
stage-managed press conferences. At one period,[2] there wer
no less than 250 requests for interviews from Irish and foreig
journalists. He was enormously *visible*; ready at all times t
attend functions and be photographed, and pleased at the ver
frequent publication of such photographs in the newspapers
And privately he was at considerable pains to maintain goo
personal relations with the whole range of press, radio an
television personnel. But his interpretation of 'personal rela
tions' had an early termination point as far as information wa
concerned. There was an undoubted cameraderie. But it lacke
solid foundation in the material for analysis which at heart wa
what the media wanted.

19

Unique Relationship

Charles Haughey had a surprisingly productive and successful autumn and winter of 1980–81. He began it well, in late September, when he marched into the offices of the Federated Union of Employers, in Baggot Street, in what was a direct intervention in national wages negotiations aimed at achieving a national understanding (this term had replaced national wages agreement, and embodied additional Government commitments on taxation and social welfare). What was actually achieved was excessive and inflationary: after a one-month 'pause' there was to be an 8-month phase one, 8 per cent plus £1, followed by a six-month second phase of 7 per cent. Even this had been gained only after protracted negotiations, two breakdowns and two Government interventions. Nevertheless, the cosmetic effect of Haughey's personal intrusion, indicating a determination to achieve a wages agreement and hopefully industrial peace, was dramatic and positive. It was also indicative of pre-election thinking.

During the summer of 1980 the Ceann Comhairle (Speaker) of the Dail, Joe Brennan, died, causing a by-election in Donegal. This was fought during October and early November, and, though a Fianna Fail majority was assured, Charles Haughey treated it as a major contest, campaigning in the county for three weeks himself and deploying virtually the whole of his Government. For Garret FitzGerald the defeat, predictable enough in terms of the relative strengths of the parties in Donegal, represented what he saw as his first major setback since becoming Fine Gael leader in 1977.

Behind the public satisfaction, however, things were n
working too well within Fianna Fail. At least three appoin
ments, those of O'Kennedy to Finance, Brian Lenihan
Foreign Affairs and Gene Fitzgerald to Labour, had bee
disappointing. And while Michael O'Kennedy was soon to l
shifted to Brussels as Ireland's Commissioner there in place
Richard Burke, whose term was to end in 1980, the reshuff
was not well-used. The basic feeling in Fianna Fail was simp
one of waiting to see if Haughey could win an election. It wa
already clear that he had not provided the necessary dynamis
and radical change demanded by his backbenchers; yet l
might still redeem the situation electorally. Part of Haughey
strategy for this lay in the realm of Northern Ireland polic
and his development of Anglo–Irish relations. The secon
summit meeting between Charles Haughey and Margar
Thatcher took place on Monday, December 8, in Dublin Cast
and was then debated in the Dail on December 11, 1980.

In the meantime the first H-block hunger strike, begun l
seven Republican prisoners on October 27, 1980 at the Maz
Prison near Belfast, had reached a sensitive stage, with at lea
one prisoner in a dangerously weak condition. Six of the me
were Provisional I.R.A., and one was Irish National Liberatic
Army, the military wing of the Irish Republican Sociali
Party. Three were serving sentences for murder; the rest fe
attempted murder, firearms offences and robbery.

The prisoners were demanding political status. The Britis
Government refused to concede a claim where the politic
motive changed the culpability of men convicted by process
law. The rights sought were not covered by the Convention c
Human Rights.

There had previously been a 'special category status' i
Northern Ireland. It had been introduced in 1972 by Willia
Whitelaw, and abolished in November 1975 for prisoners foun
guilty of terrorist offences committed after March 1, 1976. I
1980 the abolition was extended to cover all terrorist offence
whenever they were committed.

Certain provisions were made by the British Government t
ameliorate the conditions in the Maze prison during the sprin
and summer of 1980, including the changeover from priso
uniform to 'civilian-type clothing'. This and the other measure
were rejected by Provisional Sinn Fein as 'a cruel piece c

asing and political brinkmanship', in a statement on October 4, three days before the hunger strike began. There had lready been a 'dirty protest' going on for four years.[1] The October 24 I.R.A. statement said: 'They [the British Government] are more concerned with the loss of British face than the loss of Irish lives. We are not criminals and we are ready and willing to meet an agonising death on hunger strike to establish that we are political prisoners.'

'Humanitarian concern' was widely expressed as the strike progressed, not least by the Irish Government, and the British Minister responsible, Mr Humphrey Atkins, issued a detailed explanation of prison conditions, re-emphasising that the British Government would not concede the basic principle of political status.

The strike continued through December, and was on during the Dublin Castle summit meeting between Charles Haughey and Margaret Thatcher. It ended on December 18, and Humphrey Atkins announced to the House of Commons that all the strikers had taken breakfast on the morning of the 19th, including Sean McKenna, the only prisoner who had been moved to hospital. The ending of the strike did not end the dirty protest' in the Maze.[2]

The understandable tensions resulting from this hunger strike, together with the normal security precautions necessary for any visit to Dublin by a British premier, made of the day-long talks at Dublin Castle a high-profile occasion. The press were photographed and issued with special passes by the Department of Foreign Affairs, and then driven through the city in charabancs to the Castle where, from the room in which the press conference was held, they were able to watch Mrs Thatcher leaving by helicopter in the company of her Foreign Minister, Lord Carrington, the British Chancellor, Sir Geoffrey Howe, and Mr Humphrey Atkins, Northern Ireland Secretary of State.

Charles Haughey was accompanied by his Ministers for Foreign Affairs and Finance, Brian Lenihan and Michael O'Kennedy. But for a vital period the two leaders were on their own; and this was to prove significant as the divergence in what had been said and agreed developed to the point of mutual embarrassment in the months that followed.[3]

A communiqué was issued, the most important paragraphs of which were 4, 5 and 6. They read:

The Taoiseach and the Prime Minister agreed that th
economic, social and political interests of the peoples of th
United Kingdom of Great Britain and Northern Ireland an
the Republic are inextricably linked, but that the fu
development of these links has been put under strain b
division and dissent in Northern Ireland.

In that context, they accepted the need to bring forwar
policies and proposals to achieve peace, reconciliation an
stability; and to improve relations between the peoples of th
two countries.

They considered that the best prospect of attaining thes
objectives was the further development of the unique rela
tionship between the two countries.

They accordingly decided to devote their next meeting i
London during the coming year to special consideration o
the totality of relationships within these islands. For th
purpose they have commissioned joint studies, covering
range of issues including possible new institutional struc
tures, citizenship rights, security matters, economi
co-operation and measures to encourage mutual under
standing.

Effectively, two press conferences followed, as well as
number of brief interviews for radio and television. The firs
and major press conference, for the hundred or so journalists a
Dublin Castle, attempted a teasing out of the meaning behind
number of phrases in the communiqué as well as a number o
expressions used by Charles Haughey in explaining what ha
been achieved. The attempt was not wholly successful. 'Th
unique relationship between the two countries', 'the totality o
relationships within these islands', 'joint studies', 'institutiona
structures', 'measures to encourage mutual understanding
were all expanded on, but in vague if optimistic terms. T
them, Charles Haughey added a broad and persuasive gloss
the joint studies were new, and 'on a different plane than [sic
anything that has gone on so far'; 'we set no limit on wha
institutions might be brought forward' (it was not clarifie
whether the 'we' meant the Irish Government or the two head
of Government); he used the word 'historic' to describe th
meeting; he claimed that, as far as the British and Iris
Governments were concerned, the Northern Ireland problem

'is now firmly on a new plane'. In conclusion, the Taoiseach apostrophised the day's events: 'I would first take today's meeting on its own merits, as a very successful meeting, a significant meeting, a constructive meeting, a meeting which in my view had brought very considerable political movement, forward political movement, into this type of situation of Northern Ireland.'

The second press encounter, which was an off-the-record briefing for Dublin political correspondents, carried the heightened atmosphere of self-assertive significance considerably further, going so far as to anticipate the reunification of Ireland. In order to achieve this, the 'institutional structures' which were to be the subject of one of the joint studies were elevated, by implication and innuendo, to 'constitutional' ones. And in this conception were presented to the Irish reading public by senior political journalists, entirely in good faith. But it provoked an immediate process of parsing and analysing, and by the time the Dail came to debate the summit meeting the following Thursday, December 11, the degree of disagreement and bewilderment raised once again the more fundamental issue of answerability. The Taoiseach failed to clarify fully the differences which had emerged between 'institutional' and 'constitutional'. At the very end of the debate, in an attempt to achieve such a clarification, the Fine Gael leader, Garret FitzGerald, endeavoured to put words into Haughey's mouth: 'I want to express my gratitude to the Taoiseach for having clarified what I think was obscure, that the joint studies were not concerned with the constitutional issues of Northern Ireland but improving relations − ' He was then interrupted, and Charles Haughey simply said: 'I am not accepting what Deputy FitzGerald said.'

Earlier, Haughey had referred to the doubts about whether 'institutional' or 'constitutional' structures were involved when he said, 'I do not for one moment suggest that I do not avail of every opportunity that offers itself to me to talk to British politicians and anybody else that I have an opportunity of talking to about the constitutional position of Northern Ireland.' But the double negative indicated a necessary retrenchment from the risky position which the Taoiseach had adopted with the small group of political journalists during the special briefing session. Though he had set 'no limit', his concluding speech as well as certain interjections made earlier, had been quite negative. He had ruled out federation or confederation for Northern Ireland; he had denied the use of the word 'constitution'; he had also denied the use of the word 'breakthrough' to describe what he and Mrs Thatcher had achieved. Turning his back on the interpretations and speculations which his own words had substantially provoked, the Taoiseach referred deputies to the wording of the communiqué, which was 'precise and meticulous'.

On January 13, 1981, the Government brought out 'Investment Plan, 1981'. Though effectively this represented the capital programme for the year, and was part of the normal pre-Budget presentation, it was dressed up in manifesto clothing and presented with considerable publicity and drama as a 'plan' involving a total investment during the year of £1,700 million. The Budget message of January 28, 1981 bore only limited relationship to the true economic situation it was designed to correct. In his own speech on January 29, Haughey outlined an overall strategy consisting of three simple objectives: to maintain economic growth and development in order to bring the national economy 'through this current deep recession as safely as possible'. This, according to him, required a major increase in productive investment. Secondly, he said, 'we must positively protect the living standards of the under-privileged and less well-off in the difficult economic circumstances of today'; this required Health and Social Welfare provisions. Thirdly, he said that the structure of public finances had to be improved in order to provide 'a solid foundation for the greatly increased level of economic activity needed in the years immediately ahead'; he included in this provision for a phased reduction in the real level of the current Budget deficit. We had come a long way from the hard options of economic rectitude of January, 1980.[4]

This Budget was to be followed, in mid-February, by the annual conference of the Fianna Fail Party, which was to be used by the leader, in his presidential address, as a launching pad for the general election he intended to hold shortly afterwards. But in the early hours of Valentine's Day, Saturday February 14, the day on which the speech would have been made, there was a fire in the Stardust Ballroom, in Charles Haughey's own constituency of Dublin North Central, in which 48 young people died. After two postponements, the annual conference of Fianna Fail was called off. Any plans for an immediate general election had to be shelved.

As more and more things went wrong, Charles Haughey's own reaction became increasingly restless and uncertain. He was caged by the Dail, and stalked within its corridors in a restless and intolerant fashion, resentful of the tide of democratic demand coming from the Opposition. His sense of ambivalence provoked bewilderment in his own party. By his own wish he operated alone; subordinates did what he told them, generally without understanding the implications. But increasingly there was puzzlement about his intentions and motives. Frank Cluskey, the Labour Party Leader, was more forthright and pithy about the basic political character of the Taoiseach than anyone else in the Dail. Following the Stardust tragedy he said of Haughey's central problem over answering clearly and fully the questions put to him:

He regards the Dail as something to be at best tolerated. If he can avoid having to come in here and face up to the normal responsibilities of a Taoiseach . . . in a parliamentary democracy he will take every opportunity to do so . . . The Taoiseach's term of office has been distinguished by one thing more than any other, his evasiveness. Everything has come under the heading of confidentiality and secrecy. We have this with Mrs Thatcher, and we now have it with the Stardust people. Every time a legitimate question was asked in the House, and it was politically difficult and embarrassing, the Taoiseach used one of two tactics. He jumped behind procedure, or he said the matter was confidential. The confidentiality is over, and the bit in the bunker is over, because whether the Taoiseach likes it or not, the time has come when he will have to face the Irish electorate.

With each fresh development, further delay in seeking a dissolution became inevitable. That ideal moment for a swift and decisive early general election, based on a carefully constructed package of economic, social and Northern Ireland policy decisions or proposals, had passed. The first result was that the running of the economy came in for examination and criticism. It was revealed to be in more dubious health than the

January Budget had led people to believe. The second was that the 'special relationship' with Margaret Thatcher, which was to lead 'down the road to unity' was exposed to sustained examination, which undermined its seriousness. This was further aggravated by the start of the second Maze Prison hunger strike, on March 1, for which the 'special relationship' provided no answers. The Fine Gael Party, and to a lesser extent the Labour Party, were given much-needed time to prepare themselves for the general election, while the disruption of the original election timetable led Charles Haughey into making concessionary decisions in order to win support. This tended to undermine his credibility and provided his critics with ammunition. Finally, it deprived the Fianna Fail leader of an asset always of great value: surprise.

What was of critical importance was the breathing space given to the main Opposition party. After the Donegal by-election of November 1980, Garret FitzGerald had suffered a loss of confidence, and did not begin the process of recovery and the building of an effective election platform until well into 1981. He would have been thinly supplied with material had the original timetable been followed.

The result was that the general election, when eventually it was called on the afternoon of Thursday, May 21, was deprived of zest, and took place in an awkward and unhappy mood.

At a more serious level the traditional pattern emerged of the party in power attempting to establish the issues on which the election was to be fought, being challenged on this by the Opposition parties, and being forced back into the weaker position of responding to attack rather than leading it. Haughey claimed he was calling the election 'because of the grave and tragic situation in Northern Ireland', and that he was looking for a clear and definite mandate based on his policy. It was an implausible basis for an election strategy, since no one knew what Northern Ireland policy was, and since there were few if any signs that it was going to bring the hunger strike to an end, an obvious prerequisite for more fundamental change.

An alternative view of the election was at the root of both Fine Gael and Labour policies, released respectively on Friday, May 22 and Monday, May 25, and emphasising economic issues as the main ones on which the country should decide its next government. The Fine Gael programme, particularly, showed considerable work and inventiveness, and had a substantial enough impact to cause the Fianna Fail leader to react sharply. His criticisms were derisive, but his alternatives were bland. The first follow-up press conference held by Fianna Fail revealed clearly that there was party uncertainty and evasiveness about what economic measures would be taken, since there was also party uncertainty about whether or not the economy required action, or was fine as it was.

Within the first week of the campaign it was clear that the chief issue was the economy, that the measures which were being most hotly debated concerned taxation and inflation, and that the initiative had been seized by the two Opposition parties. Yet in no sense did this bring to an end the political awkwardness and public uncertainty. The principal reason for this was the absence of any clear agreement between Fine Gael and Labour as to whether or not they would be able to form a coalition government: more important was whether or not they could reconcile their fundamental differences of emphasis, over taxation reform on the part of Fine Gael and about inflation and jobs in the Labour Party's manifesto.

If the Fianna Fail leader had been less on the defensive in the first week of campaigning he might well have driven a more effective wedge between the two Opposition parties. As it was, his campaign strategy was primarily based on a country-wide, meet-the-people tour, with old-fashioned speeches on the hustings about not being deterred by demonstrators from telling the country how well it was being governed. The error was made of dismissing opponents, one at least of whom was making comparable countrywide forays calling firmly for a transfer of power to a government whose policies would be based on planning and reform. Nevertheless, there was an inherent weakness in the go-it-alone approach which both Labour and Fine Gael had adopted, and it was revealed more on television and radio than anywhere else, in debates which always became three-way tussels, generally to the disadvantage of the two Opposition parties. Much depended on the personalities involved.

The television tussles provided a background to a major media question argued over throughout the campaign: would there be a television debate between Charles Haughey and

Garret FitzGerald? Again, awkwardness was created by the insistence of the Labour Party leader, Frank Cluskey, that any such debate should include him. Knowing that a two-to-one contest on television tends to favour the solo performer (a fact which was being demonstrated on most nights anyway) the Fianna Fail leader sided with Frank Cluskey; Charles Haughey wanted all three men to meet in a studio encounter — or, at least, he wanted people to believe that this was his preferred position though, of course, the matter was in the hands of the party's director of elections, Eoin Ryan. One formula after another was tried. Eventually, all three party leaders submitted themselves separately to interrogation by a panel of newspaper journalists, each politician being allowed time in ratio to party strength in the outgoing Dail.

If one wants, in a nutshell, an image of the 1981 general election, its loss of zest, its failure to take fire, its clumsy and unsatisfactory character which would in due course be all too clearly revealed in the equally unsatisfactory outcome, then the 'Great Television Debate' provides it. It took place at the beginning of the final week. By then press and opinion polls were suggesting a neck-and-neck finish, and the cross-examination of the three party leaders did not really change this perception of how things were going to be. There was little doubt, in the aftermath of the television debate, that Charles Haughey had been the most accomplished of the three, though more in fending off questions than in answering them. Garret FitzGerald had been highly-strung and a bit uncertain. Frank Cluskey had been wooden and repetitive. The journalists involved felt they had put up a poor performance as inquisitors on behalf of the Irish people.[5]

Women played an important part in the election campaign, both as candidates and voters, and again the Fine Gael emphasis on women's issues, combined with the £9·60 tax transfer undertaking, created an electoral momentum favourable to the Opposition parties which was not matched by Fianna Fail, whose women politicians had a much more ambiguous attitude towards the women's movement, a movement which had already exercised considerable impact in two general elections, as well as in local elections and in the Euro-elections. In the 1981 general election, all three political parties clearly recognised the impact there had been in 1977, and acted on it. There were more women candidates and they won more seats. But in campaigning terms it was Fine Gael rather than Fianna Fail that made most capital out of the women's vote.

Throughout the three-week campaign, the central issue was the economy. The argument was that Fianna Fail, from 1977 to 1979, had pursued a legitimate enough course aimed at bringing down inflation, creating jobs, and putting borrowing right. It had been a difficult balancing act, but by the end of 1979 it could be regarded as reasonably successful. Up to then unemployment was below 100,000, inflation was only just into double figures, borrowing was 13 per cent of G.N.P. With the changeover from Jack Lynch to Charles Haughey the intent seemed to be the same but more firmly and more expertly administered. This was the message of the speech on television made on January 9, 1980, and it was referred to again and again to show that the right course of action had been understood, but that the nerve to implement it had not been there.

Unarguably, since the leadership change, inflation had gone up, unemployment had gone up, borrowing had gone up. Yet the unarguable was argued, the facts were challenged, the right course of action was disputed. This created uncertainty. It was clear, even from what was being said by Fianna Fail spokesmen, particularly Martin O'Donoghue, that there were two policies, one from 1977 to 1979, and one from 1980 to the calling of the election. Many people in the party, while they were prepared to defend one of these, were not concerned about the other.

It was not a satisfactory election. It was not a satisfactory result. It made the birth and early days of the new administration extremely difficult. How far the shadows were to extend over the next Dail was anyone's guess.

20

Garret FitzGerald

Instability was the overriding characteristic of the administration which came to power under Garret FitzGerald on July 7, 1981. It resulted from a number of factors, not least the election result itself. The Fine Gael Party had been by far the most successful, increasing its number of seats from 43 in 1977 to 65. Labour had dropped from 17 to 15, making a combined total of 80, a minority government in a Dail of 166 seats. Fianna Fail had won 78 seats, down from the previous general election total, in 1977, of 84 in a Dail of 148 seats. The remaining eight seats had been won by two H-Block candidates, and six other deputies: Neil Blaney, Jim Kemmy, Noel Browne, Joe Sherlock, John O'Connell and Sean Loftus.

In the aftermath of the election defeat of Frank Cluskey, the election of a new Labour Party leader led to unanimous agreement on Michael O'Leary, who had been a minister in Liam Cosgrave's coalition, and had been Frank Cluskey's somewhat disaffected deputy leader from 1977 to 1981. O'Leary then negotiated with Garret FitzGerald on a coalition deal which was subsequently put to a Labour Party conference in the Gaiety Theatre in Dublin, held on Sunday, June 28, two days before the Dail's reassembly, and carried, though not by any means unanimously, and not without quite outspoken debate and entrenched, Left-wing opposition to the idea of entering Government with Fine Gael. O'Leary himself, however, was a convinced coalitionist; the majority of deputies in the Labour Party were similarly disposed, most of them having come to power as a result of substantial votes transferring between Labour and Fine Gael.

The document for government, hammered out at the Labour Conference, inevitably became known as the 'Gaiety Theatre Document'. While this invited mild ribaldry, it nevertheless enshrined a balanced approach to government to which the Parliamentary Labour Party remained firm in its loyalty throughout the 22nd Dail. The instability derived from the uncertain dependence the coalition partners were able to place on individual Independent deputies. From the start, the new Government was dependent upon the support of at least three of them. Among those holding the balance of power were two successful candidates out of the group of nine who had stood on behalf of, or actually were prisoners on hunger strike in the Maze Prison H-Blocks. The two elected were Kieran Doherty in Cavan-Monaghan, and Patrick Agnew in Louth. They had not signed the roll, and were in no condition to take their seats; indeed, Doherty was in an advanced state of emaciation in a strike which had claimed several lives at this stage, and was to claim more, including Doherty's. This, in turn, was to raise the question of a by-election, a further twist in the screw of destabilisation. The Government successfully opposed the moving of the writ, though not without difficulties from the Ceann Comhairle, John O'Connell, who established fresh, and indeed questionable, precedents in the issue.

Contrary to the British system, while the Ceann Comhairle is automatically returned to the Dail he does not automatically resume his role as chairman. In this case Padraig Faulkner was recalled to Fianna Fail backbench status, and the house elected John O'Connell as its new chairman, without a division. John O'Connell, who was to be a key figure in this 22nd Dail, had been a member of the Labour Party but had resigned exactly five months earlier, on February 7, 1981, because of a dispute with the Labour leader, Frank Cluskey, over which constituency he would contest in the general election.[1] O'Connell was a keen admirer of Charles Haughey, particularly of what he had done as Minister for Health, but also of the Fianna Fail leader's Northern Ireland policy. He was basically not sympathetic to his own party, nor to Fine Gael, whose leader he did not admire.

The election of John O'Connell as the new Ceann Comhairle was followed by the nominations of Charles Haughey, and of the Fine Gael leader, Garret FitzGerald. There were five deputies whose voting pattern in the election of Taoiseach was significant. Each of them spoke in the short debate and they were the only members of the Dail to speak at that time.

Noel Browne was by far the most experienced politician among them. Nominally the only Dail member of the Socialist Labour Party, he had been in Irish politics for more than three decades, first entering the Dail after the election of 1948 when he became Minister for Health on his first day as a deputy and a controversial member of the first Inter-Party Government. At heart he was Labour, and sympathetic towards Garret FitzGerald, though sceptical about his political abilities. He was the first to speak in the short debate preceding the vote on the nomination of Taoiseach, on June 30, coming out strongly against Haughey, for his failures on the economy, and for what Browne described as his 'contemptuous' attitude to the Dail. But, because of the apparent 'belief in the monopoly capitalist system', he could not support the Fine Gael/Labour coalition. He therefore voted against Haughey, but abstained on the vote which nominated FitzGerald.

Jim Kemmy, the second Independent to speak, was a stone-mason from Limerick, and this was his first time in the Dail. He was a socialist, and had reservations about the Coalition not dissimilar from those of Noel Browne, but he committed himself to Garret FitzGerald.

Sean Loftus abstained on both votes. He made a lengthy if indeterminate speech, at one point suggesting that the three main party leaders should alternate in the position of Taoiseach, at another advocating a national government, and at the end thanking God and his wife Una for his seat, 'although it is a very dicey situation as I may be out in a matter of weeks or months'.

The next to speak was Joe Sherlock, the only member of Sinn Fein, the Workers' Party, to be elected in 1981, and a deputy who had contested at least two previous general elections in the mainly rural constituency of Cork East. He spoke briefly, coming down against the Fianna Fail candidate on grounds of the party's performance on behalf of working people, and promising to abstain on the nomination of FitzGerald since he could not support coalition.

The fifth Independent to speak was Neil Blaney, who talked of the choice being between bad and worse, and predictably supported Fianna Fail. He endorsed the massive construction programme (the Investment Plan of 1981) and 'a more definitely open operation' on H-Block, Mrs Thatcher and Anglo–Irish relations.

These five Independents were to assume an importance quite out of proportion to their political significance. In some cases inexcusably, they abused the balance of power which they held. So, in a different sense, did John O'Connell.

The votes were clear enough; by 83 to 79 Haughey was defeated; by 81 to 78 Garret FitzGerald was nominated to become Taoiseach and to form the next Government. In the third division on June 30, the Government was approved by 82 votes to 78, and the Dail adjourned for a week. It then re-assembled for two further weeks in July, principally to put through a supplementary Budget. Before that, however, further evidence of instability emerged in the election of a deputy speaker, when the division ended in a tie, 80 votes to 80, and John O'Connell then exercised his casting vote, contrary to Dail tradition, *against* the Government. The lengthy series of exchanges on procedure, earlier on the same day, had given clear indication both of a disruptive approach by the Opposition, and of a very loose hand on Dail discipline by its chairman. The character of the parliament was clearly going to be fractious, ill-tempered and full of confrontation; and at an early stage its chairman indicated quite openly that he was going to adopt an approach rather different from that of his predecessors.

This inauspicious start for the new Government,[2] in parliamentary and procedural terms, created additional handicaps at a time when it was already facing a revealed economic situation that was alarming, a continuation of the H-Block hunger strike which was now creating security problems in the Republic, the normal difficulties of a new Government settling down, and the background to this of the Labour Party having had to change its leader and negotiate its way into power by means of a party conference.

The figure to emerge most strongly out of all this was the Minister for Finance, John Bruton. A grim picture of the real state of the public finances had emerged following the changeover of government. The whole carefully constructed package of 'Investment Plan, 1981' in January and the Budget which had been presented after publication of the plan by Bruton's predecessor, Gene Fitzgerald, together with pre-election promises and decisions of an expansive, if not prodigal kind, began to fall apart like a house of cards. And when Bruton introduced his own midsummer Budget in July 21, he did so with the sobering introductory remark that its main objective was 'to ensure that Ireland remains an independent economy'. He was, he declared, entering on an immediate campaign to reconstruct the nation's finances, and to bring to a swift end the loose and irresponsible process by which current debt was built up for repayment by succeeding generations. Election promises involving expenditure, unlike those made by Lynch in 1977 which had proved disastrous, were abandoned by FitzGerald when the seriousness of the economic situation was fully appreciated. It was a firm approach from the start, made more impressive by the fact that it was based on an essentially minority position in the Dail. Though the Opposition described it as 'totally unnecessary', it passed swiftly enough into law, bringing in expenditure cuts and new taxes, as well as restoring transport and energy charges postponed by the previous administration for electoral reasons.

Straightaway Charles Haughey identified the Bruton approach as 'monetarist', and delivered an emotive speech the following day in the Dail about 'a harsh, uncaring economic policy' which took no account 'of the social degradation, of the waste of human talent and potential'. He saw the Government as undermining credibility, and claimed that his own administration had brought 'this small economy of ours through the worst international recession of modern times relatively safely and in far better shape than most of our European neighbours.'

This argument remained central throughout the short life of the 22nd Dail, and almost became the basis for the next general election. The whole of Charles Haughey's first period in power, from December 1979 until June 1981, with the exception of the first month, ending in his 'rectitude' speech on television, of January 9, 1980, had after all been based on the opposite interpretation of the country's economic prospects, which simply depended on the repeated anticipation of a world upturn for which Ireland had to be maintained in a 'well-poised' position and in its state of being 'basically in good shape'. Bruton disagreed, and his fundamental interpretation of the situation was profoundly at odds with that of Charles Haughey.

In extremely difficult circumstances for an incoming adminstration, sharp economic battle-lines were drawn in the intense two-day Budget debate with which the short summer session of the Dail ended, on July 23. Extra money had been borrowed, rising to something like £400 million; a switch in corporation tax had added a further £66 million to the overall burden; and, politically most serious, a combination of deferred price increases and unsanctioned expenditure had been entered into by the previous Government to gain electoral advantage. What Bruton was doing, in part, was to unravel a good deal of the economic secrecy which had surrounded the Fianna Fail administration from the period of 'Investment Plan, 1981' up to the calling of the general election.

Symptomatic of the semi-secret prodigality was Knock Airport. Knock is a small village in Mayo in which a vision was reported in 1879. Pope John Paul II visited it on its centenary, during his Irish tour. The parish priest, Monsignor Horan, sought an airport for Knock to cope with pilgrims, who were expected to come in tens of thousands, if not more, from the Pope's visit onward. Government officials were highly sceptical of this, and of the advisability of any airport at all, since there were already local airports at Sligo and Castlebar; but when it eventually came to Government, appropriately in Holy Week, 1981, and with a Department of Finance recommendation for deferral of decision, the project was approved, the State to bear the cost. What had been visualised initially as a grass airstrip escalated rapidly into one capable of taking intercontinental jets. Most of the pressure for the airport had come from a local Fianna Fail deputy, Padraig Flynn, who, as Minister for State at the Department of Transport had not only backed the project strongly, but had pre-empted Government decisions by public statements, and had sought civil service reports 'favourable' to the project. Beside a comment in the memoradum for Government saying of the request, 'This is irregular', a senior Finance official had written: 'It is outrageous.'

Nevertheless, the project was approved, and once State contracts were signed it became irreversible. Very substantial sums were spent on Knock in 1981–2, with the as yet incomplete airport likely to cost £16 million. The only profits it will ever earn are political ones: in both East and West Mayo

Fianna Fail has held two out of three seats in what were, in the past, regarded as marginals.

FitzGerald himself was preoccupied, from the moment he came to power, with the continuing and escalating problems of the H-Block hunger strike. While in Opposition, he had been very restrained. His approach then, supported in the North by John Hume of the S.D.L.P., had been to persuade the prisoners to end their strike. In power, however, and with the further deaths of Joe McDonnell on July 8 and Martin Hurson on July 13, bringing the total number of deaths to six, FitzGerald became increasingly agitated and erratic in his responses. On becoming Taoiseach he had reversed the general election priorities on which he had been elected, and made Northern Ireland his first priority; he now engaged in frenetic contacts with the British Ambassador, with the Irish Commission for Justice and Peace (a body negotiating directly with the hunger strikers), with Margaret Thatcher by telephone, stressing the need for a 'solution' and an early meeting between them, with President Reagan, to whom he appealed to intervene, and finally by a Government proposal that the British Government should deal directly with the prisoners. FitzGerald had come full circle, replacing his principled stand with a form of political panic motivated by the unnerving spectacle of a member of the Dail on the brink of a horrifying death by starvation. He was brought to his senses by the protest march which took place in Dublin on Saturday, July 18, on behalf of the hunger strikers. The mass demonstration began in an orderly fashion in St Stephen's Green, and set off for the British Embassy in Ballsbridge. The road was blocked off at Serpentine Avenue by police, and the confrontation disintegrated into violence euphemistically described by the National H-Block Committee's phrase: 'Sections of the marchers broke ranks.' Public opinion viewed it differently; it was a destabilising spillover of the North's problems, and an overwhelming majority of people wanted neither it, nor the other actions demanded by those demonstrating on behalf of the hunger strikers, which included the recall of Ireland's ambassador to London, the expulsion of the British Ambassador, the withdrawal of troops from the Border, and a Government declaration that Britain should concede the prisoners' five demands. It was too late for that. The deaths which had already taken place had tested and found lacking the public volatility required to justify the whole campaign. Though it took further days to bring it to a conclusion, during which one of the Dail's deputies on hunger strike was to die, the H-Block campaign had already failed well before the July march in Dublin.

It had nevertheless done substantial damage. The instability which was a hallmark of the 22nd Dail and its short-lived administration, was also now a central feature of the political situation in Northern Ireland. Though it was a contradiction of the basis for his election, FitzGerald was broadly right in giving it a high priority, and in seeking an early meeting with Margaret Thatcher.

This took place in early November, and the most significant outcome was the decision to publish the Joint Studies which had been initiated by Charles Haughey and Margaret Thatcher after their summit meeting of December, 1980. These revealed a sensible but limited range of options for greater Anglo–Irish co-operation, including the anticipated proposal, under the *institutional* arrangements which had been the source of so much controversy the previous December and January, that an Anglo–Irish Intergovernmental Council should be set up with a subsequent parliamentary tier and an advisory committee of experts drawn from a wide spectrum.

In addition it was proposed that the Irish Attorney General, Peter Sutherland, would discuss possible improvements in legal co-operation with his British opposite number, Sir Michael Havers, with whom he had a good personal relationship. Agreement to discuss dual citizenship, economic co-operation, security, and the possibility of some forward movement in Britain's attitude to unity, completed the fairly comprehensive list of topics covered in FitzGerald's first meeting with Margaret Thatcher. Haughey dismissed the Summit and implied that the joint studies were somehow a let-down. In his view 'the spirit and letter of the Dublin communiqué' of December, 1980, had been lost.[3]

It subsequently emerged, in direct contradiction of this, that the joint studies, as published, had been known to Haughey and approved by him before he left office in June; moreover, he had endorsed their contents, without revealing what they were, during the general election. Having raised things to 'a new plane', and then having been replaced as the central agent of implementation the Fianna Fail leader was at pains to begin a new political 'game', signalled by more scathing epithets about Margaret Thatcher — 'the woman from Finchley' — and a general dismissal of FitzGerald's Northern policy.

A parallel dismissiveness emerged from Northern Ireland, inescapably an unhappier place as a result of the hunger-strike tensions, but now still further divided by the S.D.L.P. decision not to contend the Fermanagh-Tyrone by-election. Frank Maguire's death, on March 5, 1981, had led to the by-election in which Bobby Sands, the H-Block hunger striker, had won the seat when forty days into his strike. During the campaign, Provisional Sinn Fein had talked about 'borrowing' the seat in order to save a life, presumably that of Sands. His death provoked a second by-election. Once again, the Provisionals were kind enough to describe as 'wise' the S.D.L.P. decision not to run a candidate against Owen Carron, who took the seat on August 20, leaving John Hume and his party standing on the sidelines politically in a highly marginal constituency at a particularly unstable time.

It was in this unhappy political climate, North and South, that Garret FitzGerald chose to launch his 'Constitutional Crusade'. The decision was made without Government approval, on the way to an interview for radio, and emerged before a startled public as a broad statement of intent designed to implement change and reform. Though FitzGerald was only eleven weeks into office, and was faced with massive economic and tactical Dail problems, he handled the announcement of his crusade better than could have been thought possible in the light of the complete absence of any preparation. Initially, he toyed with the idea of campaigning for a new Constitution, but he had neither the authority nor any mandate for such an approach, and there was no perceived need for it. But he did want to give some kind of all-Ireland character to his political ambitions, and, faced by the gloomy and narrow economic options inherited from the previous administration, it seemed more feasible to pursue a set of policies developed out of his own Northern Ireland policy document, 'Ireland Our Future Together'. This detailed and well-reasoned analysis of the benefits to be derived from closer North–South political co-operation was in marked contrast to the Fianna Fail policy, which started from the depressing premise that Northern Ireland had failed as a political entity. The crusade emphasised this contrast, to FitzGerald's advantage. Whether it could be made to achieve more than that lay in the future.

The accidental way in which the 'Constitutional Crusade' emerged, however, was characteristic of Garret FitzGerald. His whole-hearted dedication, which was enormously appealing, became puzzling when one endeavoured to identify the object of that dedication. It was not power or politics for their own sake; the former was an instrument he understood imperfectly, the latter a way of life he neither enjoyed nor occupied even with a rudimentary sense of comfort. It was not party, nor was it self-advancement. Though he had dedicated virtually all his energies since becoming Fine Gael leader, in 1977, to the reorganisation of the party from grassroots up, and had done so with evident electoral success, and though his whole life had had a natural Fine Gael background, which stretched back to his father's position as W. T. Cosgrave's Minister for Foreign Affairs, External Affairs and Defence, in that order, 1921–32, he was curiously detached from the party's myths and folklore, and generally dismissive of many of its traditions, particularly the emphasis on law and order. Again, it was an 'instrument' for some broader purpose or motivation towards which his restless, fervent spirit drove him. He had developed a personal creed which he expressed in terms of his parentage, father a republican Roman Catholic who had been in the G.P.O. in 1916, mother a Presbyterian Unionist who had also been there, and both of them active in the War of Independence, though at odds subsequently during the Civil War. Such roots had given FitzGerald a deep and abiding motive towards reconciliation between North and South, Protestant, Catholic and Dissenter, Unionist and Nationalist. And he was essentially emotional about the complex and frustrating range of problems towards which he turned his attention. Quite different, and much cooler, were his economic skills. Bred out of his pre-political, professional career as statistician, and augmented in its detachment by academic work, his dedication to the solving of economic ills was massively supported by command of detail. While this could be an effective weapon in debate, it was also a handicap when it came to making political judgments, one of which now faced him, in the late autumn of 1981, in the construction of a Budget.

There was no question but that, both on Northern Ireland and on the economy, FitzGerald and Haughey were diverging quite sharply from the late summer of 1981 onward. Charles Haughey's dismissiveness about the Thatcher–FitzGerald meeting was carried beyond the borderline of credibility when, on November 11, 1981, in the Dail he claimed an agreement between himself and Mrs Thatcher, made in December 1980, and now 'lost' by FitzGerald: 'The British Government then agreed to my proposal that the British and Irish Governments had joint responsibility for the resolution of the Northern Ireland problem and for bringing forward policies and proposals to achieve peace, reconciliation and stability.'[4] The claim was a gross exaggeration. Mrs Thatcher had made very clear indeed the constitutional position of Northern Ireland when she visited Belfast on March 5, 1981, that it would remain part of the United Kingdom until the people and the Parliament at Westminster decided otherwise, and to this position, which she said was fundamental to British Government thinking, she made an even stronger personal commitment: 'It is something to which I am personally and deeply committed. Let me say with all the emphasis at my command that there is no plot. There is no sell-out. Those who argue otherwise have simply got it wrong and are choosing not to understand the purpose of my discussions with Mr Charles Haughey.'

A comparable level of divergence was evident on the economy. The stringent policies adopted by John Bruton since the July Budget were attacked by Fianna Fail for their Thatcherite monetarism, with the party leader himself offering job creation as the objective to which 'absolute priority' had to be given. 'Our approach is positive and theirs is negative. We are development-investment minded, and they are committed to monetarism and deflation.'[5]

But Charles Haughey was faced with internal problems as well. Since the June defeat he had repeatedly confronted his own party with a three-pronged defence of his own position: Fianna Fail had been right all along on its policies, both economic and towards Northern Ireland; the party had been put out of power by 'an electoral quirk'; and, finally, the Coalition was in imminent danger of breaking up. Not unreasonably, if there were people within Fianna Fail who believed that the party might do better under a different leader, they were restrained from exploring the possibilities by this collective answer, and by the possibility that the last part of it might prove correct. In addition, Haughey had not faced the problem of creating a Front Bench. His team still operated, through the autumn, on the basis of their former ministerial responsibilities.

One deputy, however, did speak out. In an interview given to Geraldine Kennedy, Political Correspondent of the *Sunday Tribune*, Charles McCreevy, a Fianna Fail backbench deputy from Kildare, and one of the men who had attended the July 1979 caucus meeting, after which he had actively supported Charles Haughey for leader to replace Jack Lynch, now came out with criticisms of the leadership and of the direction the Party was taking. 'We seem to be against everything and for nothing.' Specifically asked if there was disillusionment with Haughey, he said, 'No comment'; but he went on to say, 'there is a considerable number of the Fianna Fail parliamentary party, representing the views of the organisation throughout the country, who are less than satisfied with Fianna Fail in Opposition.'[6]

It was not McCreevy's first broadside, and emphatically not his last. He had been critical, in early 1981, of what he saw as 'an auction in vote-buying', a direct reference to the economic strategy pursued by the party in power in the winter and spring before the May-June general election. After the change of Government in June he had praised the Bruton Budget in the Dail. Now he was giving expression to a rising tide of anti-Haughey feeling in Fianna Fail.

Haughey treated the confrontation with McCreevy for what it was, a challenge to his leadership. He sought McCreevy's expulsion, but even more than that he endeavoured to get badly needed unanimity within his own Front Bench over the confrontation, and failed. At a Front Bench meeting on Tuesday, January 19, less than a week after the Shadow appointments had been announced, it was clearly indicated to him that he did not enjoy unanimity over expelling McCreevy; several thought censure would be better. Haughey then requested that dissenters should abstain at the parliamentary party meeting; a further request for confidentiality was ignored, and details of the Front Bench divisions appeared in newspapers.

McCreevy himself handled the meeting at which his expulsion was sought with considerable aplomb. Forcing the situation to the brink of a vote he then made a short speech setting out his reasons for dissatisfaction — mainly that Fianna Fail had ceased to discuss issues, and therefore did not know in which direction it was moving — and left, pledging continued loyalty to the party. Charles Haughey had been cheated of the show of solidarity he so badly needed. In an interview later on radio McCreevy said: 'The leader of Fianna Fail is there for the time being.'

Haughey's own response was very tame. He announced that McCreevy, who was a substantial vote-getter in Kildare, could 'apply to rejoin at any time', or 'be invited to apply'. It was a very temporary rustication.

It needed to be. After intense deliberations, secretive and ominous, and presaged by warnings of stringencies which were inescapable, John Bruton introduced his second Budget in the Dail on January 27, 1982. Broadly correct in its five-fold objectives of reducing borrowing, increasing competitiveness, raising the living standards of the deprived and poor, reforming taxation and creating work-incentives, it nevertheless contained a fatal Achilles' heel in the imposition of VAT on clothing and footwear. By no means wrong in retrospect, it was politically ill-judged when the Coalition of Fine Gael and Labour required, for survival, the additional *minimum* of two Independents. It got the support of one, Noel Browne. Even then it could have survived with the abstention of two of the others. But Jim Kemmy, Joe Sherlock, Neil Blaney and Sean Loftus voted with Fianna Fail, giving them 82 votes against 81, and defeating the first and only Budget resolution put to the House that night. Immediately afterwards FitzGerald told the Dail, 'I will proceed immediately to Aras an Uachtarain (the President's official residence in Phoenix Park) to seek dissolution from the President'.

It seemed, on the face of it, a doomed position from which to face a general election. Yet almost immediately Charles Haughey made the tactical mistake of engaging in swift and determined attempts to *prevent* a dissolution. Under the Republic of Ireland Constitution if a Taoiseach loses the support of the majority in the Dail the President has the right to refuse him a dissolution. The power has never been invoked, partly because, in theory, it could lead to a constitutional impasse if no other person could achieve majority support; and no constitutional provision existed for that. The Fianna Fail statement, issued at 8.25 p.m., two hours after the Dail defeat, was in the party leader's name, and said: 'It is a matter for the President to consider the situation which has arisen now that the Taoiseach has ceased to retain the support of the majority in Dail Eireann. I am available for consultation by the President should he so wish.' This apparent neutrality of wording and 'availability' was at odds with three attempts by the Fianna Fail leader, or on his behalf, to make contact by telephone with President Hillery.

Politically, Charles Haughey's statement after FitzGerald's decision to seek a dissolution, indicated a combination of constitutional opportunism with reluctance to face the electorate; and it raised in some minds at least questions about the general prediction that Fine Gael, and even more so, Labour, would be more than decimated in the election brought on by the Budget.

Inescapably, the two parties had to fight the campaign on the basis of Bruton's economic programme, and as a partnership. There was no alternative option available. Their harsh 'manifesto', which had already made headlines in the evening papers as Bruton delivered it in the Dail, now appeared in the morning papers as the most detailed, and arguably suicidal election platform that ever a pair of political parties had as their campaign ammunition. Yet inevitability favoured FitzGerald's disposition, which was pragmatic to the point both of stoicism and naivety. He was followed in this by the Labour leader, Michael O'Leary. Neither they, nor any other member of either party, had the option of judging or prevaricating, and it turned out to be a much more substantial advantage than anyone anticipated in the immediate wake of the defeat which brought to an end the short, unhappy life of the 22nd Dail.

21

More Instability

Charles Haughey launched the Fianna Fail election campaign at a press conference in the Shelbourne Hotel the next day. The party leader did not have his Front Bench spokesman on Finance, Martin O'Donoghue, with him. O'Donoghue, not surprisingly, was appalled when he learned that his leader had put the whole Fianna Fail election campaign into reverse on Day One by adopting the approach that had lost the election the previous June. In other words, Charles Haughey had failed to give any clear answers on anything beyond a broad assurance that there was 'a more human way' of running the country's economy than the way laid out so harshly and so precisely in the Budget speech. Ireland had always borrowed, Haughey claimed, there was a basic need for investment, and he was refusing to be 'hypnotised' by the issue of the public finances.

O'Donoghue, to his credit, recognised straightaway that a three-week campaign following immediately after the publication of all the economic data available, simply could not be sustained on the bland foundation offered by his leader at that first press conference. He made his position plain that evening. With a massive grinding of gears the reverse movement towards the mists and prevarications of the previous May election was stopped, and the Fianna Fail campaign was re-routed on to a different but roughly parallel road of economic rectitude, reasonably closely in line with the published facts.

The tiny Irish economy, which had made such impressive strides in the 1960s and had become increasingly independent and assured in the early 1970s was now up to its ears in debt. Between 1977 and 1981, under Fianna Fail, it had borrowed £5,000 million in an economic course of self-indulgence rather than investment which had gone out of control, particularly over wages and prices, and which had failed in the central responsibility of creating jobs. The young and relatively inexperienced Minister for Finance, John Bruton, was preaching an economic doctrine based on the belief that the only jobs worth creating were those which derived from real productivity and real competitiveness. If that approach failed, then Ireland would be run by its creditors. Though Fianna Fail feigned outrage at this apparent washing of dirty linen in public, which allegedly put the country's credibility at risk, it represented an unarguable prescription in the eyes of many people. It was to O'Donoghue's credit, in the early stages of the campaign, that he managed to challenge successfully the more lunatic blandness in the party, and introduce a dose of realism which differed from Bruton's sufficiently to create a contest, but not so substantially as to undermine the credibility of his own party.

At the end of the second week, at a major press conference the leader and his Finance spokesman were almost wrestling in public for the economic soul of Fianna Fail. The party proposed the imposition of VAT on imported goods at point of entry, and the switching of corporation tax payments in a once-off book-keeping device designed to alleviate the VAT tax on footwear and clothing at no apparent cost: this was 'the more human way' of doing things. But it represented more the economic equivalent of semantics than anything else, a fairly sterile process of parsing and analysis which could not escape the basic message of stern cutting back in which John Bruton had shown the way in stark contrast to past Fianna Fail policies.

The Labour Party faced the cruellest dilemma. In the Budget vote the actual two-party coalition deal had held firm. But it left Labour candidates defending unprecedented stringency on hustings and doorsteps without having much to offer. There were deep and long-standing divisions about partnership with Fine Gael, anyway, and these emerged, not least because the party chairman, Michael D. Higgins, who was a candidate in Galway, was opposed to Labour being in Government. He said so, at the beginning of the campaign, and then went on saying so throughout.

The Labour Party leader felt free to tell the electorate, 'if we have a majority with Fine Gael, then Labour's participation in a new government with Fine Gael is certain'. But it did not satisfy either Michael D. Higgins or members of the administrative council. And O'Leary's position was further damaged by the decisions of Brendan Corish, a former leader, and Jim Tully, a long-serving deputy leader, to stand down.

It was a measure of the political sophistication in the country that a general election forced on the politicians in circumstances which initially had seemed so unbalanced, became a tightly-argued and evenly-fought confrontation, with the budgetary merits of rectitude clearly holding their own, firstly against the bland, 'more human way' offered by Charles Haughey, and then against the rationally argued alternative strategy of Martin O'Donoghue.

The basic credibility of what Fianna Fail had done with the economy since 1977, which had not been open to public consideration in the obscurantist atmosphere surrounding the May-June 1981 general election, was up for detailed consideration in the light of the quite different economic medicine being offered by John Bruton. And there were clear indications that the public favoured rectitude.

There were even clearer signs that the leaders of the two parties were at the centre of these questions of economic credibility. Furthermore, Charles Haughey had steadily declined in public appeal as a potential leader, while Garret FitzGerald's standing had increased. Besides, even within Fianna Fail, by the end of the election campaign, more than a quarter of declared party supporters preferred Garret FitzGerald as Taoiseach.[1]

There was decidedly a 'Haughey factor'. Fianna Fail politicians openly expressed the view that victory would be assured with any other leader, and went so far as to play down those aspect of the campaign which featured him personally. This 'Haughey factor' echoed down through the constituencies. Fianna Fail faction-fighting was present in about ten constituencies.[2] In one, Galway West, there had been a vote of 'no confidence' in Charles Haughey. There was also potential trouble in Roscommon, Galway East and Mayo West.

As if he did not have enough problems Haughey was sufficiently anxious about the outcome of the vote in constituencies where close aides from 1979–80 were in conflict with former neutrals or supporters of George Colley, to seek to intervene and influence the Fianna Fail vote.

No such 'FitzGerald factor' prevailed. Quite the opposite, in fact. Heavy emphasis was placed on his personal appeal, and he was made central to the campaign, a position to which he responded remarkably well in view of the Budget defeat which had been his starting point.

It was the shortest possible general election campaign. Limited funds removed any bandwagon approach, such as there had been in June 1981. The short winter days, in spite of generally mild weather, concentrated the mind on issues which were intensely debated on radio and television. The party press conferences were aggressively handled by a number of political journalists to the point where Fianna Fail accused the media of hostility. Tough arguments centred on budget provisions, and on whether the Coalition had adopted the right course for the country. The more positive election ideas, such as highlighting women's issues, and taxation reform, which had been a factor in the previous campaign, were dropped. More contentious problems came to the surface, including Knock airport, the proposed closure of Clondalkin Paper Mills, the future of the country's only oil refinery at Whitegate in Cork, and the potential and actual internal differences within the political parties.

But the underlying issue was credibility, its testing ground was the economy, the two champions confronting each other on it were the two party leaders. They met for a television debate, the first of its kind, two days before the poll.

For two years they had faced each other in an atmosphere of fundamental conflict which had worsened. The mutual consent basic to parliamentary democracy had been steadily withdrawn. In its place there was distrust and antagonism. The two men both had a vision of Ireland, but they differed profoundly on what it was; they were both reputedly adept in the economic sphere, but had profoundly different objectives, interpretations, and methods; their strong commitment to action on Northern Ireland was matched by equally strong disagreement on how to approach the problem of the Six Counties. Both men were fluent, forceful, dynamic, and determined to win. But both used these talents often in diametrically opposed directions: while FitzGerald sought to be comprehensive and detailed, Haughey managed to be extensively vague and evasive. They managed to give totally different interpretations of the direction in which they might lead the country.

Haughey won the television debate, though it is questionable whether this had any impact on voting intentions. Smoother and more assured, the Fianna Fail leader presented greater command and displayed more apparent decisiveness. FitzGerald, less good as a performer, nevertheless demonstrated a greater willingness to drag out into the open the facts and figures, and let the public decide.

The electorate chose to deliver an ambiguous verdict: more instability. Fianna Fail increased its vote by 2 per cent, over the 1981 total, to 47·26 per cent, winning 81 seats, an increase of three, but still three seats short of a majority. Fine Gael's share of the vote dropped by 0·8 per cent, but with the loss of two seats, leaving the party with 63. After Labour's gains and losses its total number of seats remained 15, though its vote declined again, also by 0·8 per cent. The balance of power in the new Dail was held by seven deputies. Three were members of Sinn Fein the Workers' Party: they were Joe Sherlock, re-elected in Cork North East, Proinsias de Rossa, who won a seat for the first time in Dublin North West, and Paddy Gallagher in Waterford. John O'Connell, outgoing Ceann Comhairle, was returned automatically. Neil Blaney won his Independent Fianna Fail seat in Donegal and Jim Kemmy retained his seat in Limerick. A new Independent deputy, Tony Gregory, won in Dublin Central at the expense of Fine Gael's Alice Glenn.

It was a phenomenal outcome. The coalition parties, which might have anticipated decimation, had achieved a stalemate which left FitzGerald with some prospect of forming the next Government. But for the country it was a decidedly gloomy result. The new Dail could only be shortlived. There was no mandate for the firm handling of public finances, for single-party rule, none for a clear coalition agreement, and no easily determined preference for a national leader.

It was Charles Haughey's failure to achieve a clear mandate, for the second time running, more than any other factor which led to an internal challenge against his leadership between the end of the election and the first meeting of the party. The belief that Fianna Fail, under another leader, would certainly have swept back to power had held firm throughout the campaign and now provoked a move against him by a group of deputies who favoured Desmond O'Malley. Vincent Browne's count, published in *Magill* magazine on February 22, named 30 anti-Haughey deputies, 17 pro-Haughey, and 34 who were neutral or whose position was unknown.

Haughey had actually told his Front Bench, at its first meeting on January 19, 1982, ten days before the collapse of the 22nd Dail, that if at any time he considered himself not an asset to the party, he would resign. He added, quickly enough, that he *did* consider himself an asset. But a month later, at the end of his second general election, the claim was in contention.

On Monday, February 22, Haughey took the unusual step of having a motion put down on the parliamentary party meeting's agenda for Thursday, February 25, for his own re-election. The meeting itself had been moved forward from its normal timing on March 9 when the new Dail was to meet, and anti-Haughey deputies suggested that this was in order to pre-empt dissent. By this stage, intense lobbying was going on by both pro- and anti-Haughey deputies. Late night and all-night meetings went on from Monday to Wednesday. On Wednesday night Desmond O'Malley decided that he would stand for the leadership of the party, and issued a statement to that effect. An immediate reply from a spokesman for Haughey said that the challenge would be met 'head-on'. The former Taoiseach, Jack Lynch, then issued a statement supporting O'Malley's decision 'to let his name go forward ... following the failure of Fianna Fail to get an overall majority', and pointedly made no comment about the present party leader. It provoked a sharp reaction from Haughey's closest aide, Ray McSharry, a former Agriculture Minister, who said that Lynch had undoubtedly been involved in some way in the attempt to remove Charles Haughey, and should not have been.

The parliamentary party assembled at 11.30 on Thursday morning. Sean Browne, its new Chairman, and Padraig Faulkner, a former Ceann Comhairle and a highly respected senior member, both appealed to deputies to avoid division while Fianna Fail still had the chance of forming a Government. But the major shock to O'Malley came when Martin O'Donoghue, who had campaigned intensely in support of O'Malley during the previous week, added his voice to those calling for unity behind Charles Haughey. It was an extraordinary about-face, never satisfactorily explained by O'Donoghue. O'Malley had no option but to withdraw his challenge, and the Fianna Fail Party decision to nominate Haughey as Taoiseach became unanimous. At a press conference which followed he described as 'the worst list of names in Irish journalism' an article which had appeared on page one of the *Irish Independent* the previous morning, identifying the areas of support within Fianna Fail.[3] Supporters of Charles Haughey admitted privately that they had used the list to conduct an intense personal and telephone campaign on Haughey's behalf; and Desmond O'Malley confessed later that his support had been eroded by this powerful and concerted campaign. The key figures in pressurising deputies were Ray McSharry, Sean Doherty and Albert Reynolds.

The following week Charles Haughey concluded a signed agreement, witnessed by Michael Mullen, general secretary of the country's largest trade union, the I.T.G.W.U., with the inner city Independent deputy, Tony Gregory, on massive development within his constituency. It secured one vital vote at an estimated cost in excess of £50 million. Neil Blaney's support was already regarded as secure, in spite of Blaney's predictable hesitations. John O'Connell's return to the Chair was hardly in doubt, in spite of his poor performance there in the previous Dail. Jim Kemmy, it was correctly assumed, would continue to support FitzGerald. This left the three members of S.F.W.P. to decide between a Fianna Fail vote which had already reached 83 and a combined Fine Gael–Labour vote of 78. They swung in behind Charles Haughey. Perhaps 'climbed in' would be a better way of putting it. They actually reached the Chamber after the doors had closed for the division, were pointed in the direction of the press gallery by a supporter of Charles Haughey, and fought and scrambled their way over the backs of journalists, across the barricade between the press and distinguished visitors' gallery, and on to the floor of the House. In this unseemly fashion the 23rd Dail nominated its Taoiseach, and for the second time, Charles Haughey became leader of the Government.

22

1982

The year 1982 was a black one in Irish politics. It began and ended with a general election. To the inevitable instability which derived from the first was added an abuse of power by the administration led by Charles Haughey which did not come to light until after the second general election. In a very real sense T. S. Eliot's lines are appropriate:

> *What might have been is an abstraction*
> *Remaining a perpetual possibility*
> *Only in a world of speculation.*[1]

The possibility and speculation, in a democracy, remain. To some extent, in spite of the secure partnership of Labour and Fine Gael, the overall situation facing the country at the beginning of 1983 ensured the survival of much of the social and economic instability which had become, in the previous two years, central to the Irish political scene.

Through 1982 the economic crisis deepened; redundancies, the collapse of companies, rising unemployment, steep increases in the level of crime, a serious urban drugs problem, and a rising tide of protest marches, brought to a welcome end the long-standing argument between rectitude on the one hand and a Micawber-like expectation that something would turn up for Ireland. On all sides, and particularly following the rejection of the politics of promises in the Dublin West by-election which came soon after the general election, 1982 was the year in which a reluctant realism eventually took over.

Its initiators, the Government team appointed by Charles Haughey, were not inspired by any collective vision.[2] After the failure of the leadership challenge, many of them were wary and suspicious. Unity of purpose and openness of approach were not high priorities.

The Dail resumed parliamentary business on March 2 when, among other things, John O'Connell, who had given his casting vote *against* the Government on the previous occasion of a tie in the election of deputy chairman, now gave it *for* the Government.[3] 'If the House thinks I am not acting impartially any member of the House is at liberty to move a motion of censure against me', was O'Connell's reply to the interruptions and criticisms which followed his decision. His attitude led later to his former Labour Party colleague, Barry Desmond describing him in the Dail as 'the worst Ceann Comhairle I have ever seen before this House. You are a public disgrace'.

Within the first week, following the introduction of the Budget to replace the one which had led to the collapse of the previous Dail, a further degree of uncertainty was created by the decision of Richard Burke, a former Government Minister under Liam Cosgrave, and his appointee to Europe as the country's second Commissioner, in January 1977, to accept the job for a further term from Charles Haughey. He prevaricated on Haughey's offer, consulting with the party which was not unanimously against the prestige and influence which would derive from Ireland's only Commissioner being not of the Fianna Fail Party. After reversing his decision once, Burke accepted the appointment and resigned from the Dail.

This increased Haughey's voting strength by one, and there was no urgency about a by-election; action was needed first to ensure victory. But the inevitability of an early contest raised another controversial issue. In the February general election, Pat O'Connor, a Dublin solicitor and Charles Haughey's election agent, had been arrested with his daughter, Niamh, and charged with personation. The two had been seen at two different voting stations accepting ballot papers, and, allegedly, using them. But the district justice hearing the case gave a controversial judgment dismissing the charges on the grounds that the secret ballot prevented anyone knowing whether anyone else had voted at all. While the case itself was to be challenged by means of the legal device of having 'a case tated' in the High Court, a legal wrangle which went on for more than a year, the district court decision provoked questions n the Dail, since a clarification was needed *before* the Dublin West by-election could be held.

The Taoiseach's understandable reluctance to discuss the situation provoked a serious row in the Dail[5] with the Ceann Comhairle endeavouring to prevent the issue being raised at all, and with the Government sitting back and watching the Opposition's frustration. But relentless parliamentary pressure combined with public anger which was augmented by other judgment in personation cases leading to prison sentences, forced a more sober debate the following day and the introduction of a Prevention of Electoral Abuses Act.

The by-election writ was moved on May 4. Though Burke's defection from party and constituency was expected to damage Fine Gael and give the seat to Fianna Fail, who ran a campaign based on promises for the sprawling suburban constituency with a popular and experienced woman candidate, Eileen Lemass, the surprising result on May 25 was a Fine Gael victory, with Liam Skelly taking the seat. It was a damaging result for the Fianna Fail leader. He had given away an important European appointment to no advantage at all and demonstrated yet again that there was no real support for the politics of promises.

From this point on the Fianna Fail Government made a firm switch towards economic rectitude, and its principal exponent became the new Minister for Finance, Ray McSharry. In the initial post-electoral euphoria, he had dismissed the Coalition's 'gloom and doom' approach, promising 'boom and bloom' from Fianna Fail. On reflection, however, he introduced a responsible Budget followed by a tough Finance Bill. It was seen as firm government at last.[6]

Firmness of a quite different kind manifested itself on two other political fronts: Northern Ireland and the Falklands. The two, as far as Ireland was concerned, were related.

Although Charles Haughey had been neutral over devolution in Northern Ireland earlier in 1982,[7] when the Prior proposals for a Northern Ireland Assembly became public at the beginning of April they were rejected by the Taoiseach. His opposition to the British White Paper[8] was positive and sustained on the domestic front, an attitude adopted equally firmly by Gerard Collins, Minister for Foreign Affairs, who claimed he had put Ireland's views about the inevitable failure of the proposed assembly to the Northern Ireland Secretary, James Prior, before the proposals were put to the British Government. Prior denied this emphatically, provoking a situation comparable to the argument about the interpretation of 'institutional' change as 'constitutional' change following the Haughey–Thatcher Summit at Dublin Castle in December 1980. Not important in itself, the prevarications were symptomatic of two things: the low state of Anglo–Irish relations, and the virtual non-existence of any Republic of Ireland alternative to Prior's proposals for devolution. Collins called for 'Anglo–Irish structures', and 'an initiative that would work' while at the same time delivering himself of such splendid advice as this: 'The situation that will develop after the initiative doesn't get off the ground will be worse than the situation if the initiative is not developed at all'.[9]

The Prior proposals, however, had been overshadowed by the Falklands crisis. The Collins–Prior meeting took place in the week of the Falklands invasion on April 2. Publication of the Northern Ireland White Paper followed on April 5. Instead of distinguishing clearly the difference between these two issues, the Irish Government fell back into the trap of traditional republican chauvinism in its response to the British position. An apparent bloody-mindedness, which provoked positive reaction against the Assembly proposals instead of silence, was followed by an equally positive interventionist stance about the remote issue of the Falklands. A swift deterioration in Anglo–Irish relations followed. To some extent the Government's response was motivated by the Dublin West by-election. Much of the constituency was working class, and assumptions were made that those holding traditional republican views, though they had produced only 3,000 first preference votes for the H-Block candidate there in 1981, might somehow respond to an anti-British line; in addition, it seemed that Irish neutrality could be presented as being under threat by aligning the Republic with other European countries in support of Britain over the Falklands.

The long-standing and emotive arguments about Ireland possibly becoming a member of NATO came to the surface. So did the much older argument about Ireland's neutrality being inked with Britain's continued presence in the North. The harmony and closeness between the two countries, so carefully encouraged after Charles Haughey's first meeting with Margaret Thatcher in May, 1980, and carried forward substantially at the Dublin Castle Summit the following December, were now firmly things of the past; and the 'unique relationship' took on a quite different meaning.

The situation reached critical proportions only in May, with the outbreak of direct hostilities between Britain and Argentina. The sinking of the *Belgrano*, on May 2, provoked an Irish Government statement which was the first official indication that Ireland was going cool on the earlier commitment to U.N. Resolution 502 in favour of Argentine withdrawal from the Falklands. On Monday, May 3, the Minister for Defence, Paddy Power, in a speech at Edenderry, and deliberately using the collective 'we' of the Government, accused Britain of being the aggressors now', and said that the Government would be adopting a 'neutral' stance. Everything in his speech indicated that it would be a neutral stance *against* Britain, and his reception from his rural audience was rapturous.

The Taoiseach described the outburst as 'spontaneous ... personal ... understandable'. It was also embarrassing. At the time a British submarine had become entangled in the nets of an Irish trawler, and the trawler had sunk. There had been no British Government acknowledgement or apology. This episode, too, was woven by Power into a complex argument in which British troops in Northern Ireland, neutrality, the Falklands, the E.E.C., Ireland's role within the United Nations (Ireland was on the Security Council, and Noel Dore, the Irish Ambassador to the U.N. was due to become the Council's president in August) were somehow to be taken together. The Sunday statement was followed by one on Tuesday, May 4, which began with the words, 'The Government are appalled ... ' went on to suggest that world peace was threatened, and proposed a U.N. involvement 'to secure an end to the present conflict'. Ireland's method for achieving this was an immediate cessation of hostilities and 'the negotiation of a diplomatic settlement under the auspices of the U.N.'. Given the intensive, month-long negotiations which had proved abortive, together with the fact that the U.N. had been deeply involved since the Argentine invasion on April 2, this statement carried little weight, and was substantially modified later the same day, in the Dail,[10] where Ireland's support for U.N. Resolution 502 was confirmed, and the country's apparent intention to withdraw unilaterally from European economic sanctions was changed to reservations about the value of such sanctions. While there was room for debate about this, greater potential danger surrounded the attitude Ireland might adopt in the U.N. Security Council. There Ireland could easily find itself in direct conflict with Britain. Over an issue in the distant South Atlantic which had virtually no Irish dimension this could be at best counter-productive at a time when ostensibly, at least, Irish interests closer to home might be served better by adopting a stance supportive of Britain. The point was made more than once in the debate, but ignored. Clothing the issue in arguments about neutrality, it remained the Fianna Fail objective to adopt a position which at least domestically would be seen as 'combative'. Had there been any wave of hysteria in Britain against 'Irish treachery', this approach might have yielded some marginal dividend. But Margaret Thatcher's reaction was extremely careful. The most she would acknowledge publicly was 'disappointment', and this was also the attitude of the Northern Ireland Secretary of State, James Prior. Dublin's policy over the Falklands, at the U.N. and in Europe, would not alter her intention of going ahead with further meetings with the Taoiseach.

Ireland was seen to be puffing and blowing inordinately over an issue which had virtually nothing to do with the country's domestic or foreign interests. The Government fumbled badly over U.N. policy, and then reverted to support for the basic Resolution 502. Withdrawal from E.E.C. sanctions followed, though the impact of Irish economic relations with Argentina could not have been great. The net result as far as defence policy was concerned was confusion. And even greater confusion emerged over neutrality, which had been invoked as a central issue. The most serious aspect of all, however, was the negative effect of this muddled policy on North–South relations, and on the complex series of joint issues which had been undertaken in project form following the December, 1980 summit, and were now seen to be more or less in disarray. It was as if the Government had gambled on Britain not being able to sustain a Falklands campaign, gambling also on an international repudiation of war which would leave Argentina in control of the islands. This was to misread totally the character of the British Prime Minister.

A second by-election took place, this time in Galway East in July. Though comfortably won by Fianna Fail in a constituency in which the party had enjoyed a 13 percentage points' advantage in the general election in February, the result showed a 5 per cent drop. Translated into national terms, it represented defeat and loss of power for Fianna Fail in the event of a general election; and given the inbuilt instability, a general election was always on the cards.

An entirely domestic crisis displaced Northern Ireland, the Falklands, and even the economy, in mid-August, when Malcolm Edward McArthur was arrested in the flat of the Attorney General, Patrick Connolly, and charged with the murder of Bridie Gargan, a nurse, in the Phoenix Park three weeks earlier. The arrest was made on Friday, August 13, in the middle of the row provoked between the Government and the unions over the decision to defer the 5 per cent final phase of the national agreement. The Attorney General had flown away on holiday, first to London and then on to New York, within 24 hours of the arrest. He had left Ireland knowing that for nine days McArthur had been living in his flat and now faced serious charges. Connolly had three conversations with the Taoiseach by telephone between McArthur's arrest and his own return to Dublin. In the subsequent statement of resignation he said: 'The Taoiseach contacted me in London and suggested I should return. I informed him I would prefer to discuss the matter from New York and that any arrangements which might be necessary could be made from there. When I arrived in New York the Taoiseach again contacted me and asked me to return to Dublin to discuss the situation that has arisen.' Because of the embarrassment caused to the Government, Connolly resigned. It later transpired that the Taoiseach and his Attorney General had spoken together on the Friday night, before Connolly left for London. Widespread doubts about the political judgment of the Taoiseach in handling the affair over the first weekend were expressed. In the absence on holiday of Sean Doherty, responsibility for the Department of Justice had been assumed by Haughey. If there were questions about his judgment there were also questions about the level of information passed to him by civil servants on a highly delicate issue. Referring to the crisis as 'grotesque, unprecedented bizarre, unbelievable', the Taoiseach attracted to himself the soubriquet GUBU from Conor Cruise O'Brien; and the mnemonic stuck. The unlucky GUBU principle entered the Irish language and gave expression to a degree of public disquiet not justified by the facts. Further expression of this gloomy for the Government, was given in the monthly opinion poll surveys by Irish Marketing Surveys, which showed that satisfaction with the way the Government was running the country, and with Charles Haughey as Taoiseach, was declining with relentless speed. A comparable increase in satisfaction with FitzGerald's performance was absent, but with the ever present possibility of the hung Dail collapsing, should the Workers' Party or one or other of the Independent deputies withdraw support, the prospects for Fianna Fail were anything but good.

It was in this demoralising atmosphere that Charles McCreevy tabled a motion of no confidence in Charles Haughey's leadership of Fianna Fail at the beginning of October. He consulted few colleagues, and there was certainly no campaign in advance of the meeting of the Fianna Fail Parliamentary Party, on October 6.

Haughey handled the confrontation badly. In a radio interview on Sunday, October 3, he made it clear that, in facing up to the challenge, he would be looking for the following, controversial commitments: an open roll-call on the motion of no confidence, each deputy in the party standing up, in alphabetical order, and declaring his or her position; secondly, that members of the Government should commit themselves beforehand to supporting him; thirdly, that the party's National Executive should declare support for his leadership; fourthly that the organisation throughout the country should exercise a mandate over individual deputies as to how they should vote

This pre-emptive approach turned out to be so provocative as to be counter-productive. Two members of the Government Martin O'Donoghue, Minister for Education, as well as the previous challenger for leadership, Desmond O'Malley, Minister for Trade, Commerce and Tourism, declined to give the undertaking demanded, and resigned. On the National Executive, Haughey also failed to win unanimous backing when a senior and powerful member of the party hierarchy, Senator

Eoin Ryan, not only refused to support Haughey as Taoiseach and leader, but then announced that Haughey was an electoral liability and should resign. The effect of the other two demands, within the parliamentary party and throughout its country-wide organisation, was to induce a mood of bitter division and rivalry between factions. Deputies resented the proposal that their attitude on the party leadership, traditionally a parliamentary party issue, should be laid open to constituency pressures. More fundamentally, many of them opposed strenuously the 'pocket-borough' voting system by roll-call and demanded a secret ballot, and debate on this took up much of the time during the party meeting which considered Charles McCreevy's no confidence motion.

Haughey's closest advisers underestimated the seriousness of the challenge and the intensity of feeling against him. The meeting, on Wednesday, October 6, went on from 11 a.m. until 10.50 p.m. There were many outspoken attacks, and many surprise critics who had not been previously identified as hostile to the party leader. Throughout the day close aides of the Taoiseach were obliged to revise upwards their estimate of the size of the challenge; and when the vote eventually came 22 deputies (including the two former cabinet ministers, and one minister of state) stood up to support the motion and 58 voted in favour of Haughey.[11]

It was a pyrrhic victory. The event was unprecedented in any parliamentary party, in power or in opposition. A substantial bloc of dissidents within Fianna Fail had been created and identified, and their reaction, after the meeting, was triumphant. By contrast, Haughey cancelled a press conference, made a brief statement, and then withdrew. It was the single most shattering experience he had undergone since becoming party leader and Taoiseach in December 1979. Far worse than his electoral defeat in the general election of June 1981, the open challenge to his leadership by a quarter of the party revealed a division within Fianna Fail which would represent a major handicap in any early general election.

An election was in fact imminent for reasons which were not apparent at that time. Ironically, Haughey himself had intended to call one to resolve his own minority dependence on a mixed group of Workers' Party and Independent deputies in the Dail; this was the explanation for his economic strategy in the summer. But, while the McCreevy challenge caused him to think again, it became increasingly apparent that he had set in train his own greater electoral vulnerability. He had already taken economic actions of a stringent kind which were alienating previous supporters, like the three elected representatives of the Workers' Party. He had already set in motion the economic strategy document which would serve as an election manifesto.

Not for the first time Haughey had placed himself in a position where he was assailed by the inevitability of Greek tragedy. In a Dail of 166 members, with all Fianna Fail seats filled, he commanded 81. In addition, he had relied throughout the previous five-month sitting, from March 9 to the end of July, on Neil Blaney. He had exacted a price for his support: more outspoken pressure for a united Ireland and British withdrawal, and it was this which had altered Haughey's policy, mainly towards Britain, during his second term. Some dependence could be placed on Tony Gregory, with whom Haughey had negotiated an extraordinary signed and witnessed 'inner city' development deal for Dublin in exchange for his support in forming a Government the previous March; but it was by no means a secure relationship. Even less secure was the support of the three Workers' Party deputies who had tumbled into the Chamber in March to elect him as Taoiseach, against the rules and procedures of the House, so eager had they been for Haughey's nomination then. It was different in October, following the changeover by Fianna Fail to harsh economic rectitude.

By any standards, it was not a time to take risks or to gamble on precarious support. Yet in a sense the dice had already been thrown. It was as if they were suspended in mid-air, spinning and turning in agonising slow motion, when news of Bill Loughnane's death, followed by details of Jim Gibbon's two heart attacks, arrived to foreshorten dramatically the life of the 23rd Dail. The carefully orchestrated momentum of economic rectitude, forward planning, unequivocal opposition to the Northern Ireland Assembly, coolness towards Britain, which would all have constituted a reasonable electoral platform if the party had remained united and more time had been available to force open the potential divisions between Labour and Fine Gael over the economy, was now abruptly challenged.

The package of stern measures announced at the end of July were given much more extensive form in a major economic policy document, 'The Way Forward', which charted Government strategy for the next five years along basically tough lines, and which was published in October. It was imprecise in details, but austere in its message. It was released in anticipation of the reassembly of the Dail, when it was to be debated. But with the Fianna Fail no confidence motion, the death of Loughnane, and the illness of Gibbons, a softer line was adopted towards the debate. It would be an open-ended 'noting' of the document's contents rather than an open confrontation leading to a vote. An attempt was made to filibuster; then to refer 'The Way Forward' to a select committee of the House. Both failed. What was seriously worrying Haughey was not just the loss of Loughnane and Gibbons; this could still have left him with a majority of one. It was the loss of support from the three members of the Workers' Party who could no longer see any future gains out of propping up so divided an administration. The open challenge of the 22 Fianna Fail dissidents had also given a new authority to the two main Opposition parties, in their challenges to the Government.

FitzGerald, who had regarded Haughey as unworthy and unsuitable to be Taoiseach, now saw an opportunity to challenge and defeat him. He believed that he himself would be the better leader, and that a dose of his brand of politics, however unconventional, was what the country needed. He was deeply sceptical of Haughey's convictions, either on the economy or on any other issues, including Northern Ireland.

This mood inspired the majority of Fine Gael politicians as well as the Labour Party when the Dail resumed on October 27. There was some division in Fine Gael; deputies who believed that the Government's self-inflicted wounds might well be left to fester favoured waiting for an election until the 1983 Budget the following January. But wiser counsel recognised that the Government's conversion to a policy of economic rectitude would lead, well before Christmas, to the ground being cut from under Fine Gael, and policy differences between them and the Labour Party would become pronounced.

There was another precipitating force. It concerned the Workers' Party; yet it derived from Fine Gael. The three Workers' Party deputies in the Dail had very ambivalent feelings towards Fine Gael and Labour. At the same time they were heartened by the fact that consistently, in the opinion polls since the summer, their support had grown. Conventional opinion was that they would gain further if they waited. But if they did this their odd voting behaviour in supporting the new Government rectitude would be seen as counter-productive. Then, in a private limited constituency poll conducted in Dublin West, it emerged that Tomas MacGiolla, the leader of the Workers' Party who did not have a Dail seat, had gained sufficient electoral support to win one. The information was 'leaked' and played a part in the bringing together of the Workers' Party with Fine Gael and Labour in the critical division on the evening of November 4.

When it became clear, on November 2, that the Government was not prepared to conclude the debate on 'The Way Forward' at the agreed time, with a division, Garret FitzGerald put down a motion of no confidence, and a two-day debate on the survival of the Government was fixed for Wednesday and Thursday, November 3 and 4. The Workers' Party announced on Tuesday night that they would oppose the Government. Tony Gregory said he would abstain.

On the evening of Thursday, November 4, the 23rd Dail came to an end. Conceived by accident, born in confusion, nourished amid epidemics which regularly threatened it with extinction, it was doomed from the start to a short life. The sickly creature wailed its way from one affliction to the next. Artificially supported and nursed by eccentric political midwives, it struggled from vote to vote, challenge to challenge, issue to issue, never very far from crisis in its eight-month life. In the end it succumbed to its primary ailment: instability. And though it died in uncertainty, and was buried without much grief, it left behind, as a form of election testament, the fundamental question for the electorate: how was the country to acquire a stable Government out of the undignified collapse of the 23rd Dail?

23

The 'Unwanted' Election

Throughout 1982 Garret FitzGerald felt that he had unfinished business to do in Irish politics and that he could provide the stability required. His first period as Taoiseach had lasted from June 1981 to the end of January 1982, and had then been rudely interrupted by his defeat over the Budget. This defeat had been put down to his unprofessionalism as a politician, in allowing that Budget to contain provision for taxation on children's footwear and clothing. And undoubtedly it represented a streak of political naivety which had manifested itself in other ways and was bound to remain as part of his political character. Yet this very fault was central to his enormous appeal which had achieved a vital, united political party, well organised nationally, and with clear policy objectives. It was also responsible for his high personal popularity. Looked at another way, the Irish electorate had, over the years, learned a measure of scepticism about that very professionalism in politics, the absence of which was regarded by political pundits as a defect in FitzGerald's make-up. He was admired by many for being the antithesis of the norm. And in this very arena of professionalism he stood in the sharpest contrast to his opponent, Charles Haughey, who was, above all else, a machine politician who relied on well-tried Pavlovian responses from those around him.

The general election divided fairly naturally into three phases of a week each. From the dissolution of the Dail, on the night of Thursday, November 4, until the following Wednesday, November 10, was taken up with constituency conventions, launching party programmes, and defining real issues as the door-to-door canvas got under way. By Wednesday the predictable and traditional confrontations in Irish politics had been firmly established: Fianna Fail under Charles Haughey were faced by a potential, if undeclared, partnership of Fine Gael and the Labour Party. The main issue was one of credibility between the two leaders.

Initially, Haughey, who was naturally irate at the timing, although he was himself moving towards a dissolution anyway, made the calling of the 'unwanted' general election one of the three main issues on which the campaign would be fought. The other two were his economic plan, 'The Way Forward', and abortion. Abortion is not legal in the Republic of Ireland and, under the 1861 Act, is punishable by penal servitude for life. But, before the general election of June 1981, a small pressure group calling itself the Pro-Life Amendment Campaign, had obtained from the leaders of Fianna Fail and Fine Gael undertakings that they would bring in an amendment to the Constitution protecting the unborn child. It was feared that a constitutional case might be brought before the courts by which abortion could be established in Ireland as a human right. It had subsequently proved extremely difficult to word an appropriate amendment, and nothing had been done until the week in which the November 1982 general election was called. A Bill containing the proposed amendment had been published and was to have been brought before the Dail. On the night of the dissolution, Haughey issued a statement containing the words: 'We will seek the support of the people also on the basis of our proposed amendment to the Constitution to protect the life of the unborn.'

At his first press conference of the campaign, Haughey said he could not trust the Fine Gael leader to go ahead with the proposed constitutional change. This charge was angrily refuted by FitzGerald, who had given a clear undertaking that he would put such a referendum before the people. But the question of which leader one could trust on this and other matters was to become central to the campaign. Certain themes emerged from questions by journalists: the leadership of Fianna Fail, Haughey's low rating in the opinion polls, his credibility rating when compared with the Fine Gael leader. This line of questioning provoked from Haughey the claim

22, 23 and 24   Jack Lynch (*left*) campaigns towards his greatest triumph: the 1977 general election victory. Charles Haughey contemplates similar challenges, but with different outcome. Frank Cluskey (*below*) leads Labour into the 1981 Coalition victory, in which he could not share because he lost his own seat.

ARTY LEADER

25, 26 and 27   Desmond O'Malley (*left*) whose challenge against Charles Haughey for the Fianna Fail leadership failed in February 1982. George Colley (*right*) was his close associate and opponent of Haughey. *Below*: the Fine Gael leader, Garret FitzGerald, confers with his former rival, Jack Lynch, during the 1981 general election.

28 and 29　The 'Unique Relationship': Margaret Thatcher and Charles Haughey meet for their second summit at Dublin Castle, December, 1980. They were accompanied (*from left*) by Lord Carrington, Sir Geoffrey Howe, Michael O'Kennedy and Brian Lenihan. *Below*: Dick Spring and Garret FitzGerald win the November 1982 election and go into partnership Government.

30 and 31   The Workers' Party deputies in the 1982 Dail were (*above, from left*)
Joe Sherlock, Proinsias de Rossa and Paddy Gallagher. The Party was excluded
from the New Ireland Forum. Four political leaders who attended the Forum are
here at the first meeting, with their chairman. *Below, from left*, John Hume, Garret
FitzGerald, Colm O hEocha (chairman), Charles Haughey and Dick Spring.

that he was the victim of 'a well-orchestrated campaign of vilification'. He declined to be specific but blamed Fine Gael and the media, singling out in particular the *Irish Independent.*

Garret FitzGerald held his first press conference of the campaign on Monday, November 8. The anticipated phenomenon of the Fine Gael leader confounding his questioners with facts and figures was absent. An injection of the very professionalism which had played so limited a part in FitzGerald's make-up in the past, seemed to have been administered. The handicap of not having access to the facts and figures on the economy was turned to an advantage. The idea of the general election being 'unnecessary' was brushed aside. The abortion referendum as a serious bone of contention was dismissed.

That the Fine Gael campaign was kept deliberately under control was largely due to the party's strategy committee, which consisted of a group of businessmen who had first come together in the aftermath of the Donegal by-election of November 1980. Sensing that an election might be imminent, they had begun intense preparation for it some months earlier. By the second weekend the opinion polls published in three national newspapers showed a swing towards a FitzGerald-led administration.

As far as the Labour Party was concerned the general election of November 1982 was potentially one of the most traumatic in its history. Dick Spring, a thirty-two-year-old deputy with only eighteen months' Dail experience, had taken over his father's North Kerry seat in the 1981 general election. A barrister, he had been capped several times at rugby for Ireland. He had been elected leader on Monday, November 1, 1982. On Thursday afternoon he made his first major speech as leader in the Dail, in the debate on the motion of confidence in the Fianna Fail Government. Two hours later the Dail had been dissolved, and Spring was leading the Labour Party into its third election in eighteen months. In each of those two previous elections support for the party had fallen. In first preference votes, and in Dail seats, the Labour Party had been in decline since the general election of 1969. Dick Spring was its fourth leader in just over five years. It was a highly inauspicious time for the party to be going to the country. Indeed, it was courageous of them to come out firmly against Haughey in the Dail confidence debate, joining not just with Fine Gael but with the

Workers' Party as well, whose members were confident they would benefit from Labour's disarray.

The catapulting of Spring into the leadership of the Labour Party had come about as a result of the attempts made by the former leader, Mr Michael O'Leary, to obtain coalition endorsement at the party's annual conference in Galway on October 23. This had been defeated. The Labour Party had decided on the electorally questionable mechanism of a post-election delegate conference which would consider whatever coalition proposals had been worked out between potential partners, and then decide. The compromise was judged by the centre of the party as essential for unity at a time of general doubt and disillusionment among members, engendered in part by the growing strength of the more radical Workers' Party.

It was regarded by Michael O'Leary, however, as a defeat; and correctly so. On Thursday, October 28, without consultation, and late at night, he resigned the leadership of the party and membership of it as well. The following Sunday, October 31, he had the first of three meetings with Garret FitzGerald. On Tuesday, November 2, a joint statement was issued by the two men saying that O'Leary wished to join Fine Gael, and that FitzGerald was recommending this to his party. By the time this statement was made a general election was already inevitable.

These were hardly the kind of auguries under which a political leader wishes to start. Spring and the Labour Party had been ill-served by the former leader's precipitate rush into Fine Gael, reflecting badly as it did on Labour's chances at the polls. But his more serious concern was with the Workers' Party. A key issue in their decision to withdraw support from the Government was the fact that the Workers' Party, in the opinion polls, was apparently increasing support, while Labour remained static. Gains made by the Workers' Party were largely at the expense of Fianna Fail, of course, and Government unpopularity was a key factor. But the apparent disarray of Labour, following its Galway conference, was an additional factor in the Workers' Party decision to bring about the early collapse of the Government. If anything, Spring's election as leader of the Labour Party seemed to be an added bonus.

Spring, however, took to leadership with a coolness and strength of purpose that was quite astonishing. On the threadbare material left to him by his predecessor he constructed and presented an election manifesto on the Tuesday afternoon following the dissolution. It showed substantial differences of emphasis from both of the larger political parties, and Spring himself was given a certain amount of rough treatment over these policy differences and the resultant unreality of looking towards a Labour Party for the stable government which could only derive from a willingness within the party to go into partnership. This was emphasised further by differences in Spring's attitude to the abortion referendum. He had reservations about the proposed wording, and issued a separate statement on the subject at the end of the electoral manifesto presentation. He also announced that the Labour Party would be instructing its supporters to continue their preference voting in favour of the candidates most closely reflecting Labour policies and objectives. This was a variation from previous leaders' instructions, in favour of transferring directly to Fine Gael, and the subtle difference in approach was noted, if anything, with approval.

Ostensibly, this did not seem to offer the best recipe for the only outcome in which Labour could expect to play a part in providing stable government, one in which between them, Labour and Fine Gael would hold a majority of seats in the Dail. Yet in reality Spring had already established with absolute clarity that he and his party were committed to the removal of Haughey and Fianna Fail from power, and that they preferred an administration led by FitzGerald for which, one way or the other, they would vote when the new Dail met. Their main subsidiary purpose was to ensure sufficient seats to hold the balance of power in a parliament to which there might just be returned a Fine Gael overall majority. Labour, after all, was being given poor prospects at this early stage in the election. Yet the Labour leader soon reversed this.

Deriving in part from the personal impact Spring had already made in his first week as party leader, and in part from the visible and palpable evidence of solid party unity presented at the first press conference on Tuesday, November 9, the party offered a reasonable option for moderate Left-wing support which was actually enhanced by O'Leary's departure. Having established the required electoral platform, and presented himself as the personable leader of a newly united Labour Party, Spring had to concentrate on the difficult task of ensuring the return to the Dail of at least the fourteen members which it had on dissolution. The party shared uneasily the working class vote with Fianna Fail, however, and the trade union movement was undoubtedly ambivalent in its political attitudes as between Labour and Fianna Fail. When it suited the unions, as in set-piece spectaculars like the annual conferences, they asserted a role within the Labour Party, though often it was an obstructive one. But when there was a question of delivering a vote, as in a general election, the trade unions became curiously silent. One of the oddities of the November 1982 election, in fact, was that the Irish Congress of Trade Unions made no contribution whatever during the campaign, and then, when it was all over, came out with a statement of demand for whichever incoming administration would take over, a statement which, coming before the Labour Party Conference, closely identified I.C.T.U. with Fianna Fail!

The Workers' Party, which had dropped its fuller and more emotive name — Sinn Fein the Workers' Party — in mid-1982, had grown steadily in strength politically and was optimistic about increasing its representation in the Dail. This belief was endorsed in opinion polls. To retain their position in the Dail, they needed to back Fianna Fail rather than a Fine Gael–Labour coalition, where their strength would be shared with other Independents. This meant voting for legislation which was directly against party policy, and from February to July 1982, their performance had been damaging to the party's image in the country. Their manifesto, presented to the press on the same day as that of the Labour Party, was socialist, with strong emphasis on jobs. The manifesto of the Democratic Socialist Party was similar, though with emphasis on tax reform. This party had one deputy in the Dail, Jim Kemmy, from Limerick. The other two out-going Independents were Neil Blaney, and Tony Gregory, whose contribution to politics had been vigorous and stimulating.

The coming of Dick Spring affected the whole electoral picture, including the Independents, with the exception of Neil Blaney, in whose Donegal North East constituency there was for Labour only negligible support. Elsewhere, it was as if the new Labour leader had pulled his party together to such an extent that it entered upon the election campaign with its own internal crises firmly behind it.

The unhappy progress of the first phase of the general election campaign, for Fianna Fail, resulted in greater emphasis on the playing of the 'Green Card' of anti-British republicanism. An indication that this would be an element in the election had been contained obliquely in the statement issued by Charles Haughey on the night of the dissolution. He had referred then to the preservation of Ireland's 'traditional policy of military neutrality' and of Ireland's 'position in world affairs as a sovereign independent nation', references which, if they had any electoral relevance, needed to be taken in the context of the frosty state of Anglo–Irish relations deriving from the opposition of the Government to the Northern Ireland Assembly, and the stance adopted at the time of the Falklands campaign.

On the evening of Wednesday, November 10, in Newcastle West, a small town on the road from Limerick to his home in Abbeyfeale, the Foreign Minister, Gerard Collins, reportedly made a speech accusing the Fine Gael leader of having allowed himself to be used as the instrument of British policy in Ireland. The approach was indirect: a British newspaper report was quoted as suggesting that FitzGerald had been used by the British Secretary of State for Northern Ireland, James Prior, to lobby the Duke of Norfolk on behalf of the Northern Ireland Assembly, and Collins then went on to challenge the Fine Gael leader to say how many other British politicians he had approached on James Prior's behalf. Later, he was to allege that R.U.C. men (who carry arms in Northern Ireland) would 'turn up in the company of the Gardai on the doorsteps in Kerry, Donegal, indeed anywhere in the country'. Though patently absurd, the allegations were widely reported under headings such as 'FitzGerald Backs Britain Row'. Officials of the Department of Foreign Affairs in Dublin denied responsibility for the speech, and it was traced to a Fianna Fail tactician at party headquarters. It coincided with at least one major article on Northern Ireland initiatives which FitzGerald would undertake should he be returned to power. But it was well ahead of the single speech on Northern Ireland which the Fine Gael leader had promised he would make later in the campaign.

The next day the Taoiseach, at a press conference in Leinster House, told Britain to keep out of Ireland's election. He suggested that British radio and television, as well as certain influential Fleet Street newspapers, were interfering in Irish affairs. He developed his Foreign Minister's accusations about FitzGerald being used by the British, but softening the sharpness of the previous day's attack and shifting the emphasis to the question of Ireland's independence, neutrality and foreign policy generally. Instead of the emphasis being on the confrontation between himself and FitzGerald on Northern Ireland policy, where the latter's consistency was better than his own, Haughey implied a British attack on himself as a result of the 'independent' stance Ireland had adopted over the Falklands crisis. By implication, Fianna Fail were being punished by the British media, motivated in turn by the British Establishment. Using more vigorous language at an election meeting that night in Trim, County Meath, one of the marginal seats, Haughey went so far as to say that the issue 'on which the election turned' was Ireland's sovereignty and independence:

> The Irish people asserted their sovereign right to independence in the past, and today they must reassert that right. I am once again saying, as I said at a press conference earlier today, that we want the British to stay out of the election. We arranged their departure from our country 60 years ago, and we don't want them coming back in 1982. We want a resounding victory in this election as an indication of your support for the freedom and independence of Ireland as a whole.

That weekend saw the publication of various opinion polls, the relentless message being that Northern Ireland and foreign policy generally were of such minor importance as hardly to merit a single percentage point one way or the other. For the Green Card to win any tricks at all, something more dramatic was required.

It came from James Prior, at a press conference in Washington on Tuesday, November 16, in which he referred to a forthcoming speech, which the Fine Gael leader was actually scheduled to make the following Thursday. An article in *The Times* of Tuesday by George Brock had spelt out in some detail what Garret FitzGerald would be likely to say. Based in part on the Richard Dimbleby Lecture which the Fine Gael leader had delivered on B.B.C. television on May 20, under the title 'Irish Identities', Brock had identified two possible proposals which might be forthcoming; those for an all-Ireland court and an all-Ireland police force. Prior had suggested that these would be proposed by FitzGerald, and might be considered, in spite of his having expressed opposition to them earlier. (He had been present in the studio audience for the lecture in May.)

The Irish newspapers the following day carried only confused accounts. The *Irish Press* referred to the Prior press conference, and also carried a story about the all-Ireland court and police force proposals taken from *The Times* article the previous day. The *Irish Times* carried the story on an inside page and emphasised Prior's praise for the work of the F.B.I. against the I.R.A. Well down in the story was a reported reference to the all-Ireland court and a tripartite council, though nothing about policing. Only the *Irish Independent*, in a very brief story, at the top of an inside page, and more in its heading than in the body of the text, hit at the heart of the potential controversy: 'Prior: FitzGerald wants Garda–R.U.C. merger.'

The reaction of the Fianna Fail leader was extreme. He issued a four-paragraph statement accusing FitzGerald of 'collusion' with the British Government and of Fine Gael collaboration which amounted to 'the most serious threat to the Republic of Ireland's independence since the Second World War'. Haughey repeated the accusations, and elaborated on them during a radio interview which took place at the same time as FitzGerald was giving a press conference at which he was pointing out the proposals had been common knowledge for months and the accusation of collusion 'nonsense'.

On radio Haughey said that the British interference and Fine Gael's position were 'completely alarming' for anyone concerned about Ireland's independence. 'The British Government and Mr Prior are actively intervening in our internal affairs and trying to influence this election.' When it was suggested to him that he was playing the Green Card, he said: 'If it involves asserting Ireland's right to independence, to run our own affairs without interference from the British, if that is playing the Green Card, yes, I am playing it.' And he repeated his call: 'Britain, stay out of our election.'

The episode undoubtedly had an immediate and adverse impact on the Fine Gael campaign. It was defused, however, by FitzGerald calmly dismissing the claims, by the text of his Northern Ireland speech, delivered on the evening of Thursday, November 18, and by the patent over-reaction of Haughey.

The 'British Connection' was to remain part of the election campaign, however. On the Thursday morning, at a press briefing, Haughey was questioned at one point by a B.B.C. journalist, and a staff writer from the *Financial Times*. 'I can only take one foreigner at a time', he said, and proceeded to deal critically with the *Financial Times*, treating it as antipathetic to his Government's economic programme without realising the journalist he was speaking to came from the paper. Two days later, at his Saturday press briefing before the final weekend of the campaign, Haughey attacked individual journalists for collaborating with Fine Gael, and issued a press statement allegedly showing that the Duke of Norfolk was 'a trained British spy'. Between Thursday and Saturday Haughey had been campaigning in the two marginal constituencies of North and South Kerry, emphasising strongly all the time the British Connection with Fine Gael, and he reported on the Saturday the success of his own campaign experiences. It was still being seen as such by Fine Gael party workers. But on the Friday night the Fine Gael leader had done two things to challenge, head-on, this lurch into verbal republicanism. Firstly, in a fine show of temper he had rejected the attacks by Haughey as deliberate lies, nailing one by one the allegations in the course of a widely reported radio interview. Secondly, he had deliberately gone off to a function, also widely reported, held by the British–Irish Association in Dublin for the purpose of awarding the Ewart-Biggs Memorial Prize to the staff of a Northern Ireland publication called *Fortnight*. It was a provocative public endorsement by FitzGerald of where he stood, in terms of British–Irish relations. Though also invited to the function, Charles Haughey was otherwise engaged.

These smears were followed by the appearance of 'Kitchener'-type leaflets, suggesting that Margaret Thatcher 'needed' FitzGerald, and on that evening by an unusual, if not unprecedented, intervention in the election campaign by the Attorney General, John Murray, who issued a long public statement about the FitzGerald proposals for North–South security co-operation. For perhaps the first time in any general election, however, the traditional verbal republicanism of Fianna Fail, which sought an undefined, eventual unity of Ireland, without spelling out the intermediate actions designed to achieve that goal, was being challenged by a man whose credentials offered the best alternative in terms of policy and commitment. Nevertheless, there was talk of Garret FitzGerald 'snatching defeat out of the jaws of victory', and a strongly held belief that the proposed all-Ireland police force would not only cost votes but might, in Border constituencies, cost vital seats as well. The impact was reflected in the weekend opinion poll findings, which had been taken in mid-week. But, though more favourable to Fianna Fail than the previous polls, they still indicated that Garret FitzGerald would lead the incoming administration.

One of the findings of at least some of the opinion polls held during the general election was of a marked discrepancy in swing between different regions. While it was clear that Fianna Fail was losing support in Dublin, it was equally clear that the party was gaining in Connaught and Ulster. From Fianna Fail's point of view there were certain constituencies requiring a minute swing to cause them to go their way, and these had been carefully targeted during the campaign, particularly with 'Green Card' statements. Two of them were constituencies with seats held by the Workers' Party, Cork East and Waterford, and a third was Kerry South, thought to be responsive to the Green Card. After that, though in theory the party needed a much less significant swing in its favour to gain an overall majority, in practice the likelihood of the relevant seats going their way was ruled out by constituency or personality problems.

In one other important area, monitored by the strategy committee, but dreamed up by two advertising men, Fine Gael ran a remarkably successful campaign: this was in advertising, particularly on television. The party scored most sharply with a film which highlighted the divisions within Fianna Fail. To the background music of Frank Sinatra singing 'Love and Marriage' (i.e. 'You can't have one without the other') film of the dissident deputies was juxtaposed with film of deputies loyal to Haughey. It was an eloquent and economical lesson in credibility and stability, the two issues Fine Gael had made central to their campaign. It stayed the right side of giving more than political offence: but only just.

Towards the end of the campaign, it became clear that Fine Gael, and more particularly its strategy committee, had consistently run a more professional campaign at every level. Guarded over policy, but confident and positive in selling themselves, with a clear presentation of a popular leader leading a united team, their strategy had been aimed at the inherent differences and contrasts within Fianna Fáil. It paid off.

In sharp contrast, the general uncertainty of the Government's handling of the election campaign had been demonstrated by the erratic turnout of ministers for press conferences and television debates. While individual ministers did well in media debates, their collective assembly for press conferences was dominated too much by the Taoiseach. He then subsequently took conferences on his own, with the party's general secretary in attendance, and it was only on the last Thursday, two days after the James Prior 'intervention', that the whole Cabinet assembled for what was to be a press conference of very mixed benefit.

At his first press conference, Haughey had given an undertaking that he would publish the Book of Estimates before the end of the campaign so that people would have an idea of where public spending cuts would be made. The 'Green Card' row was in full spate but the publication of the Book of Estimates went ahead on Thursday, November 18. Though it was the middle of a general election, virtually all the permanent secretaries of Government departments were present, many of them privately critical, not only of their own presence, but also of the political use of an occasion normally carried out in the absence of politicians.[1] The objective, as far as the general election was concerned, was to give an honest outline of the Government's intentions on cuts. This kind of openness had been an inescapable part of the general election in February 1982. But that was a unique election, deriving from defeat in an actual Budget debate, and the openness had been beneficial to Haughey's opponent, the then Taoiseach, Garret FitzGerald. It was not unreasonable, with the tables turned, for Haughey, with things not going well, to try the same approach with the Book of Estimates.

It did not work. Many of the cuts provoked sectoral outcry. Many specific issues, such as increased bus and train fares, and the ending of free school transport, enraged people. And the two Opposition parties, apart from adding their voices of criticism, refused to co-operate further by offering their alternative proposals, and merely undertook to accept the broad budgetary implications. All Haughey was left with was an appeal to be seen as honest. In gaining whatever approbation there was on this score he had lost popularity; in addition he had spiked his own guns by interrupting the Green Card stoking of anti-British feelings which had become a significant, if geographically mixed, asset.

All that really remained, that last weekend, was the television debate on the Monday night between the two leaders. This was the climax to the campaign. Within one hour of the dissolution of the Dail, on November 4, Charles Haughey had issued a statement in which he challenged Garret FitzGerald 'to debate with me immediately on television the reasons why he has forced this General Election upon the country and the issues on which the people must decide when they go to the polls.' In a reply on the same night, FitzGerald declined immediately to take up the challenge, saying that it was a matter which would be sorted out during the course of the campaign, and its sorting out became itself an issue, provoking much comment and speculation.

FitzGerald was the darling of the media. Always open with journalists, always available to them, he spoke freely — many would say far too freely — on every subject with extraordinary breadth of vision and depth of knowledge. Quite often he had shown himself to be at his best in a totally unprepared, un-rehearsed situation. This was a major worry to his advisers. In the embattled arena of a television studio, where his main electoral opponent was fighting for his political life, a quite different set of rules applied, rules which were not sympathetic to the open willingness with which the Fine Gael leader had learnt to deal with the media.

Haughey was a complete contrast to FitzGerald. His association with journalists was tense at all times, and had steadily worsened in the two-year period of his leadership of Fianna Fail, during eighteen months of which he had been Taoiseach. He liked best of all photographers, who were silent; and he had an inexhaustible appetite for photo-calls which manifested itself in innumerable pictures in the newspapers. He was less happy answering questions. He gave almost no interviews. And he liked least of all the commentators who monitored his political performance and who had increasingly exposed the limited quality of his leadership of the country. Nevertheless, he was an enormously resourceful politician and a great survivor. He was perfectly capable of handling a hostile press with skill and with wit; the worse things became, the better he seemed able to perform.

Private preparation for the encounter was intense on both sides. Teams of advisers, 'with busy hammers closing rivets up', completed their advice on the issues and carried out final rehearsals. Garret FitzGerald arrived at the studios thirty-five minutes later than proposed, accompanied by a team of advisers who stuck close to him throughout all subsequent arrangements. He refused to shake Mr Haughey's hand in front of the cameras, and after the most perfunctory of encounters with senior officials of the broadcasting station, went in to make-up. From then on he was isolated from all but his own advisers. When called into the studio for the opening shots in the programme, he was accompanied by them. And as soon as the Dick Spring interview began they removed him again to avoid the twenty minutes sitting facing his opponent. They returned to their own hospitality room from which R.T.E. personnel were summarily dismissed. Only minutes before the end of the interview with Spring did the group bring FitzGerald back to the studio, and leave him ready and waiting for the encounter. None of this had been anticipated, either by Haughey or his advisers, and he was left bewildered by the succession of unscheduled departures from the proposed sequence of events. This was precisely what had been intended by FitzGerald's team, members of which had thought out in great detail every aspect, including the matching of the colour of his suit to the studio background, the washing but not the cutting of his hair, and the adjusting of his glasses so that they would not slip down his nose. He had been schooled not to gesture with his hands, to speak slowly, not to consult notes, not to touch his glasses or his face, and above all not to smile.

The opening of the debate was critical. The first issue, which took up half the programme was the economy. The position adopted by the Taoiseach was that he had brought forward a comprehensive economic plan for the country, 'The Way Forward'. Early on he referred to the 'endorsement' of the plan by the E.E.C. Commission, by the Central Bank and by the Economic and Social Research Institute. He was politely but firmly corrected by FitzGerald, who coldly told him that no such endorsements had been given. An individual Brussels Commissioner, François-Xavier Ortoli, had sent a personal letter endorsing it; but the Bank as such and the Council of the E.S.R.I. had in no sense given endorsement, and as for the Commission, FitzGerald was able to quote his own encounter with Gaston Thorn, a personal friend, as evidence supporting the dismissal he was making of any claim by Haughey that the E.E.C. were behind 'The Way Forward'. The document was never discussed by the Commission. It was a palpable hit, one of those occasions in television encounters, particularly hostile ones, where a clear advantage is gained and where the impact is equally clearly apparent.

The attack by the Fine Gael leader shifted to Fianna Fail economic inconsistencies during their period in power from 1977. This line of argument provoked a second, and major tactical error from Haughey when he named and blamed the former Fianna Fail architects of economic strategy, men who were now his opponents in the party, George Colley and Martin O'Donoghue. It was a form of disloyalty which lodged in the mind, to be resurrected later in the programme when the disunity of Fianna Fail was raised, immediately after the economy had been set aside.

On the dissidents within Fianna Fail Haughey's defence was that they *now* supported the leader, and had voted solidly in the Dail debate of confidence. For the first and only time in the hour's exchanges FitzGerald allowed himself a smile before dealing with this 'tradition of voting together' and contrasting it with the 'roll-call' vote in the party rooms, and the inconsistency of the 22 dissidents subsequently supporting a man in whom they had demonstrated a clear lack of confidence. It was no basis either for credibility or for stability.

Northern Ireland did not enter the television debate until the second half of the programme and then, contrary to expectation, the various bitter allegations about collusion and collaboration were not raised. Far more devastating, however, was the single dramatic gesture by FitzGerald, when he handed his Northern Ireland speech across to Haughey and asked him to find in it any reference at all to 'a British–Irish force', which Haughey claimed was in it. Haughey took the script, but laid it aside, declining to pursue the issue of what had actually been said on the previous Thursday evening.

From a difficult position FitzGerald had won on Northern Ireland, and won convincingly on the economy as well. He had raised serious questions about the internal stability of the Fianna Fail Party, and more generally about its credibility. Before the debate finally concluded he was already shuffling together the cue-cards which he had not needed to use, and was allowing the ghost of a second smile to cross his features. As one commentator wrote the next day, FitzGerald had had most of the best lines, while Haughey, 'defensive, leaning forward, aware it was a battle for his survival,' by the end 'was almost out of his chair, like a jockey standing in his stirrup at the end of a race'.

Only the *Irish Independent*, of the three Dublin morning papers, gave FitzGerald a convincing win. The *Irish Times* and the *Irish Press* said it was a draw. As one Fianna Fail deputy said, 'staunch party supporters would say their man won, on either side, but no one could say that Dr FitzGerald lost.' And he went on to explain that, if the Fianna Fail newspaper, the *Irish Press*, said it was a draw, that meant the other side won.

The opinion polls had revealed intense interest in the debate combined with an overwhelming number of people saying that it would *not* alter their voting intentions, on which they had already decided. It was viewed by huge numbers. Where it did have an impact was on party morale during the final day of the election, and this was reflected in the press conferences given by the two leaders. Haughey remained embattled to the end, still dismissing the idea of his leadership being challenged, should he lose, still asserting that he would form the new administration. But there was an absence of confidence, and he was accompanied only by his director of elections. FitzGerald, with a cross-section of his Front Bench team, was in confident mood, predicting an overall but shared majority for Fine Gael and Labour and the subsequent coalition agreement which would give the required stability.

The final press conferences were given in the same ballroom of the Burlington Hotel, one at three o'clock and one at five. The same bar facilities were twice trundled in and then out again. The large crop of journalists who had covered the campaign compared notes and came to the same conclusion: there would be a change of government.

The early turnout, on Wednesday, November 24, was good. Rain swept different parts of the country during the morning, and adversely affected the vote, though it picked up in the evening. At an average of 72·82 per cent it was down on the 74 per cent figure of February 1982, and the 76 per cent figure the previous June.

On Friday, November 26, with all counts completed, Fianna Fail had 75 seats, Fine Gael 70, Labour 16, the Workers' Party 2, and there were three Independents. A Fine Gael–Labour coalition, with a clear majority, would form the next government.[2]

24

'Programme for Government'

The only formal obstacle to a coalition between Fine Gael and the Labour Party was the commitment made by Labour at its annual conference in Galway a month before the election that it would stick with its existing arrangements for a special delegate conference following an election where it held the balance of power. The conference would then decide on whether to support a minority government or to go into power as part of a joint arrangement. Since Fianna Fail had ruled out partnership, this latter course was only an option with Fine Gael.

The cynical saw the process of inter-party negotiations as a piece of necessary 'theatre' to fulfil the requirements of the Labour commitment to consult the party before entering on any arrangement for the new Dail. That it had to be coalition if it were to last a full term, was widely recognised. Nevertheless, there were several reasons why the process had to be treated seriously. Dick Spring himself was the first of these. His political future needed to be measured well beyond the 24th Dail. He could not sustain credibility while at the same time committing himself to an unreal or superficial arrangement. In this he was supported by his three closest associates in the parliamentary party, Liam Kavanagh, Frank Cluskey and Barry Desmond. All of them serious and committed politicians, with many years' experience, part of it ministerial, their united support for the party leader, fifteen or more years their junior, had been a bold piece of strategy which had paid off handsomely, and now offered the prospect of power for between four and five years. The Labour Party itself badly needed time in power to reorganise itself. It could do this only under a leadership which, in a period of recession, offered a measure of socialism. Frail as the prospects for such genuine socialism had been in the Republic of Ireland in the past, the leader of Fine Gael did realistically offer the best prospects for the kind of compromise which would satisfy the mixed strands of political belief which constituted the moderate socialism of the Labour Party.

As soon as it was clear that the combined overall majority was there, on the night of Friday, November 26, plans were made for negotiations between Garret FitzGerald and Dick Spring. They had exactly two weeks. By the night of Saturday, December 11, a joint agreed document would have to be ready for presentation to the Labour Party's special delegate conference in Limerick the following day, and to a meeting of the Fine Gael parliamentary party in the Burlington Hotel on the Sunday afternoon. The Dail was to meet on the Tuesday, December 14. The main areas for discussion involved the pace at which the current budget deficit would be eliminated, the measures to be adopted to create employment, and the taxation proposals aimed at greater equity including some measure of tax on property or wealth.

The first meeting between the two leaders was held in a secret Dublin venue on Wednesday, December 1. These preliminary talks were followed by a further meeting on Friday, December 3. Position papers were exchanged, and the preparation of more detailed documents went ahead over the weekend, at which stage 'confidence' about a coalition deal was being expressed. On Monday, December 6, Garret FitzGerald cancelled a trip to Paris for the joint conference of Fine Gael's European partners, and stayed in Dublin instead to continue the talks.

Curiously, it was just at this time, Tuesday, December 7, that the Irish Congress of Trade Unions decided to spell out, in a document containing ten demands, its requirements from the incoming government. It had remained silent and passive during the general election, providing no public endorsement of the Labour Party's electoral programme. Now this strangely-timed intervention, before the special delegate conference, from a body representative of unions which, for the most part, were committed *against* the partnership which was being discussed by Spring and FitzGerald, was received coolly. Even more strange was the degree of similarity in many of the vaguely-worded 'demands' to the Fianna Fail Party's election manifesto, 'The Way Forward'.

Undeterred, the parties completed their deal. 'The Fine Gael/Labour Programme for Government', to be put before the conference in Limerick, was the outcome of intense and lengthy exchanges between the two potential coalition partners. It was the third such document in the 1968–82 period. While it covers all issues including foreign policy and Northern Ireland, the main deal between the two parties hinged on tax concessions, including a residential property tax and increased capital taxation, the setting up of a National Development Corporation as a major job creation agency, and a softening of the Fine Gael election policy on the pace of eliminating the current budget deficit.

The emphasis was on unemployment, particularly of the 50,000 of the 170,000 without jobs who were under 25 years old. As an agency to cope with this, the National Development Corporation, for which an initial equity capital of £200 million had to be found, with further substantial borrowing rights, to a ceiling of £500m, was essentially a compromise between Fine Gael's prior insistence in its own economic policies that the only real jobs were competitive, free enterprise ones, and the Labour Party's long-established insistence on greater State participation in employment creation. It was a compromise on both sides. The Labour Party were presiding over 'profitable commercial projects geared to import substitution and to export markets', objectives which could well leave the Corporation frozen at birth. And Fine Gael could reassure themselves with the frequent use in the document, both in the context of the Corporation and elsewhere, of the word 'competition' and its derivative, 'competitive'. In conference terms, of course, it answered many problems.

The taxation sections were preceded by a preamble headed 'Equity'. Geared to a recent major report on taxation, the document proposed a residential property tax on houses worth more than £65,000 owned by those with incomes in excess of £20,000. Though likely to yield only £20 million, the principle established by this tax, and its potential for extension and adaptation, was important. Rates in Ireland on private property had been abolished by Jack Lynch as part of his fulfilment of election commitments made in 1977. It was a retrograde step, though not altogether unfair, since the basis was at least a century old, and fell equally hard on the wage earners and the retired or widowed. The new proposal was a less severe, more equitable version of rates.

Other tax provisions included service charges for development land, a tax on derelict sites, and the gradual introduction of a number of income tax reforms. Housing, health and education provisions were prominent; so, too, were social and institutional reforms. A clear and long-standing solidarity between Fine Gael and the Labour Party on Northern Ireland was reiterated. This included the question of constitutional reform, economic and social co-operation between North and South, improved Anglo–Irish relations, and reconciliation within Northern Ireland preferably gaining expression through 'devolved political institutions'.

The Labour Party met to confer in Limerick at noon on Sunday, December 12. The Party chairman, Michael D. Higgins, spoke for fifteen minutes. He was opposed to coalition. The Party leader, Dick Spring, also spoke for fifteen minutes in favour of coalition with Fine Gael, and presented the joint document as the programme in office. Of the parliamentary party only one man, Mervyn Taylor, spoke against. Each speaker had five minutes, with the leader winding up at around 5 p.m. The decision to enter into coalition by 846 votes to 522, a majority of 324, was relayed to Dublin, where a meeting of the Fine Gael Party had also endorsed the programme, with one dissenting voice, that of John Kelly, a former Minister and Attorney General.

An obviously relieved Fine Gael leader gave a press conference shortly after 7 p.m. and predicted a full term of five years for the new administration. Further talks on the formation of the Government were held the following day and on Tuesday the new Dail met at 3 p.m. The comparatively tedious formalities of entering the names of members, electing a chairman, and then nominating a Taoiseach, were completed. The Dail adjourned to allow Garret FitzGerald to receive his seal of office from President Hillery, and at 6.15 p.m. he led into the Dail Chamber his new Government and announced their portfolios.[1] The country's fifth coalition since the Second World War had come to power.

Postscript

Patrick McLaughlin, the Police Commissioner, and Joseph Ainsworth, the Deputy Commissioner, offered their resignations to the Government on Thursday, January 20, 1983, to take effect on February 1. The resignations, following the discovery of the tapping of the telephones of two journalists, were blamed by Fianna Fail on the 'irresponsibility' of the Coalition Government. The former Ministers, Ray McSharry and Sean Doherty, resigned from the party's Front Bench. Doherty later resigned the party whip. Pressure increased on Charles Haughey to resign as leader. During the last week in January he was visited by a number of deputies urging him, in the interests of the party, to resign. He listened in silence to their appeals. The same message came from the National Executive, with one member, Joe Farrell, telling him he was an embarrassment.

In the Senate elections, which took place at the beginning of February, several close Haughey aides were defeated, including a former junior minister, Lorcan Allen, who had lost his Dail seat. On Wednesday, February 2, 40 deputies signed a petition for a party meeting on Haughey's leadership. A party meeting held on that day broke up in confusion after Jim Tunney, the party chairman, had adjourned it, ignoring attempts to raise issues, and, literally, running from the room. He adjourned because of the death of a Donegal deputy, Clement Coughlan. On Monday, February 7, the Fianna Fail Party voted, by 40 to 33 in favour of Charles Haughey's continued leadership.

On Wednesday, Alan Dukes introduced an extremely tough Budget, raising value added tax, imposing a 1 per cent levy on incomes, abolishing or reducing reliefs, introducing a new property tax, bringing all farmers into the income tax net, and reducing mortgage relief. Petrol, oil, road tax, telephone charges, television licences, all went up. The curious 'honeymoon' period for the new Government, augmented and made more agreeable by the intense public wranglings within the Fianna Fail Party over its leadership, had come to an abrupt end. In addition, a further controversy arose over the proposed constitutional amendment on the protection of 'the unborn'.

During the 1981 general election campaign, the two main leaders, Charles Haughey and Garret FitzGerald, had given undertakings to a small, extreme Catholic pressure group calling itself the Pro-Life Amendment Campaign, that they would introduce a constitutional referendum allowing for an amendment protecting 'the unborn'. The Labour Party, both then and later, resisted the appeals to it, and, although ultimately divided in its views, held out against making any pre-election commitments, either in 1981, or before the two elections of 1982.

It was not possible to work out and bring before the people a wording, either during the second half of 1981, or during 1982. But on the day of the collapse of the Dail, November 4, 1982, the Haughey Government brought in a wording.[1] On February 15, the Attorney General, Peter Sutherland, announced that the published wording was imprecise and potentially dangerous.

On Wednesday, March 23, an alternative wording was announced by Fine Gael. Five members of the party immediately said that they found the alternative wording unacceptable. On March 29 the Irish Catholic bishops came out against the new wording, favouring the first version which had been put forward by Fianna Fail. A week later the Protestant, Church of Ireland Primate, Dr Armstrong, came out strongly against the wording favoured by the Catholic bishops, saying that it favoured the teaching of one church, and was not acceptable to Protestants.

It was revealed on April 21 that a third wording had been proposed by the Government, more firmly 'pro-life' than the one announced, but that this had been dropped 'because of Catholic hierarchy objections'.

217

In the Dail on Wednesday, April 27, the alternative, published Government wording was defeated by 87 votes to 65, and the first wording, which Fianna Fail had solidly supported in the Dail, was passed by 87 votes to 13. The Bill, which provided for a referendum in which the new wording for the Constitution would be put to the people, was passed by 85 votes to 11. The Taoiseach advised people to vote No because of the dangers inherent in the wording. After a three-week campaign of great bitterness and division, based on legal, medical, moral, and constitutional differences of opinion, as well as widespread confusion and doubt, the wording was approved by a two-to-one majority. There was, however, wide divergence between urban and rural areas, and several Dublin constituencies had majorities against the amendment.

It involved differences between Church and State redolent of the 1950s. It divided political parties, communities, professional groups, even families. It contrasted oddly with a parallel event: on Friday, March 11, the three main political parties in the Republic, together with the S.D.L.P., agreed to take part in a Forum to discuss how peace and stability could be established in 'a new Ireland'. The Forum met for the first time on Monday, May 31, and continued its deliberations through the rest of 1983. As a starting point for some future examination of what kind of country the Irish people want for themselves, the awkward conjunction of these two debates will offer some historian at the close of the twentieth century food for thought.

Notes

The Impact of Northern Ireland

Until this reform, Northern Ireland still retained a householder qualification for local government elections.

An auxiliary police force, roughly 8,000 in number in 1968, and made up of part-time volunteers. They were trained, uniformed and armed, keeping their weapons at home. Overwhelmingly Protestant, they were a traditional local militia, knowledgeable about republicans, and generally a divisive force.

More correctly, the Civil Authorities Act (Special Powers), it gave wide powers of arrest, search and detention without trial to the police, and had been in force since 1922, maintained as a response to the periodic outbreaks of terrorism.

The Irish Labour Party, the oldest of the three parties in the Dail during the late 1960s, was led by Brendan Corish; it was an untypical socialist party, part republican, part deeply conservative.

The second largest party in the Dail, led by Liam Cosgrave.

The I.R.A. was not responsible. It had not, at this stage, divided into the 'Official' and 'Provisional' wings, with comparable political organisations. It had become active within the Civil Rights Movement. The attack was carried out by loyalist paramilitaries.

R.T.E. television interview, January 18, 1974.

3 Reaction in the Republic

1 At no time, either before the arms crisis of 1970 or later, did Blaney rely on, or was relied on by, key Northern Ireland politicians such as John Hume, Paddy Devlin or Gerry Fitt, for North-South liaison. And he is remembered by some colleagues in government presenting the civil rights activists as 'partitionists'.

2 Closest to Lynch, in the administration he inherited from Sean Lemass, were George Colley (Industry and Commerce), Paddy Hillery (Labour), and Erskine Childers (Posts, Telegraphs, Transport, Power). He would, in addition, have had the unquestioning loyalty of Padraig Faulkner (Lands and Gaeltacht), Joe Brennan (Social Welfare), Michael Hilliard (Defence), and Frank Aiken (External Affairs); Aiken, in addition, was Tanaiste (Deputy Prime Minister). The remaining ministers, Brian Lenihan (Education), Sean Flanagan (Health) and Micheal O Morain (Justice) were somewhere between the two factions. The latter two subsequently moved closer to the Haughey-Blaney-Boland faction, though for different reasons; Flanagan was personally close to Haughey at this time, O Morain was to some extent intimidated by their strong republican views. One significant change was occasioned by the death of Donogh O'Malley, on March 3, 1968. His job at Education was taken by Brian Lenihan, who moved there from Justice, making way for O Morain, and letting Faulkner into the Government for the first time.

3 Among other things, Fine Gael and Labour had seriously considered the possibility of merging the two parties. Between October 1967 and January 1968 various meetings were held between leading politicians in both parties, including a January meeting between Liam Cosgrave and Brendan Corish. But the idea was dropped, mainly because of Labour Party reservations.

4 The statement contained a key principle, as far as Haughey was concerned: 'I don't mind being praised or blamed for my actions in public office. I object to my private affairs being used in this way.' (*Irish Times*, June 4, 1969.)

5 Two former ministers, Frank Aiken and Michael Hilliard, retired to the backbenches. Two new men were appointed, P. J. Lalor (Posts and Telegraphs), Jim Gibbons (Defence). Hillery moved to Foreign Affairs and was succeeded at Labour by Brennan.

Lenihan went to Transport and Power, and Faulkner to Education. Erskine Childers became Tanaiste. Others retained their pre-election portfolios. On July 9 Lynch appointed seven parliamentary secretaries: Desmond O'Malley (Taoiseach's Department), Jeremiah Cronin (Agriculture), Gerard Collins (Commerce, Industry, Gaeltacht), Robert Molloy (Education), John Geoghegan (Social Welfare), Noel Lemass (Finance) and Paudge Brennan (Local Government).

'The Historic Unity of Our Country'

Taca was a semi-secret fund-raising body of Irish businessmen (Kevin Boland, *Up Dev!*, Dublin, 1977, p. 8).
The relevant Articles are as follows: 'Article 2: The national territory consists of the whole island of Ireland, its islands and the territorial seas. Article 3: Pending the re-integration of the national territory, and without prejudice to the right of the Parliament and Government established by this Constitution to exercise jurisdiction over the whole of that territory, the laws enacted by that Parliament shall have the like area and extent of application as the laws of Saorstat Eireann and the like extra-territorial effect.'
Boland, op. cit., p. 13.
Ibid., p. 14.

The Blaney Factor

Irish Times, August 20, 1969.
The Hunt Committee, which reported in 1969, recommended various changes in Northern Ireland policing, and a new structure was introduced in 1970 which, among other things, led to the replacement of the B Specials with the R.U.C. Reserve, and the setting up of the Ulster Defence Regiment. It became operational on April 1, 1970.
The Scarman Tribunal was set up in 1969, following the Derry and Belfast riots. Its report, *Violence and Civil Disturbance in Northern Ireland in 1969*, published in 1972, found that neither the I.R.A. nor any Protestant organisations were responsible.
The Cameron Commission, whose inquiries went back to the Derry riots of October 1968, was the most wide-ranging of the inquiries set up by the British Government, and investigated a range of injustices and grievances covering housing, local govern-

ment powers, police, B Special and Special Powers Act partisa
ship. The report, published in 1969, was instrumental in t
urgent reforms introduced by O'Neill.

5 Kevin Boland, *Up Dev!*, Dublin, 1977, p. 16.

6 'We Asked for Guns'

1 Evidence to the Arms Trial.
2 James Kelly, *Orders for the Captain*, Dublin, 1971, p. 8.
3 Arms Trial evidence.
4 John Kelly: unsworn statement in court in Dublin, Wednesda
   October 14, 1970.
5 Vincent Browne, 'The Arms Crisis', *Magill* magazine, Ma
   1980.
6 James Kelly, op. cit.
7 Neither appropriate, nor legally necessary.
8 The transformation of the I.R.A. from being an organisation wit
   a Marxist-based doctrine, related to some vague and distar
   overall revolution of the people, to an urban, or communit
   based movement, cellular in its structure, was in the process
   taking place. It shifted non-democratic republicanism towards
   more insular, more introverted, more Right-wing set of princ
   ples. Nevertheless, it was more directly a response to the neec
   and dangers which emerged in the early confrontations of 1968
   9. The basically sectarian struggle of Catholics against the la
   and order forces, including the B Specials, which were e
   clusively Protestant, and then their successors, which were a
   most exclusively so, was one which gave birth to the ne
   community protection association called Provisional I.R.A.

7 Arms and the Men

1 *Magill* magazine, May, June, July, 1980.
2 *Magill* magazine, May 1980, p. 38.

8 The Arms Crisis

1 Included is Micheal O Morain, Minister for Justice, who ha
   resigned the previous week on health grounds. His health prok
   lems had kept him absent from the Department of Justice a
   crucial times, eventually resulting in the Secretary, Berry, goin
   directly to Lynch with security matters, as well as to othe
   ministers.

2 Albert Luykx was a naturalised Irishman, originally from Belgium, who had settled in Ireland in 1948. He was a business-man, introduced to Kelly by Blaney. He accompanied him as interpreter when negotiating for arms in Antwerp.

9 The Arms Trials

1 Frank Aiken was deeply shocked by the arms crisis revelations. He decided at the next general election that, because Charles Haughey had been endorsed as a candidate for Fianna Fail, he would not stand. He intended to make public his reasons, but was persuaded by Lynch to give 'health reasons' instead. The details of his thinking at the time were published only after his death, in an account given by his son to Geraldine Kennedy, and published in the *Sunday Press*, June 1983.

10 The Aftermath

1 In reality, Wilson's Dublin visit had a covert motivation: a meeting held secretly with representatives of the I.R.A. in the organisation of which the Irish Labour Party deputy, John O'Connell, played a part.

2 *The Future of Northern Ireland; A Paper for Discussion*, H.M.S.O., 1972. The paper contains useful annexes, including the position papers of five Northern Ireland political parties, an outline of the reform programme, an assessment of North–South relations and how they had developed, and a summary of the Government of Ireland Act, 1920.

3 The legislation included an Emergency Prisons Bill, the bringing into force of Section Five of the Offences Against the State Act of 1940, setting up the Special Criminal Court (still in operation for terrorist offences), and the amendment of the same Act, allowing for the easier conviction of members of illegal organisations.

4 Speech at the annual conference of the Irish Labour Party, January 1969.

5 With the exception of Paddy Donegan, Liam Cosgrave was virtually isolated within the Fine Gael Party which, before the bombs, had decided to abstain. After the explosions the impres-sion was given that the party had been won round to support for the Bill, ruling out any immediate possibility of the leadership challenge which had been imminent.

11 Cosgrave's Men

1 The overall effect of Proportional Representation, using the single transferable vote, is best illustrated in the following table

Year	Fianna Fail		Fine Gael		Labour	
	Seats	% Votes	Seats	% Votes	Seats	% Votes
1969	75	45·66	50	34·1	18	17·02
1973	69	46·24	54	35·09	19	13·67

The more detailed working of the STV system of Proportional Representation is best shown in respect of one constituency. The three seats in Kildare were critical in 1973. In 1969, with only 43·4 per cent of the vote, the party had won two out of three seats. In 1973, with 50·2 per cent of the vote, it was reduced, by the effective operation of P.R. between Fine Gael and Labour, to one seat, one each going to the other parties. This is how it happened:

Key statistics: Population, 67,332; Electorate, 40,065; Total Poll, 30,678; Spoiled Votes, 357; Valid Poll, 30,321 (or 75·68 per cent of the electorate.) The quota was 7,581. This is found by dividing the valid vote by one more than the number of seats (i.e. divided by four in a three-seat constituency), and then add one. There were six candidates for the three seats, and five counts were needed to decide the issue. The counts were as follows:

	Name	Counts: One	Two	Three	Four	Five
(Lab)	Bermingham, J	6791 +	81=6872 +	365=7237 +	309=7546 +	204=7750
(FF)	Boylan, T	4898 +	704=5602 +	31=5633 +	7=5640 +	1549=7189
(FF)	Dooley, P	1441 +	449=1890 +	43=1933 +	8=1941 −	1941
(FG)	Malone, P	6581 +	56=6637 +	1268=7905 −	324	
(FG)	McEvoy, J	1716 +	23=1739 −	1739		
(FF)	Power, P	8894 −	1313			

A total of 220 were non-transferable.

Figures in italics indicate where they exceeded the quota. Of the crucial 560 by which Bermingham won the seat, 285 came to him from Fianna Fail transfers, whereas the transfers in the other direction, from Fine Gael to Fianna Fail, were negligible. In addition, the majority of non-transferable votes were from Fianna Fail. The transfer from Fine Gael to Bermingham was over 95 per cent.

The way in which the Single Transferable Vote itself works is also best illustrated in relation to this count. Papers are numbered 1, 2, 3, in order of preference against candidates' names. In the case of Power, P, who had a surplus of 1,313 over the quota, this was distributed *in proportion to* the overall number of second preferences. Clearly a majority of the overall 8,894 voters gave their number two preference to Boylan, and this same proportion is reflected in the 704 votes, just over half of the total available for transfer. This represents the second count. The third is simpler, involving the transfer of *all* of McEvoy's votes, with the exception of 32 which did not transfer, and account for the discrepancy in totals. The big transfer to Malone gave him a surplus, transferred next in the same way as Power's had been. Dooley was then eliminated, and his total vote (less 108 non-transferable) then failed to bring his Fianna Fail running mate, Boylan, sufficient to overtake Bermingham, who exceeded the quota on this fifth and final count on transfers which crossed traditional party lines.

Liam Cosgrave was nominated Taoiseach by the Dail on March 14, 1973, by 72 votes to 70, and formed a National Coalition Government with Labour. Its membership was as follows: Brendan Corish (Lab., Tanaiste and Minister for Health and Social Welfare), Patrick Donegan (F.G., Defence), James Tully (Lab., Local Government), Richie Ryan (F.G., Finance), Mark Clinton (F.G., Agriculture, Fisheries), Garret FitzGerald (F.G., Foreign Affairs), Michael O'Leary (Lab., Labour), Tom O'Donnell (F.G., Gaeltacht), Tom Fitzpatrick (F.G., Lands), Conor Cruise O'Brien (Lab., Posts, Telegraphs), Justin Keating (Lab., Industry, Commerce), Peter Barry (F.G., Transport, Power), Richard Burke (F.G., Education), Patrick Cooney (F.G., Justice). Declan Costello was Attorney General. Seven parliamentary secretaries were appointed: John Kelly, Richard Barry, Henry Kenny, Michael Begley, John Bruton (all Fine Gael), Michael Pat Murphy and Frank Cluskey (Labour).

Mark Clinton was absent on E.E.C. agricultural business when the Dail voted.

12 The Economy

These were both forced on him. At the end of Patrick Hillery's term as Ireland's E.E.C. Commissioner, Cosgrave appointed Richard Burke, who was Minister for Education. And, following Patrick Donegan's resignation as Minister for Defence, in 1976, Oliver J. Flanagan was appointed.

13 Sunningdale

1 Garret FitzGerald, Patrick Cooney, Richie Ryan, James Tully, Conor Cruise O'Brien, Brendan Corish and Declan Costello.

2 The Republic of Ireland took a case against the United Kingdom at the Court of Human Rights for the inhuman and degrading treatment of prisoners under interrogation by the R.U.C. in Northern Ireland. The judgment, several years later, was in Ireland's favour.

3 Following the imposition of direct rule, and the resignation of the Northern Ireland Government in March 1972, the seven parliamentary political parties of Northern Ireland were invited to a conference at Darlington, held from September 25–27, to discuss the future of Northern Ireland. The Unionist, Alliance, and Northern Ireland Labour Parties attended. In addition, the S.D.L.P. and the Ulster Liberal Party submitted documents, as did the New Ulster Movement.

4 For the text of these articles see Chapter 4, note 2, above.

5 The perfidy was not in the speech, in which Harold Wilson called the Loyalist strikers 'thugs and bullies' who were 'sponging on British democracy'; it was in the subsequent failure to act in response to the Northern Ireland Executive's ultimatum to him, demanding, on Thursday, May 23, that he break the eight-day strike.

14 Security

1 The Littlejohn brothers, Kenneth and Keith, had links with the I.R.A. and British Intelligence as well as being involved in various bank roberries, the last of which in Ireland, at the Allied Irish Bank in Grafton Street, led to the arrest and conviction of both men. The fullest outline of their tangled and cavalier activities appears in Jonathan Bloch and Patrick Fitzgerald, *British Intelligence and Covert Action*, Brandon Books, Kerry; Junction Books, London, 1983.

2 Senator William Fox had been a Fine Gael Dail deputy from 1969 to 1973, when he was an unsuccessful candidate, subsequently winning a seat in the Senate.

3 A Constitutional body which includes Taoiseach, Tanaiste, Chief Justice, President of the High Court, Chairman of the Dail and Senate, Attorney General, former office holders and 'such . . . as may be appointed by the President'.

4   Eamon de Valera in a Dail debate on the Constitution, 1937.
5   Cearbhaill O Dalaigh was Attorney General, 1946–8 and 1951–3, and thereafter a Supreme Court Judge, becoming President of the Supreme Court as well as Chief Justice in 1961. From 1973 he was a Judge of the E.E.C. Court of Justice.

15 The Opposition

1   It was eventually published by Keating's successor, Desmond O'Malley in 1978. Bula Resources have not, so far (1983) developed the resource.

2   Jack Lynch was nominated Taoiseach on July 5, 1977, by 82 votes to 61. He announced the following Government: George Colley (Tanaiste, Finance, Public Service), Charles Haughey (Health, Social Welfare), Brian Lenihan (Fisheries), Padraig Faulkner (Tourism, Transport, Posts, Telegraphs), James Gibbons (Agriculture), Desmond O'Malley (Industry, Commerce, Energy), Robert Molloy (Defence), Gerard Collins (Justice), Michael O'Kennedy (Foreign Affairs), Sylvester Barrett (Environment), Gene Fitzgerald (Labour), Denis Gallagher (Gaeltacht), John Wilson (Education), Martin O'Donoghue (Economic Planning, Development). Anthony J. Hederman was Attorney General. Seven parliamentary secretaries, who were made Ministers of State (junior ministers) the following November, were also appointed: Patrick Lalor, David Andrews, Jim Tunney, Tom Fitzpatrick, Pearse Wyse, Tom Hussey, and Maire Geoghegan-Quinn.

16 Commitments

1   Article 28.1 reads: 'The Government shall consist of not less than seven and not more than fifteen members who shall be appointed by the President in accordance with the provisions of this Constitution.' And Article 28.2 reads: 'The executive power of the State shall, subject to the provisions of this Constitution, be exercised by or on the authority of the Government.'

2   The agreements were: in 1970 and 1972 for 18 months; 1974 and 1975 for 12 months; 1976 for seven months.

17 Changing the Pilot

Those who attended the caucus meeting in July were: Bertie

Ahern, Lorcan Allen, Liam Aylward, Vincent Brady, John Callanan, Sean Calleary, Hugh Conaghan, Ger Connolly, Bernard Cowan, Brendan Daly, Noel Davern, Sile de Valera, Sean Doherty, Jackie Fahey, James Fitzsimons, Padraig Flynn Christopher Fox, Sean Keegan, Tim Killeen, Liam Lawlor Eileen Lemass, Jim Leonard, Terry Leyden, Charlie McCreevy Thomas McEllistrom, Tom Meaney, Tom Nolan, Timothy O'Connor, Rory O'Hanlon, Paddy Power, Albert Reynolds Michael Smith, Joe Walsh. (Source: *Magill*, January 1980.)

2   The new Government: Taoiseach, Charles Haughey; George Colley (Tanaiste, Tourism, Transport), Brian Lenihan (Foreign Affairs), Desmond O'Malley (Industry, Commerce, Energy) Gerard Collins (Justice), Michael O'Kennedy (Finance), Gene Fitzgerald (Labour), John Wilson (Education), Ray McSharry (Agriculture), Padraig Faulkner (Defence), Maire Geoghegan Quinn (Gaeltacht), Michael Woods (Health, Social Welfare) Patrick Power (Fisheries, Forestry), Albert Reynolds (Posts Telegraphs), Sylvester Barrett (Environment). Anthony Hederman remained Attorney General. The five new Ministers were McSharry, Woods, Reynolds, Power, Geoghegan-Quinn, who was also the first woman appointed to an Irish Government. In addition, the following Ministers of State were appointed Raphael Burke, Tom Hussey, Jim Tunney, Sean Moore, Jackie Fahey, Lorcan Allen, Ger Connolly, Tom McEllistrom, Sean Calleary, Mark Killilea; and the following March Tom Nolan Brendan Daly, Tom Meaney, Padraig Flynn and Sean Doherty were added.

3   Personal inquiry at the time by the authority (April 23, 1980).

18 Charles Haughey

1   The Labour Party leader was formerly an assistant in a butcher's shop.

2   Information from Government Press Secretary, Frank Dunlop March 11, 1980.

19 Unique Relationship

1   Prisoners refused to wear the clothing issued, draping themselves in blankets; they smeared their cells with food and excrement.

2   A second hunger strike began on March 1, 1980, led by Robert (Bobby) Sands, who was serving a four-year sentence for firearms offences. This time the prisoners announced that the pre

vious protest had been called off because they had been 'morally blackmailed'.

3 A more detailed account of this summit and the events leading up to, and surrounding it, is given in my essay on 'Political Constraints: Dublin' in *The Constitution of Northern Ireland: Problems and Prospects*, edited by David Watt, London, 1981.

4 See p. 146 *et seq.*

5 The interrogation was done by *Today, Tonight*, the main television current affairs programme. Its editor, Joe Mulholland, invited Vincent Browne, editor of *Magill*, Michael Mills, Political Correspondent of the *Irish Press*, Paul Tansey, economist working with the *Irish Times*, and the author, Parliamentary Correspondent of the *Irish Independent*, to form the panel.

20 Garret FitzGerald

1 O'Connell was asked by the Administrative Council of the Labour Party to transfer to Dublin West, in which part of his former constituency had been, and leave Dublin South Central to the Party leader, Frank Cluskey. O'Connell refused, resigned, ran as an independent in Cluskey's constituency, and took the seat; this cost Cluskey his own seat and the leadership of the Labour Party.

2 Garret FitzGerald's Government was formed on June 30, 1981; Michael O'Leary (Lab., Tanaiste, Industry, Commerce), Peter Barry (F.G., Environment), James Tully (Lab., Defence), Tom Fitzpatrick (F.G., Fisheries, Forestry), Eileen Desmond (Lab., Health, Social Welfare), John Bruton (F.G., Finance), Liam Kavanagh (Lab., Labour, Public Service), Patrick Cooney (F.G., Transport, Posts, Telegraphs), John Kelly (F.G., Trade, Commerce, Tourism), John Boland (F.G., Education), Paddy O'Toole (F.G., Gaeltacht), Jim Mitchell (F.G., Justice), Alan Dukes (F.G., Agriculture), James Dooge (F.G., Foreign Affairs). Peter Sutherland was Attorney General. Dooge was a Senator, and his appointment was not ratified until after the Senate elections. Between June 30 and October 21, therefore, John Kelly was Minister for Foreign Affairs in addition to his other appointment. The following Ministers of State were appointed in June and July: Gerard L'Estrange, Edward Collins, Fergus O'Brien, Donal Creed, Mary Flaherty, Patrick Harte, Michael Begley, Michael Keating, Michael D'Arcy, Ted Nealon, Jim O'Keeffe,

all Fine Gael; Joseph Bermingham, Barry Desmond, Dick Spring, Labour.

3 Dail Report, November 10, 1981, Col. 1586.
4 Dail Report, November 10, 1981, Col. 1587.
5 Dail Report on adjournment debate on the economy, December 18, 1981, Col. 2836.
6 *Sunday Tribune*, December 27, 1981.

21 More Instability

1 *Satisfaction rating:*

	June '81	Dec. '81	Feb. 7, '82	Feb. 14, '82
FitzGerald:	44%	44%	51%	56%
Haughey:	43%	36%	31%	33%

(Figures taken from Irish Marketing Surveys opinion polls.)
2 Carlow-Kilkenny, Cork South West, Dublin Central, Dublin North West, Dublin South, Galway West, Kildare (McCreevy's constituency), Tipperary North, Waterford and Wicklow.
3 *Irish Independent*, Wednesday, February 4, 1982. My article listed 28 supporters of Desmond O'Malley, further possible supporters, and a group loyal to Haughey.

22 1982

1 T. S. Eliot, *Burnt Norton*, I, ll. 6–8.
2 Charles Haughey was nominated Taoiseach by 86 votes to 79, on March 9, 1982, when he announced the following members of the Government: Ray McSharry (Tanaiste, finance), Brian Lenihan (Agriculture), Desmond O'Malley (Trade, Commerce, Tourism), Gerard Collins (Foreign Affairs), Gene Fitzgerald (Public Service, Labour), John Wilson (Transport, Posts, Telegraphs), Martin O'Donoghue (Education), Michael Woods (Health, Social Welfare), Patrick Power (Defence), Albert Reynolds (Industry, Energy), Raphael Burke (Environment), Brendan Daly (Fisheries, Forestry), Padraig Flynn (Gaeltacht), Sean Doherty (Justice). Attorney General was Patrick Connolly, subsequently replaced by John Murray on August 17, 1982. The following were appointed as Ministers of State in March and in June: Bertie Ahern, Sylvester Barrett, Lorcan Allen, Bernard Cowan, Terry Leyden, Maire Geoghegan-Quinn, Denis Gallagher, Ger Connolly, Gerard Brady, Tom McEllistrom.

3 That is, on both occasions, a casting vote in favour of the Fianna Fail candidate, Jim Tunney.

4 Dail Report, March 30, 1982, Col. 862.

5 Dail Report, April 28, 1982, Cols. 1635–75. The argument, including a half-hour suspension, went on for three hours.

6 Public Service employment restrictions, the postponement of special pay increases, and departmental cuts were announced in a Government statement at the end of July.

7 Dail Report, March 24, 1982, Col. 328.

8 *Northern Ireland: A Framework for Devolution*, H.M.S.O., Cmd 8541, Published April 5, 1982.

9 Radio Interview with Gerard Barry, R.T.E. lunchtime news, Wednesday, March 31, 1982.

10 Dail Report, May 4, 1982, Cols. 35–40.

11 The members of what became known as the 'Club of 22' were: David Andrews, Sylvester Barrett, Tom Bellew, Seamus Brennan, Hugh Byrne, Sean Byrne, George Colley, Hugh Conaghan, Padraig Faulkner, Tom Fitzpatrick, Sean French, Jim Gibbons, Mary Harney, Charlie McCreevy, Tom Meaney, Robert Molloy, Ciaran Murphy, William O'Dea, Martin O'Donoghue, Desmond O'Malley, Joe Walsh, Pearse Wyse.

23 The 'Unwanted' Election

1 Technically, there were *two* press conferences, at the insistence of the Secretary of the Department of Finance. One followed immediately after the other. The first, in theory, was to release the Book of Estimates. After it, the senior civil servants left. In practice, the event, with most Government Ministers present, was an election press conference, distinctly political throughout.

2 There were 41 constituencies returning 166 deputies to the Dail. There were 15 5-seaters, 13 4-seaters, 13 3-seaters. One of the 5-seat constituencies, Dublin South Central, was effectively a 4-seater because it returned automatically the outgoing Ceann Comhairle, John O'Connell. Of the 2·3 million voters on the register, 1·7 million, or 72·86 per cent, voted. When the 23rd Dail was dissolved, one seat was vacant. Fianna Fail had 80, Fine Gael 64, Labour 14, the Workers' Party 3, 3 Independents, and the Ceann Comhairle. When the 24th Dail met on December 14, Fianna Fail had 75, Fine Gael 70, Labour 16, Workers' Party 2, and there were two Independents as well as John O'Connell, who became an Independent backbencher. This substantial change

had been brought about by the following swings: 2·05 per cent from Fianna Fail, 1·92 per cent to Fine Gael, 0·23 per cent to Labour, and 0·96 per cent to the Workers' Party. Regionally, the position was rather different. In Dublin City and County the swing against Fianna Fail was 4·29 per cent and towards Fine Gael it was 2·23 per cent. The Workers' Party gained a swing of 2·94 per cent and took a seat from Fine Gael. In the rest of Leinster the swings were more marginal: against Fianna Fail 2·24 per cent, towards Fine Gael 1·67%, and towards Labour 1·79%. In Connaught-Ulster the opinion polls were not borne out in practice, since Fine Gael gained a swing of 2·61 per cent while Fianna Fail's gain was only 0·29 per cent. And in Munster the swing away from Fianna Fail was 1·51 per cent, and towards Fine Gael 1·38 per cent.

24 'Programme for Government'

1 Garret FitzGerald was nominated Taoiseach on December 14, 1982, by 85 votes to 79. His Government was as follows: Dick Spring (Lab., Tanaiste, Environment), Peter Barry (F.G., Foreign Affairs), John Bruton (F.G., Industry, Energy), Liam Kavanagh (Lab., Labour), Patrick Cooney (F.G., Defence), John Boland (F.G., Public Service), Paddy O'Toole (F.G., Gaeltacht, Fisheries, Forestry), Jim Mitchell (F.G., Transport, Posts, Telegraphs), Alan Dukes (F.G., Finance), Frank Cluskey (Lab., Trade, Commerce, Tourism), Barry Desmond (Lab., Health, Social Welfare), Austin Deasy (F.G., Agriculture), Michael Noonan (F.G., Justice), Gemma Hussey (F.G., Education). Attorney General was Peter Sutherland. Twelve Fine Gael Ministers of State were appointed: Sean Barrett, Nuala Fennell, Ted Nealon, Jim O'Keeffe, Paddy Hegarty, Paul Connaughton, Edward Collins, John Donnellan, George Birmingham, Fergus O'Brien, Donal Creed, Michael D'Arcy. Three Labour appointees were Ruairi Quinn, Joseph Bermingham and Michael Moynihan.

Postscript

1 The proposed wording was: 'The State acknowledges the right to life of the unborn, and, with due regard to the equal right to life of the mother, guarantees in its laws to respect, and, as far as practicable, by its laws to defend and vindicate that right.'

Index

Adams, Gerry, 82
Agnew, Patrick, 163
Aiken, Frank, 77
Ainsworth, Joe, 216
Allen, Lorcan, 71, 216
Alliance Party: Darlington conference, 82; N.I. Assembly (1973), 106, 107; and power sharing, 108, 111
Anglo-Irish Free Trade Area Agreement, 12, 30, 31
Aontacht Eireann Party, 112
Arms Trials, 14, 74–8, 116
Armstrong, Dr John, opposes abortion amendment, 217
Assembly (1973), 106, 108–16; prorogued, 114
Assembly (1982), 185, 201
Atkins, Humphrey, hunger strike statement, 153

Barret, Sylvester, 128
Barry, Peter, 93
'Battle of the Bogside', 35
Beit, Sir Alfred, 118
Belgrano, 187
Bell, Martin, 82
Berry, Peter, 55–6, 61; Arms Trial evidence, 74–6; and *Magill* articles, 150; resigns, 89

Blaney, Neil, 20, 21, 29, 30, 32, 38, 41, 53, 62, 83, 162, 180, 200; and arms crisis, 59–63, 71, 77, 78; dismissal of, 60, 63–6, 69; expulsion from Fianna Fail, 71, 88; Letterkenny speech (November 1968), 22; Letterkenny speech (1969), 48–50; and Northern Ireland, 23, 25, 28, 29, 31, 35, 37, 39, 42–52, 69–70, 72, 76, 85, 120; and Sunningdale, 113, 114; supports Haughey, 164–5, 182, 192; wins European seat, 136
'Bloody Sunday', 2, 81, 116
Boland, Gerry, 71
Boland, Kevin: and arms crisis, 60, 62, 68–9; challenges Lynch's leadership, 71, 77; and Electoral Amendment Bill, 13, 33; expulsion from Fianna Fail Parliamentary Party, 71; and Fianna Fail policies, 40–1, 42, 50–1, 53; forms new party (Aontacht Eireann), 88, 112; legal action over Sunningdale, 112–13, 114, 115, 118; on Northern

Boland, Kevin: *continued*
  Ireland, 35, 41, 42, 47–8,
  68–9, 70; as Party organiser,
  30, 32; resignation as
  Minister, 60, 63, 65, 68–9;
  resigns from Dail, 71, 78;
  resigns from Fianna Fail, 71,
  83, 88; Skeffington on, 72;
  24-hour resignation of, 37–8,
  41, 47; and united Ireland, 20,
  29
Brennan, Joseph, 37, 53, 67;
  death causes by-election, 151
Brennan, Paudge, 64, 71;
  expelled from Fianna Fail, 88
Brennan, Seamus, and 1977
  manifesto, 129
British Commonwealth, 80
British-Irish Association, 204
Brock, George, 202–3
Browne, Noel, 31; walk-out at
  Cork conference, 85, 162; as
  Socialist Labour Party
  member, 164
Browne, Sean, 181
Browne, Vincent, 60 and n.,
  61, 181
Brugha, Ruairi, 126
Bruton, John, 165–7, 172, 173;
  budget (January 1982) 174,
  175, 177
B Specials, 18, 42
Bula, 127–8
Bunting, Ronald, 24
Burke, Richard, 93; and
  contraception Bill, 97, 152;
  and E.E.C. commissionership,
  184, 185
Burntollet Bridge, 24

Caledon, 16
Callaghan, James, 34, 35, 44, 46
Cameron Committee, 46 and n.
Campaign for Social Justice in
  N.I., 16

Carrington, Lord, 79, 153
Carron, Owen, wins
  by-election, 170
Castlereagh, 25
Central Bank, 209
Channon, Paul, 82
Chichester-Clark, James, 26,
  33, 34, 35; resigns as
  N.I.P.M., 79
Childers, President Erskine, 125
Claudia, 117
Clinton, Mark, 93; views on
  contraception, 97
Clondalkin Paper Mill, 179
Clonmel, 1968 speech by
  Lynch, 21
Cluskey, Frank: on Haughey,
  157; as Leader of Labour
  Party, 129, 142, 149; loses Dail
  seat, 162; television debate,
  160; supports Spring, 212
Coalisland, 16
Colley, George: as Finance
  Minister (May 1970), 67, 68;
  as Finance Minister (1977–8),
  130–1, 132–3, 134, 209; in
  Haughey's Government, 142–
  3, 149; on Northern Ireland,
  113; in Opposition, 126–8; as
  potential successor to Lynch,
  135, 141
Collins, Gerard, 67; attacks
  FitzGerald, 201; as Minister
  for Foreign Affairs, 186
Committee of Public Accounts,
  86–8
Connolly, Patrick, resigns as
  Attorney General, 189
Constitution, 88; abortion
  referendum, 217–18; and
  Criminal Law (Jurisdiction)
  Bill, 119; and Dail Committee
  of Public Accounts, 87; and
  Emergency Powers Bill,
  121–5; in McGee case, 6–7;

parliamentary review committee on, 12–13; President's right to refuse dissolution, 174–5; referendum to amend, 90; and Sunningdale Agreement, 112–13

Cooney, Patrick: appointment as Minister for Justice, 93; and contraception legislation, 97; and Emergency Powers Bill (1976), 122; loses Dail seat, 129

Corish, Brendan, 31, 67, 80, 87; on coalition, 85–6 and n.; refuses to stand again for Dail, 178; resigns as Party leader, 129; becomes Tanaiste, 93

Cosgrave, Liam, 184; and arms crisis, 38, 60, 66–7, 86; and coalition, 85, 86, 101; and constitutional duty, 124–5; and emergency powers, 121–2; and general election (1969), 31; and general election (1977), 128–9; Government of, 92–8, 99–105; and Northern Ireland, 80, 87, 106–9, 110, 115, 116, 148; political views of, 18–19, 86, 90, 95–6, 102, 103, 106–7, 120, 121; resignation of, 129; and West Mayo by-election, 120, 121

Cosgrave, W.T., 18, 171

Costello, Declan: 'Towards a Just Society', 86; Attorney General, 93, 96

Coughlan, Clement, 216

Council of Ireland, 105, 108–9, 110, 120

Coyle, Marian, 121

Craig, William, 16, 26, 81, 105, 106; stands for Unionist leadership, 79

Criminal Law Act, 121–5

Criminal Law (Jurisdiction) Act: proposed, 110; Dail debates, 118, 119–20

Cronin, Jeremiah, 67

Crowley, Flor, 71, 137

Crum, General Erskine, 79

Currie, Austin, 16, 19

Darlington conference, 82–3

Democratic Socialist Party, 200

Democratic Unionist Party, 106

de Rossa, Proinsias, 180

Derry Citizens' Defence Committee, 35

Desmond, Barry, 85; censures Ceann Comhairle, 184; supports Spring, 212

de Valera, Eamon, 71, 81; Boland on, 40–1; and Boland's resignation, 41; dismissal of Haughey and Blaney, 60; dissolves 18th Dail (May 1969), 31

de Valera, Sile: challenge to Lynch, 139–40; supports Haughey, 141

de Valera, Vivion, 126

Devlin, Bernadette (see McAliskey)

Doherty, Kieran, 163

Doherty, Sean, 137, 182, 189; and phone-tapping, 1; resigns from F.F. Front Bench, 216; resigns Party whip, 216

Donegan, Paddy, 93, 97; and president O Dalaigh, 123–5

Dore, Noel, 187

Dugdale, Bridget Rose, 118

Dukes, Alan, introduces Budget (1983), 217

Dunne, Sean, 33

E.E.C.: Hillery as Commissioner, 89; Ireland's entry, 6, 12, 82; and oil crisis, 101; and

E.E.C.: *continued*
'The Way Forward', 209
Emergency Powers Act, 121–5
Enright, Tom, 97
E.S.R.I., 209
European Monetary System,
    decision to join, 134–5
Ewart-Biggs, Christopher,
    assassination of, 121, 139;
    Memorial Prize, 204

Fagan, Anthony, 75
Fahey, Jack, 137, 138
Falklands invasion, 2, 185–9,
    201, 202
Farrell, Joe, 216
Faulkner, Brian: his Govern-
    ment replaced, 82; and
    internment, 80, 108; leaves
    O'Neill's Government, 24, 26;
    resignation (1974), 112, 114;
    and Sunningdale, 106, 108,
    110, 111–12, 113–15; tipped as
    future premier in N.I., 25; and
    violence in N.I., 81
Faulkner, Padraig, 37, 53, 181;
    and postal strike, 135; returns
    to backbenches, 163
Financial Times, 204
Fitt, Gerry, later Lord, 16, 22,˙
    108; veto on talks during
    internment, 81
FitzGerald, Garret, 33, 84, 116;
    'Constitutional Crusade', 170–
    1; as Foreign Affairs Minister,
    93, 96, 103–4; general election
    (February 1982), 174, 175,
    179–80; general election
    (November 1982), 195–211;
    leader of Fine Gael, 129;
    negotiations with Spring, 213–
    14; and Northern Ireland, 19;
    opposes Haughey, 142, 149,
    155, 193, 194; personal
    popularity, 178–9; political

character, 171, 195; in power
    (1981), 162–75; summit with
    Mrs Thatcher, 169–70; as
    Taoiseach, 164–5, 195;
    televised debates, 159–60, 179,
    207–8
Fitzgerald, Gene, 152, 166
Fitzpatrick, Tom, 93
Fitzpatrick, Tom, (F.F.), 126
Flanagan, Oliver, J., 97
Flanagan, Sean, 35, 77
Fleming, Chief Supt. John, 55–6
Flynn, Padraig, 167
Foley, Des, 71, 83, resigns from
    F.F., 89
Fortnight, 204
Fox, Senator Billie, 118
Freeland, General Sir Ian, 35,
    42; resignation, 79

'Gaiety Theatre Document',
    162–3
Gallagher, Denis, 142
Gallagher, Eddie, 121
Gallagher, Paddy, 180
Gargan, Bridie, 189
Gibbons, James: arms crisis
    (Minister for Defence), 35, 37,
    54, 55, 56, 67, 70, 75, 88;
    Arms Trials, 75, 76; evidence
    to Committee of Public
    Accounts, 88; leaves
    Haughey's Government
    (1979), 142; Minister for
    Agriculture, 67; political effect
    of heart attacks, 192, 193
Glenn, Alice, 180
Goulding, Cathal, 42, 56
Gregory, Tony, 180; signs deal
    with Haughey, 182, 192;
    abstains in no confidence
    debate (November 1982), 194;
    fights Nov. 1982 election, 200
Guardian, 4
GUBU, 3, 190

Haughey, Charles: ambitions of, 29, 84, 86–7, 137–8, 141, 148–9; Anglo-Irish Free Trade Area Agreement, 30; arms crisis, 30, 53–4, 56, 57, 59–63, 64–73, 88, 143; Arms Trial, 74–8; Budget (1969), 31; Cluskey on, 157; confrontations with McCreevy, 173–4, 190–1; contest for Taoiseach (1981), 163–5; and contraception, 97; dismissal of, 60, 63, 64–6, 68; and the Falklands, 186–9; FitzGerald challenges, 193; general election (January 1982), 176–80; general election (November 1982), 195–211; his Government (1982), 183–94; 'Green Card', 201–4, 207; land deals, 32; his leadership challenged, 180–2, 190–1, 216; and McArthur affair, 189–90; and the media, 150, 154–6, 176, 191, 196–7, 202, 204, 207–8,; and Mrs Thatcher, 147–8, 152–6, 169–70, 186, 187, 188; and Northern Ireland, 20, 35, 37, 38, 39–40, 41, 147–8, 152–3, 169–70, 172, 185–6; in Opposition (1981), 166, 169–70, 172; as party organiser and tactician, 30, 32, 152–6, 172–3, 174–5, 195; and phone-tapping, 2; policies in power, 146–7, 148–51, 156; Pro-Life Amendment, 196, 217; returns to Fianna Fail Front Bench, 118, 120, 131; signs agreement with Tony Gregory, 182, 192; supported by S.F.W.P. members, 182, 192, as Taoiseach, 141–3, 146–50, 157, 182; television performances, 159–61, 179, 180, 207–10

Haughey, Padraig, 87
Havers, Sir Michael, 169
H-Block, 2, 3; Ballsbridge protest march, 168–9; election candidate (1981); first hunger strike, 152; influence on Dail, 165
Healey, Denis, 35
Heath, Edward, 79, 101; Baldonnel meetings, 107; calls general election (February 1974), 113; meetings with Faulkner and Lynch, 80, 81, 91; and Sunningdale, 105–15
Hefferon, Colonel Michael, 54–7, 88
Henchy, Mr Justice, 74, 75
Herrema, Tiede, kidnapped, 121
Higgins, Michael D., 31, 177–8; at Limerick conference, 215
Hillery, Patrick, 77; E.E.C. Commissioner, 89; President, 175, 215
Horan, Monsignor, 167
Howe, Sir Geoffrey, 153
Hume, John, 19, 168; condemns Blaney's Letterkenny speech, 49
Hunt Inquiry, 43 and n., 46
Hurson, Martin, 168

I.R.A. (see also Provisional I.R.A.), 14, 42, 98
Irish Congress of Trade Unions, 200, 213–14
Irish Independent, 4, 182, 197, 203, 210
Irish Marketing Surveys, 189
Irish National Liberation Army, 152
Irish Press, 203, 210
Irish Republican Socialist Party, 152

Irish Times, 1, 32 and n., 72, 203, 210

Kavanagh, Liam, 212
Keating, Justin, 31, 33, 84, 85, 93; assessment of, 94, and Bula, 127–8; loses Dail seat, 129
Kelly, Captain James, 53–8, 60, 66, 71, 74–6, 88
Kelly, John, 54–8, 71, 75, 76
Kelly, Professor John M., 95, 215
Kemmy, Jim, 162, 164, 180, 182, 200
Kennedy, Geraldine, 1, 2; interview with McCreevy, 173, 223
Kenny, Enda, 120
Kenny, Henry, 120
Killilea, Mark, 137
Knock Airport, 167, 179

Lalor, Paddy, 67
Legge, Hector, 66–7
Lemass, Eileen, 185
Lemass, Sean, 27, 29; economic pragmatism of, 40–1; resigns, 12
Lenihan, Brian, 35, 152, 153
Littlejohn brothers, 118 and n.
Loftus, Sean, 162, 164
Loughnane, Bill, 192, 193
Luykx, Albert: Arms Trial, 71 and n., 74–8
Lynch, Jack: and arms crisis, 56, 59–63, 64–71, 88; assessment of his political contribution, 143–4; backbench revolt against (1979), 137–8, 142; becomes Taoiseach (1966), 12; on Criminal Law (Jurisdiction) Bill, 119–20; early challengers of, 29, 37–8, 126; and E.E.C., 89, 90, 91; general election (1969), 30–3; general election (February 1973), 91; Haughey challenges after Arms Trials, 76, 77, 78, 84; and I.R.A., 42; meets Heath, 80, 107; and Mountbatten's murder, 139; and national emergency (1976), 122; and Northern Ireland, 20–3, 35–6, 37–8, 44–5, 46–7, 49, 51–2, 64, 80, 81, 82, 85, 88, 106, 110, 112, 119–20, 121, 139, 148; and O'Neill's resignation, 27–8; his political character, 38–9, 45, 61–3, 83, 90–1, 106, 116, 129; reinstates Haughey, 118; resigns, 140–5, 149; returns to power (1977), 130–6, 214–15; sets up Dail Committee of Public Accounts, 86–7, 88; speech to Ard Fheis (1970), 51–2; supports O'Malley for F.F. leadership, 181; timing of handing over leadership, 131, 134–5, 138, 140–1

McAliskey, Bernadette, wins Mid-Ulster, 25
McArthur, Malcolm Edward, 189
McAteer, Edward, 22
McCreevy, Charles: attacks Haughey, 173–4, 190–1, 192; *Sunday Tribune* interview, 173
McDonnell, Joe, 168
McEllistrom, 137
McEntee, Sean, 41, 77
McGee case, 6, 96
McGiolla, Tomas, 142
McGlinchey, Bernard, 137
McGuinness, Martin, 82

McKenna, Sean, 153

McLaughlin, Patrick, 216

MacSharry, Ray, 137, 181; as Minister for Finance, 185; and phone-tapping, 1; resigns from F.F. Front Bench, 216

MacStiofain, Sean, 82

Magill magazine: Arms Trial articles, 150; on Fianna Fail leadership challenge, 181

Maguire, Frank, death causes by-election, 170

Maher, T.J., 31, 136

Maudling, Reginald, 79, 80, 81

Molly, Robert, 67, 142

Moore, Sean, 144

Morgan, William, 24

Mountbatten, Lord Louis, 139

Mountjoy Prison, 1973 protest, 117

Mullen, Michael, 182

Mullins, Tommy, 71

Murphy, E.B., 66

Murray, John, intervenes in election (1982), 204–5

Napier, Sam, 25, 26

National Development Corporation, 214

National Farmers' Association, 31

New Ireland Forum, 218

Noonan, Michael, 1

Norfolk, Duke of, 201, 204

Northern Ireland Civil Rights Association, 16, 17, 23

O'Brien, Conor Cruise, 31, 33; background of, 94; critical of Lynch and F.F., 119; and GUBU, 190; and human rights, 18, 84; influence of in Labour Party, 18, 85, 116; loses seat, 129; as Minister, 93, 94; and national emergency, 122; on Northern Ireland, 18, 49, 67, 70, 94; and R.T.E., 94; and Sunningdale, 115, 116; views of, 32

O'Connell, Daithi, 82

O'Connell, Dr John, 18, 162,180; as Ceann Comhairle, 163, 182, 184

O'Connor, Niamh, 184

O'Connor, P.J., 68; arrested for personation, 184

O Dalaigh, President Cearbhall: and emergency legislation, 123; presidential crisis, 124–5

O'Donnell, Tom, 93, 97

O'Donoghue, Martin: changes sides over Haughey's leadership, 181–2; as economic strategist, 131–6, 146, 161, 176–7, 209; general election (January 1982), 176–7; Haughey drops, 142; in 'inner cabinet' (1977), 130; and leadership struggle, 141; and phone-tapping incident, 1; prepares election manifesto (1977), 129; resigns, 190

Offences Against the State Act, 122

Official Sinn Fein (*see* Workers' Party)

O'Higgins, Tom, 67

O'Keeffe, Mr Justice Andreas, 74

O'Kennedy, Michael, 152, 153; as Foreign Affairs spokesman, 120–1; as Minister for Finance, 149–50

O'Leary, Michael, 84, 93, 94; and Labour leadership, 129, 162, 198, 199

O'Malley, Desmond: appointed Justice Minister, 67; in 'inner

O'Malley, Desmond: *continued*
cabinet', 130, 141; Opposition
performance, 126–8; resigns,
190; stands against Haughey,
181–2
O'Malley, Donogh, 19
O Morain, Micheal, 37, 56, 65,
72, 73, 77
O'Neil, Captain Terence, later
Lord, 33; fight for survival, 14,
24, 25, 26; his Northern
Ireland policy, 21, 22, 23, 27–
8; his resignation, 26, 27–8
Ortoli, François-Xavier, 209

Paisley, Ian, 28, 49, 105, 106;
removal from Assembly, 113
People's Democracy, New
Year's march (1969), 23–4
Pope John-Paul II, 167
Power, Paddy, 138; Edenderry
speech, 187
Power-sharing agreement, 108
Prevention of Electoral Abuses
Act, 185
Prior, James, 2, 105; and
Falklands, 188; and 'Green
Card' election (November
1982), 201, 202–3, 206; and
Northern Ireland Assembly,
185–6, 201
Pro-Life Amendment campaign,
7, 196, 217
Proportional Representation,
13, 82, 92 and n.
Provisional I.R.A., 14, 42, 82,
94; helicopter hi-jack, 117;
involvement in hunger strike,
152
Provisional Sinn Fein, 152

Radio Telefis Eireann (R.T.E.),
94
Reagan, President, 168
Rees, Merlyn, 114

Reynolds, Albert, 137, 182
Robinson, Mary, 73, 118
Ryan, Eoin, 160, 190–1
Ryan, Richie, 67, 84, 93; and
management of economy, 99–
104, 133

Sands, Bobby, 170
Scarman Tribunal, 43 and n.
Schleuter, Otto, 58
S.F.W.P. (*see* Workers' Party)
Sherlock, Joe, 162, 164, 180
Sherwin, Sean, 71, 83, 88
Sinclair, Betty, 16
Sinn Fein, 14, 94, 120
Skeffington, Owen Sheehy, 72–
3
Skelly, Liam, 185
Special Powers Act, 18 and n.,
80
Spring, Dick, 197–200, 201,
212; negotiates with
FitzGerald, 213–14; supports
Coalition, 215
Stardust Ballroom fire, 156–7
Strasbourg torture case, 110
Sunday Independent, 66
Sunday Press, 1
Sunday Tribune, McCreevy
interview, 173
Sunningdale, 106, 109–16, 119–
20; communiqué, 111
Sutherland, Peter, 169, 217

Taca, 40 and n.
Taylor, John, 106
Taylor, Mervyn, 215
Thatcher, Margaret: first
meeting with Haughey, 147–8,
187; and 'Green Card' election
(November 1982), 204; Irish
attitude to Falklands, 188–9;
second meeting with Haughey,
152, 153–6, 157, 158, 168–9,
172, 186; summit with
FitzGerald, 169–70

Thorn, Gaston, 209
Thornley, David, 31, 33, 84, 85
Times, The, 113, 202–3
Tully, James, 93, 178
Tunney, Jim, 216
Twomey, Seamus, 82

Ulster Vanguard Movement,
 81
Ulster Volunteer Force, 50
Ulster Workers' Council, 114,
 117
United Nations, 14, 35–6, 42,
 43, 46, 50, 76, 94

Vanguard Party, 106

'The Way Forward', 193, 194,
 209, 214
West Belfast Loyalists, 106
Whitegate Refinery, 179
Whitelaw, William: meets
Provisional I.R.A. leaders, 82;
postpones referendum and
elections, 83; and power-
sharing, 105; as Secretary of
State, N.I., 81–2, 105
Wilson, Harold, later Lord:
calls general election in U.K.
(1970), 71; meets Provisional
I.R.A. leaders, 82; and
Northern Ireland, 21, 22, 34,
80, 91; and 'spongers' speech,
114; and Sunningdale, 113–
14, 115; and Ulster Workers'
Council strike, 114, 115; wins
general election (February
1974), 113
Windlesham, Lord, 82
Woods, Ernest, 74
Workers' Party (formerly Sinn
Fein the Workers' Party), 182,
191, 192, 193, 194, 198, 200,
205